IMAGES
of America

CASA GRANDE

On the Cover: Notwithstanding the misspelled word "Salloone," everyone knew that this small adobe building served as Thomas Meehan's latest enterprise, the Hard Luck Saloon. After a catastrophic fire tore through downtown Casa Grande on April 28, 1914, and destroyed his original business, the Gilt Edge Saloon, Meehan—ever the entrepreneur—quickly set up this newly named enterprise on Main Street. Among the men pictured are several well-known citizens of the town: Ray Woolport, Jim Megson, Ramon Armenta, a Mr. Breckenridge, Ben Morrin, T.R. Peart, Fred Cuttler, Sam Bailie, George Bennett, Mark McNatt, Tom Meehan, Chindo Lopez, Chomo Arujo, Ray Slick, a Mr. Vasquez, John Lewis, and Ray Armenta.

IMAGES
of America

CASA GRANDE

Dawn Snell and the
Casa Grande Valley Historical Society

ARCADIA
PUBLISHING

ISBN 978-0-7385-7953-5

Published by Arcadia Publishing
Charleston, South Carolina

Printed in the United States of America

Library of Congress Control Number: 2011916698

For all general information, please contact Arcadia Publishing:
Telephone 843-853-2070
Fax 843-853-0044
E-mail sales@arcadiapublishing.com
For customer service and orders:
Toll-Free 1-888-313-2665

Visit us on the Internet at www.arcadiapublishing.com

Thank you to everyone who has helped the society fulfill its goal of collecting, preserving, and disseminating the history of the Casa Grande Valley.

Contents

Acknowledgments		6
Introduction		7
1.	Passing Through	9
2.	What Hath This Railroad Wrought?	17
3.	Hard Rock and Hard Times	29
4.	Add Water and Stir	39
5.	Becoming a Town	61
6.	Growing Pains of a Desert Community	85
7.	The Historical Society	121

ACKNOWLEDGMENTS

The society would like to especially thank Kay Benedict, Merrilyn Ridgeway, and Dawn Snell, the creative forces behind this publication. Archivist Kay Benedict, one of the original founders of the society, perused thousands of photographs in the museum's collection in order to select those that best tell the story of Casa Grande. Education director, grant writer, and former librarian Merrilyn Ridgeway conducted research into the people and events depicted herein. Retired archaeologist and current volunteer collections manager Dawn Snell wrote the text. All three of them are dedicated volunteers who regularly give many hours to the museum.

Special thanks go to Don Bufkin for permission to use maps from his book *Historical Atlas of Arizona,* Second Edition, and Bill Hogan of Tucson for permission to use the sketch of Pauline Cushman. The author is especially indebted to Susan Randall of the *Casa Grande Dispatch* for the many fine articles about Casa Grande she has written through the years. Those articles provided a firm basis for my approach to this book. I would also like to thank the ever-helpful office staff, Virginia Middleton and DeeRinda Heinle, for their assistance whenever I asked, regardless of what I asked.

And of course, thank you to the citizens of Casa Grande and Pinal County who have supported the museum through the years with their donations of artifacts, photographs, and all types of archival material. Among their most important contributions have been their time, money, and helpful comments. Not to be forgotten are the thousands of visitors who have toured the museum through the years and provided valuable commentary about their experience.

Unless otherwise noted, all images appear courtesy of the Casa Grande Valley Historical Society.

INTRODUCTION

Today, Casa Grande is a growing city located along Interstate 10 in south-central Arizona. Interstate 10 is the latest trail in the area, but through the years, trails meant many things, ranging from the footpaths of prehistoric inhabitants to historical trade routes, and from cattle trails to railroads. Although early Casa Grande was not yet a city, or even a final destination, the area was well traversed through the centuries.

Before man inhabited the Casa Grande Valley, it was covered with water and then with a grassland environment that provided forage for a variety of large fauna—among them bison, wolf, giant sloth, mammoth, and camelops. Thus, animal paths were the first trails created in the Casa Grande Valley.

About 9500 BC, Paleo-Indians wandered into this desert grassland, sustaining themselves by hunting the big game that flourished here. Eventually, the Hohokam (an Akimel O'Odham word meaning "those who have gone" or "all used up") moved into the region. The Hohokam or Huhugam were sedentary farmers who lived in the Sonoran Desert from about 300 BC to roughly 1450 AD. Their territory extended from Mexico to Prescott and from Yuma to Apache Junction. These desert dwellers created a complex society whose most amazing accomplishment was their hand-dug irrigation canal system. This system was one of the first man-made "trails" in the area. To date, more than 1,000 miles of their canals have been found. Many of today's canals follow the same system that the Hohokam created all those centuries ago.

The Pima Indians, descendants of the Hohokam, traveled to the Gulf of California primarily to gather salt, and in the process, they collected seashells that they made into jewelry. These early traders followed a path that ran between Table Top in the Maricopa Mountains and the western portion of what would eventually be Casa Grande.

Early historical trails to and through Casa Grande were largely north-south trade routes from Mexico and places farther south. Turquoise, obsidian, pottery, and exotic bird feathers were common exchange items along the trails. Even a liquor trail has been identified coming through Casa Grande and on to Maricopa Wells.

The 1500s through the 1700s saw the arrival and passage of explorers such as Fray Marcos de Niza, Fr. Eusebio Kino, Fray Francisco Garces, and Juan Bautista de Anza. They were followed by fur trappers and traders in the 1800s. These mountain men established the first routes that ran east to west as they plied their trade between the mountains of New Mexico and the Pacific Coast. They are thought to be the first Anglo Americans to arrive in Arizona territory.

In the early 1800s, several military outposts were established to protect settlers from marauding Indians. The presence of these posts precipitated the need for consistent communication services, thus, the military telegraph system was built. The telegraph system connected military posts in southern New Mexico through Casa Grande and as far north as Prescott and Camp Verde before continuing west to San Diego. This was another type of trail that was instrumental in the establishment of new cities in the Wild West.

By the 1830s, several small mines were being developed in the area. Supply and ore wagons pulled by horses or mules traveled old Indian trails and established trails of their own as they transported material throughout the region.

By the mid-1800s, stagecoach lines, several of which followed old Indian trails, linked cities in the East with the West Coast. Many of the lines ran through or near Casa Grande. The Butterfield Overland Mail run, which began semiweekly mail and transport service between Missouri and California, passed through the Casa Grande Valley. Eventually, the stage coach business was relegated to short lines that connected settlements to each other.

In 1846, a war with Mexico began. The Mexican-American War provided an opportunity for the Corps of Topographical Engineers to map the Gila Trail, which in future years became a major route for gold seekers as they made their way to California.

After the war with Mexico ended (1848) and the Gadsden Purchase was completed (1854), American explorers and surveyors traversed the region. One of their more important undertakings was a survey to determine a southern railroad route from California to the East. Following the completion of two major east-west oriented transcontinental railroads, there remained a need for additional rails. This was especially true for mining companies and their suppliers, who had to travel great distances using horse- or mule-drawn wagons to haul supplies and ore.

Following the creation of the Arizona Territory in 1863, settlers began to establish homes in the area. The first modern irrigation canal in the Casa Grande Valley was constructed in 1864, and as irrigation increased, so too did the amount of land devoted to farming.

In 1879, the largest trail through the region was created as the Southern Pacific Railroad line from Yuma to points east halted construction in the middle of the desert. As a temporary stop, the place was called Terminus just like other temporary stops had been. In 1880, this particular stop was named Casa Grande after the prehistoric Hohokam Indian ruins located about 20 miles away. Once the railroad was established, horse- and mule-drawn wagons largely gave way to the expediency of trains. A few stage lines remained active as short runs, bringing customers to newly constructed depots.

The railroad hastened the growth of the town as it became a major supply point for the mines. The railroad transported mining supplies and equipment into the city, and ore from the mines was sent elsewhere for processing. In addition, as more wells were dug and farming increased in importance, Casa Grande was becoming known as a farming community. Farm equipment was brought to the city, and excess food was shipped out via the railroad.

World Wars I and II played a large role in the development of the region, especially as cotton became an important crop. The military listed about 11,000 uses for cotton products. Because food was also needed by the military, the farming community around Casa Grande expanded and grew more crops to support that need.

Livestock became a major growth industry after World War II, with more than 35 feed lots in Pinal County. Cotton growing and processing continued to be of prime importance. With the increase in farming and the growing demand for water, the issue of water accessibility became of concern. In 1916, the US Congress passed a law providing for the creation of the Florence-Casa Grande Irrigation Project. Unfortunately, water rights and availability continue to be an issue to this day.

As the population increased, new businesses opened to provide a variety of products and services common to every growing community. Today, Casa Grande is a city of more than 45,000 people from all over the country. The town is studded with historical and new residential areas, schools, churches, malls, stores, restaurants, libraries, and entertainment and sports venues. A large influx of winter visitors contributes to the local economy. Because of cultural diversity and new business demands, the city continues to grow, although it still retains the best qualities of a small town.

One

Passing Through

Trails to, from, and through the Casa Grande Valley were created and expanded by megafauna, prehistoric Indians, explorers, traders, settlers, and entrepreneurs. Among the early inhabitants of the region were the Hohokam Indians, who farmed the area by building an extensive canal system. A little is known about their culture from the petroglyphs they left behind. Animals, human forms, and geometric designs tell tales that remain unverifiable mysteries. Salt, shells, liquor, exotic bird feathers, and semiprecious minerals came through or near Casa Grande from Guadalajara, Mexico, and beyond along what Dr. Henry Dobyns called the Western Turquoise Trail.

The first non-Indian thought to have made an appearance in the area was a black slave named Estaban, who was a member of Nunez de Vaca's 1536 expedition. In 1539, Franciscan friar Marcos de Niza was believed to be the first white man to visit the region. In 1774–1775, Fray Francisco Garces traveled with Juan Bautista de Anza as he sought a route to the Pacific Ocean. Fr. Eusebio Kino, a Jesuit priest from Italy, would prove to have the longest-lasting impact on the area.

Soon, mountain men were creating new trails through the territory as they trapped for fur along the then-flowing rivers. As more settlers traveled west, the military established forts and camps to provide protection. For those brave new settlers, getting here was not half the fun. But come they did, on horseback, by wagon, and in uncomfortable stagecoaches. The West was on its way to becoming settled.

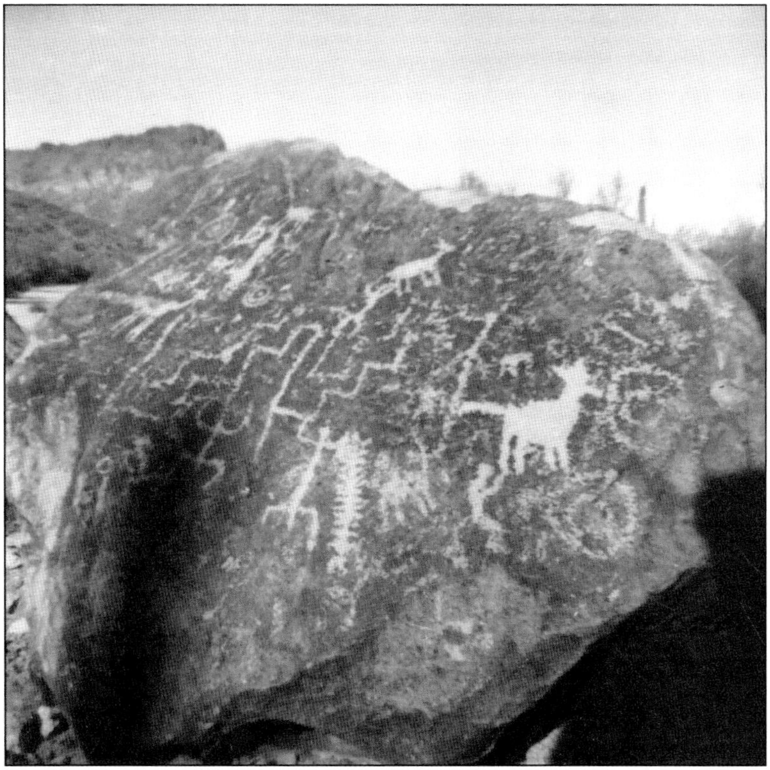

Patina, or desert varnish, which formed on rock faces over time, was carved, pecked, and abraded away to create a variety of designs. This panel contains many of the elements used by the prehistoric Hohokam Indians. Easily discernible are geometric patterns, animals in the form of coyotes and centipedes, and human forms as seen in the stick figures, as well as what may be a hump-backed flute player.

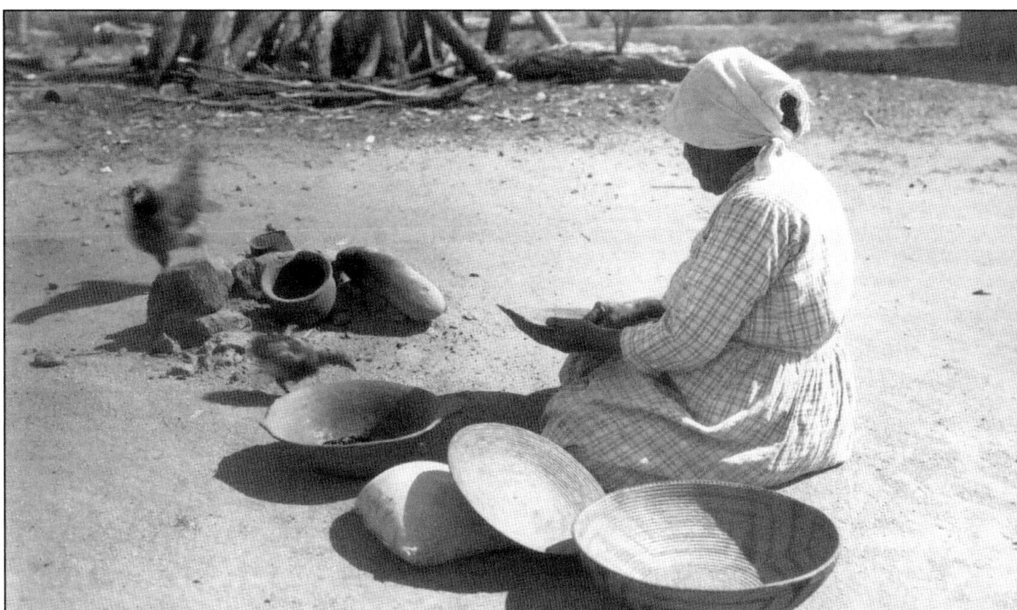

A Pima woman in Blackwater, Arizona, is seated by baskets woven from grasses and reeds gathered from the fields. Following traditions established by their Hohokam ancestors, Pima and Papago basket weavers incorporate patterns seen on rock art left generations earlier as they maintain ties to their heritage. In one of the baskets, this woman is preparing pinole, ground corn often made into mush.

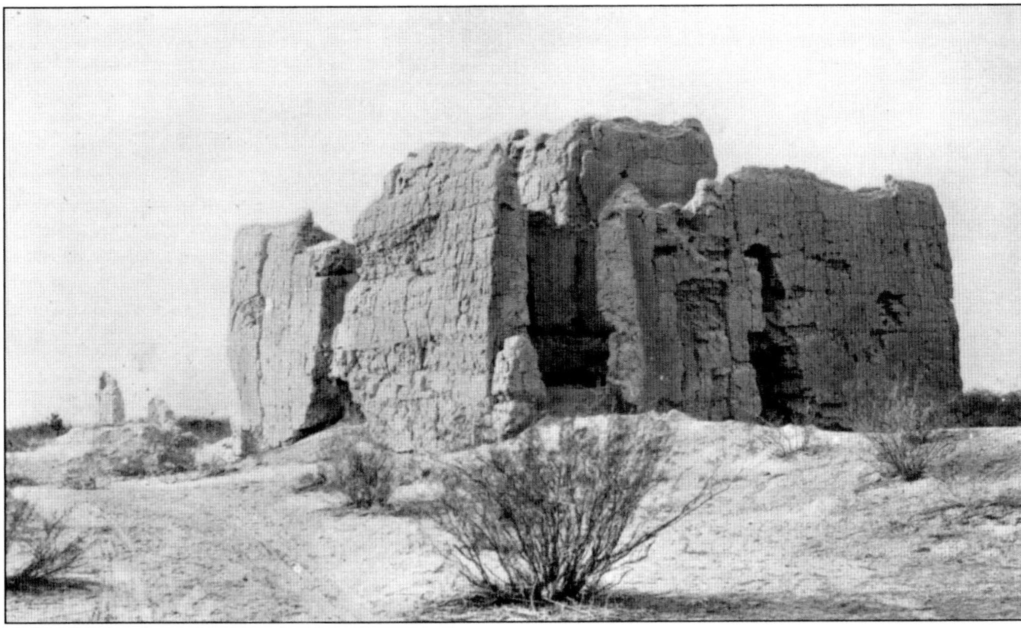

Casa Grande, or Big House, was built and abandoned by the Hohokam Indians, who had created a community comprised of a four-story great house, at least one ball court, plazas, and various structures surrounded by irrigated fields. In 1890, when this picture was taken, the great house had fallen into disrepair, although it probably looks much as it did when first seen by Fr. Eusebio Kino in 1687.

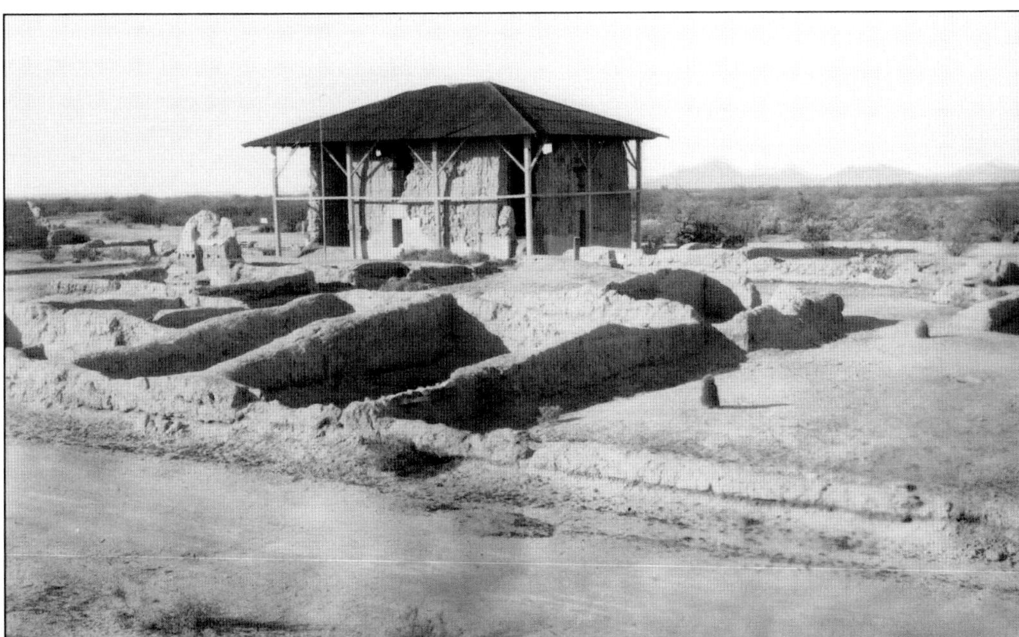

Casa Grande is one of the largest prehistoric structures ever built in the United States. It became the first archaeological site to be preserved when Pres. Benjamin Harrison established a one-square-mile protective reserve around the ruins in 1892. Pres. Woodrow Wilson proclaimed Casa Grande Ruins the nation's first national monument in 1918.

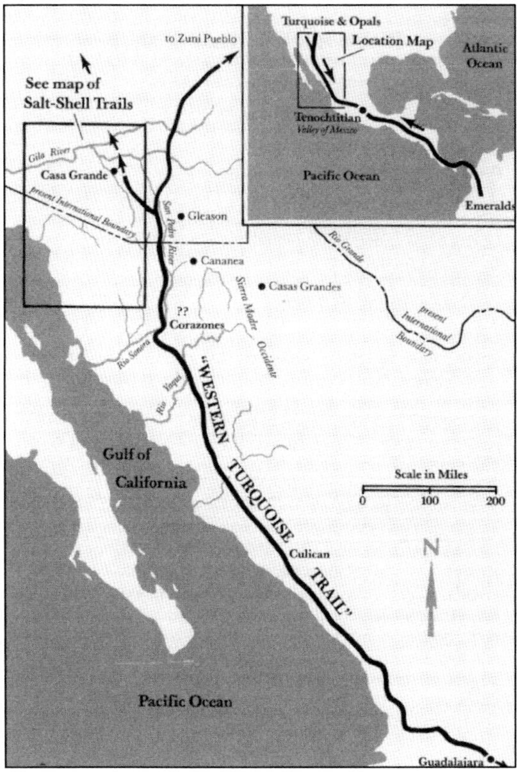

Salt was an important ingredient in the diet of the early inhabitants of the region, but acquiring it required a considerable walk to the Gulf of California. While there, the natives collected seashells to make bracelets, earrings, and other ornaments that are found in archaeological excavations to this day. Liquor (one can assume this was mescal or tequila) was also traded along the trails.

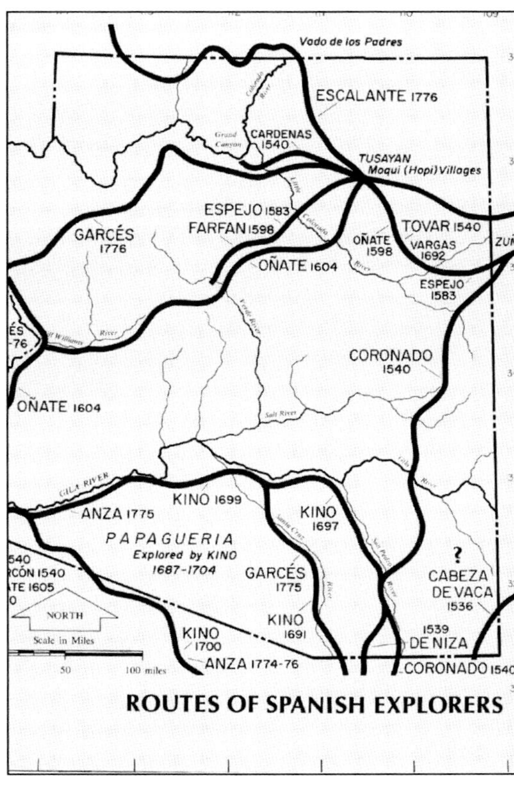

Early Spanish explorers were primarily interested in finding gold or silver for their king. Although the trails through Arizona were eventually oriented east-west, they generally began in Mexico. Most of the early visitors came and went quickly, but Fr. Eusebio Kino spent many years with the Pima and Papago Indians around Casa Grande. (Courtesy of Don Bufkin, *Historical Atlas of Arizona*, Second Edition, p. 13.)

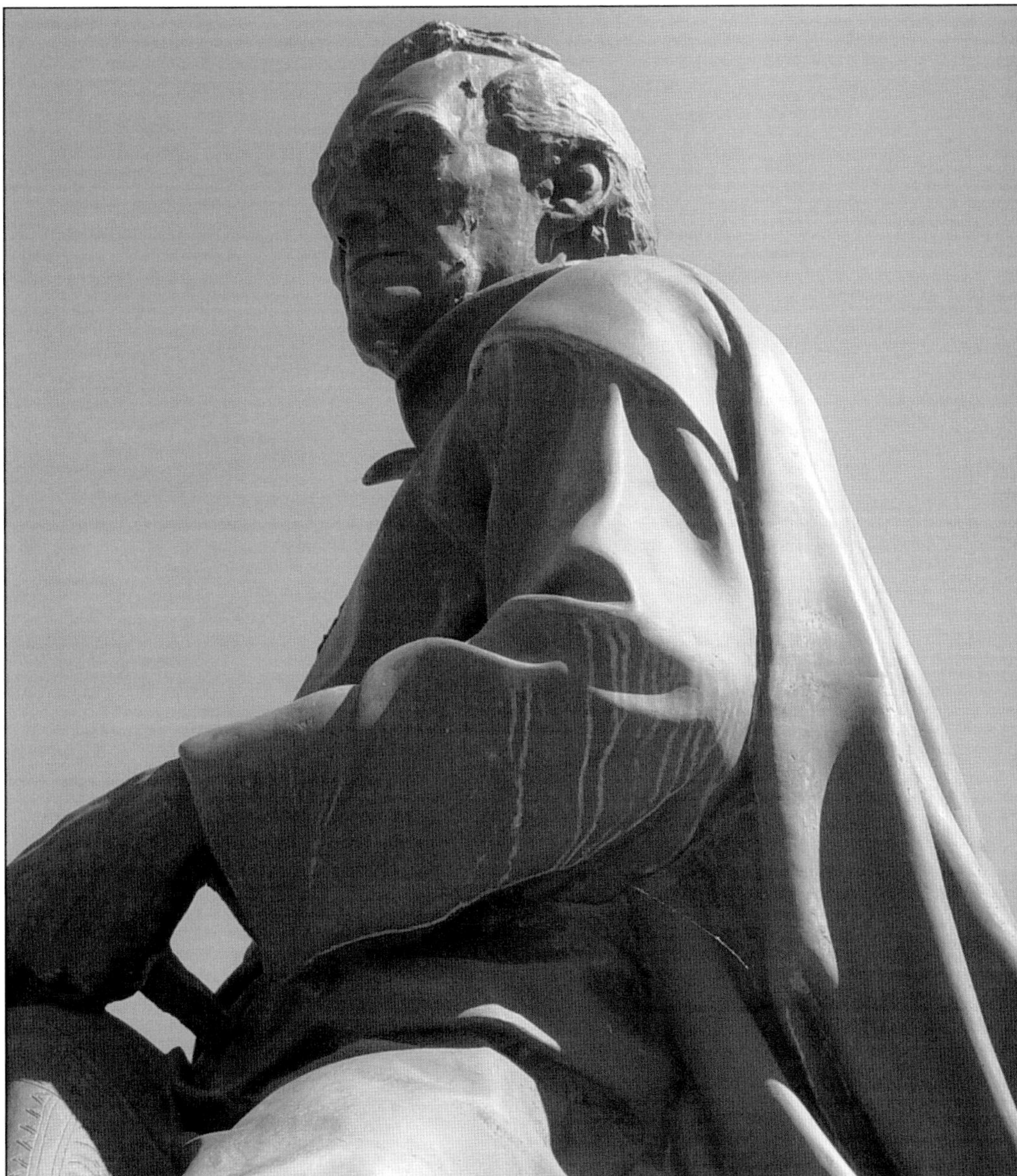

It is believed that Fr. Eusebio Kino, a Roman Catholic priest, made the first of his 40 explorations in 1691 in what was to become Arizona. Father Kino was an explorer, astronomer, mathematician, author, cartographer, and humanitarian. Arguably, his most important impact on the Casa Grande area was the introduction of cattle, horses, mules, and sheep to the native population. His original herd of 20 cattle grew to 70,000 during his time in northern Mexico and the deserts of southern Arizona. He also taught the Indians new techniques related to agriculture. Father Kino established 24 missions throughout southern Arizona and began to convert the locals to Catholicism. Although his role as a missionary priest was to convert the various indigenous tribes with whom he came into contact, he often disregarded the laws of Spain and the church leadership to oppose forced labor of the Indians in the silver mines. He was the first white person to write about Casa Grande Ruins, and in 1694, he performed mass there. His statue can be seen across from the Arizona state capitol in Phoenix.

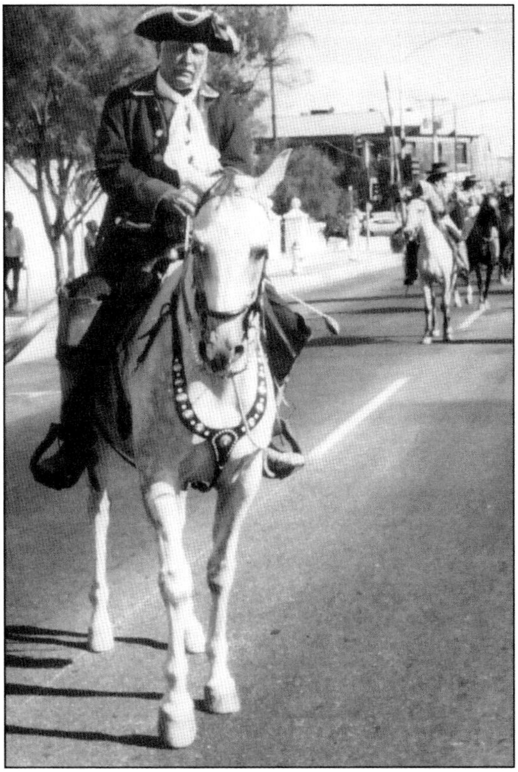

A De Anza bicentennial reenactment was held at Casa Grande Ruins in 1975 to honor explorer Juan Bautista de Anza. In the photograph on the left, De Anza is portrayed by Don Yijinio Aguirre, a local rancher whose family arrived in northern New Spain in the late 17th century. Born in Mexico of Basque descent in 1736, Juan Bautista de Anza was the first person to establish an overland route from Mexico through the Sonoran Desert to the Pacific Coast. In 1775, as his troops camped just southeast of the junction of the Santa Cruz and Gila Rivers, he visited Casa Grande Ruins. Interstate 10 closely follows the De Anza trail from Tucson, although the original trail slightly bypassed Casa Grande as it continued to Sacaton before turning sharply west to Yuma. This statue (below) honoring De Anza is located in San Francisco, California.

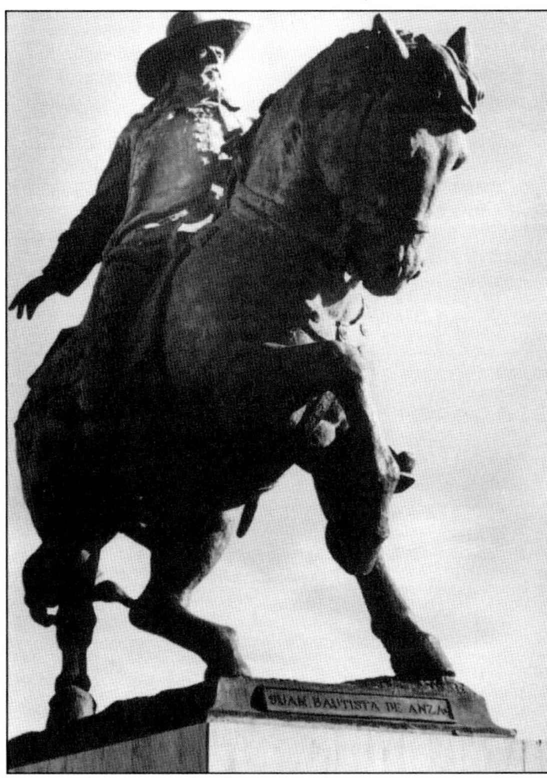

Following the era of Spanish exploration, the first Anglo penetration into the area was by the mountain men led by James Pattie. He trapped a section of the Gila River in 1825. In 1826, Ewing Young trapped the Salt and Gila Rivers all the way to the Colorado River. By 1846, the Gila Trail was a well-known east-west route across what would become the state of Arizona. The mountain men passed their knowledge about the territory on to subsequent surveyors and engineers. (Courtesy Don Bufkin, *Historical Atlas of Arizona*, second edition, p. 17.)

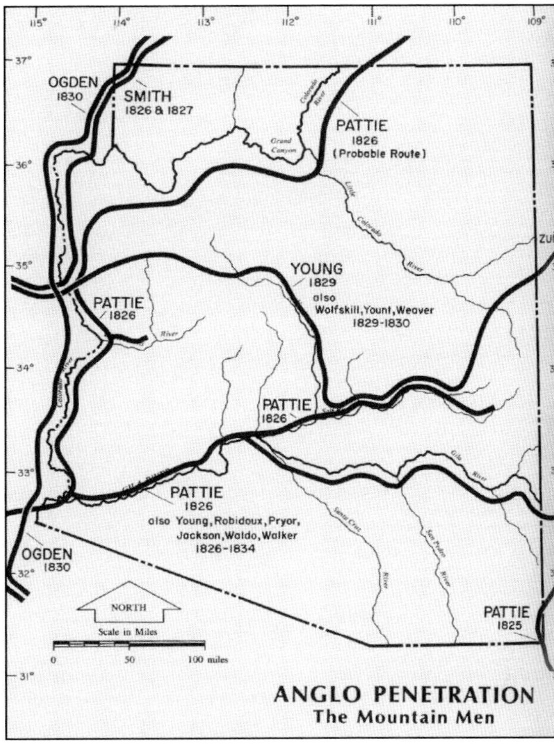

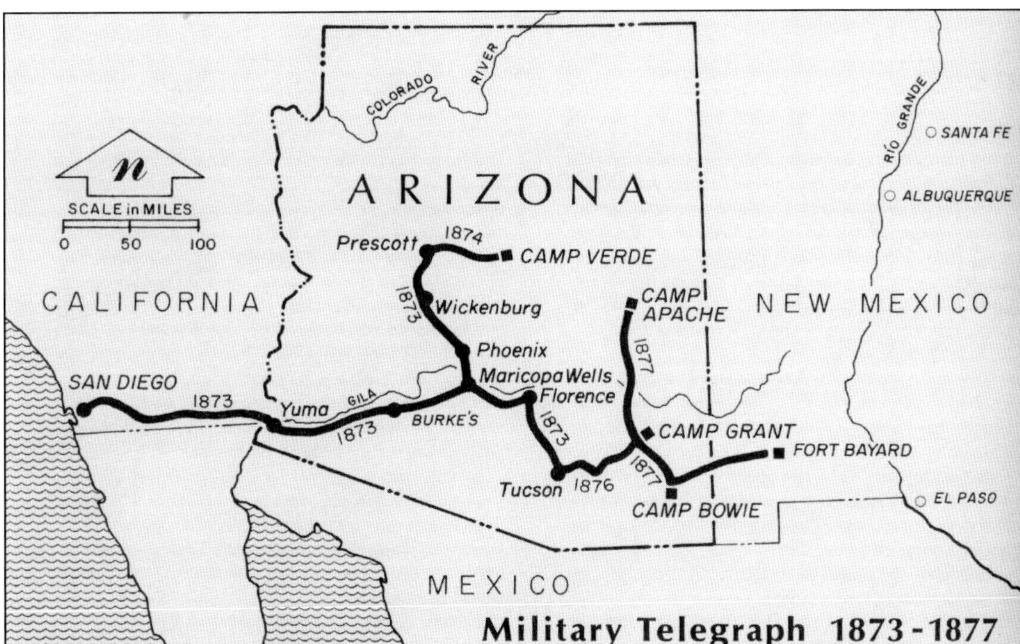

Military outposts were established to protect the few intrepid settlers in the region. This created the need for another kind of trail, a telegraph system across the territory that would enable soldiers at the scattered posts to respond more quickly to trouble spots. In 1873, Congress approved $120,000 to build a line from Los Angeles to Yuma, Prescott, and Tucson. (Courtesy Don Bufkin, *Historical Atlas of Arizona*, second edition, p. 27A.)

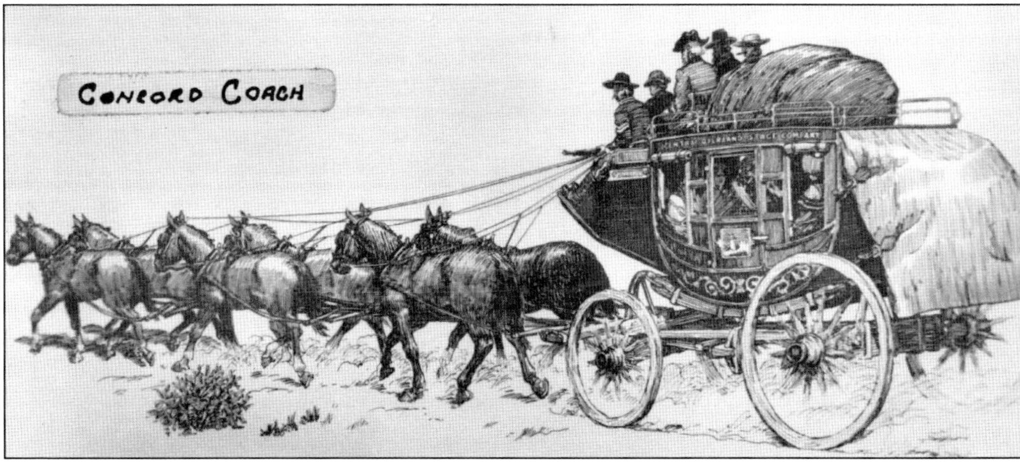

Once the idea of settling the West took hold, transporting travelers from the East became big business. Other than horseback or wagon, the most common mode of travel was by stagecoach. The Concord Coach (above), built in Concord, New Hampshire, weighed one ton and cost $1,050 in 1827. These coaches were the backbone of the Butterfield and then the Butterfield Overland Mail routes that traversed southern Arizona. The Butterfield Stage passed through southern Arizona every Sunday and Wednesday from 1858 to 1861, carrying mail and passengers from Texas to California. The old Butterfield Stage Road was later used by the Confederate and Union armies. A few trail remnants can still be seen locally. In addition to traditional stagecoaches, four-to-twelve-passenger celerity wagons (below)—also known as mud wagons, passenger wagons, and mail wagons—were used for short hauls, branch routes, or mountainous roads.

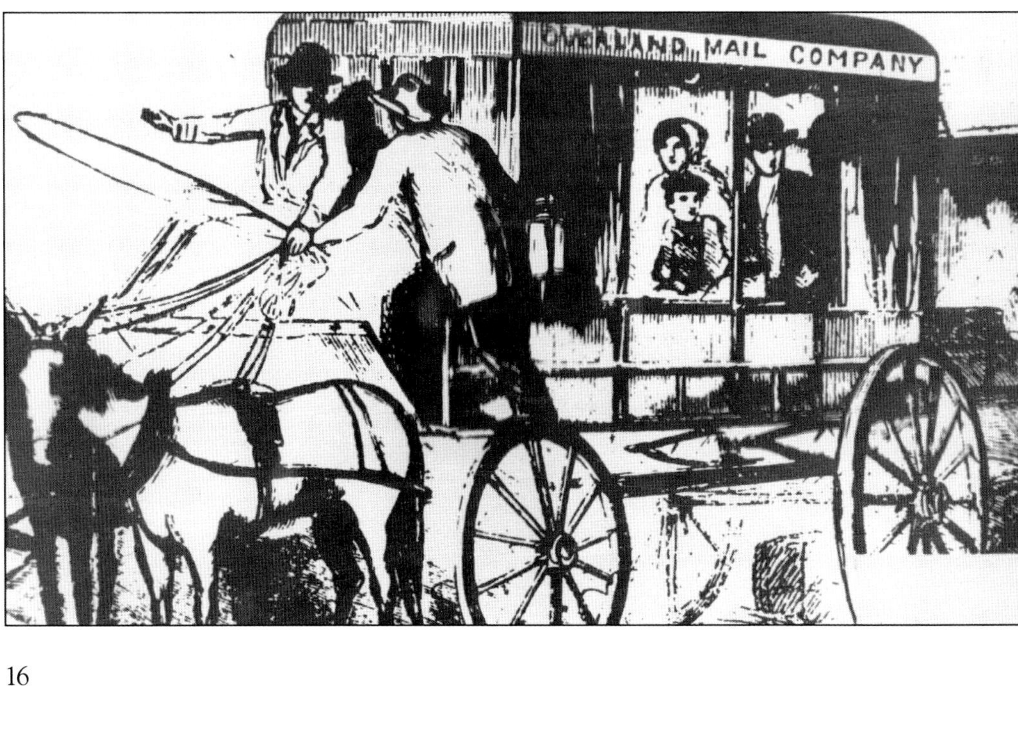

Two

What Hath This Railroad Wrought?

In 1877, the Arid Land Grant Act was passed, encouraging farmers to try their hand at sustaining crops and creating a life in the desert. Most arrived by horseback or mule- or ox-drawn wagons. Many of them came with nothing more than a dream of owning land. Little did they know that by 1879 this small spot in the desert would be on its way to becoming a town. In 1879, the Southern Pacific Railroad was building a new trail across the southern United States. Proceeding east through the vast desert from Yuma in the summer of 1879, railroad construction came to a halt because the mainly Chinese workers said the rails were too hot to handle. The spot where they stopped was called Terminus, as were dozens of other temporary stops along the railroad route.

From all reports, five men were in Terminus when construction ceased. By the time construction resumed in January 1880, the town had 33 people. Later in the year, executives of the Southern Pacific Railroad decided to call the stop Casa Grande after the Indian ruins located about 20 miles east. On September 10, 1880, Casa Grande acquired a new post office and a postmaster. And 1880 was also the year that Rutherford B. Hayes, the 19th president of the United States, stopped briefly in Casa Grande as he traveled by train from California.

The railroad played a prominent role in the growth of Casa Grande. When the first official town map was recorded in 1890, the original townsite consisted of 40 blocks, with streets running parallel to the railroad tracks. While several mines were already operating nearby, the arrival of the railroad enabled them to proliferate and expand. Because of the railroad, the town grew as a supply point for the mines, but it also soon became a shipping and shopping center for the growing population and the farms that had sprung up around the town.

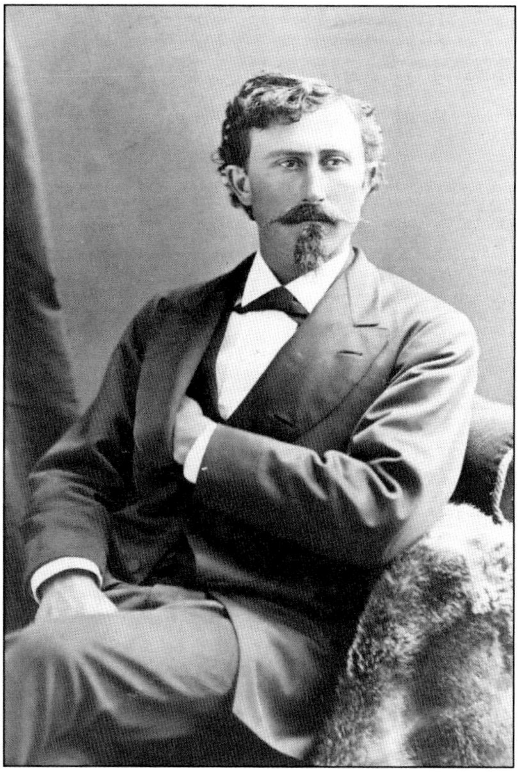

One of the first five inhabitants of Terminus, soon to become Casa Grande, was a dapper, flirtatious gentleman known as Jeremiah "Jere" Fryer. Hotel owner, postmaster, and sheriff, Fryer was perhaps better known as the husband of Pauline Cushman, who had been a spy for the Union army during the Civil War. Cushman was captured and sentenced to death before being rescued by Union forces. For the next 10 years, she capitalized on her fame in a series of speaking engagements across the country, eventually marrying Fryer and moving to Casa Grande. Together, they operated the Fryer Hotel until she left town in 1890. Cushman died of a morphine overdose in San Francisco in 1893. Debate continues as to whether her death was an accident or suicide. (Below, courtesy Bill Hogan.)

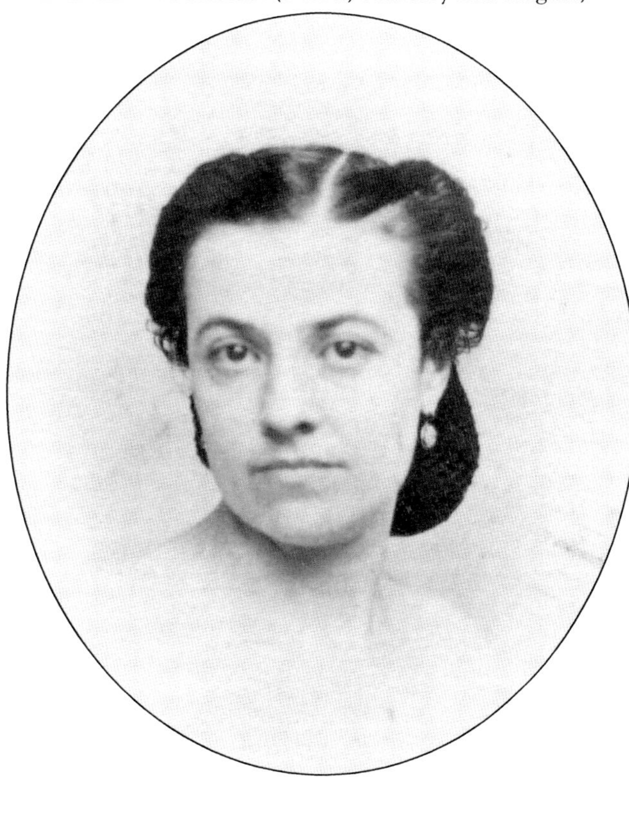

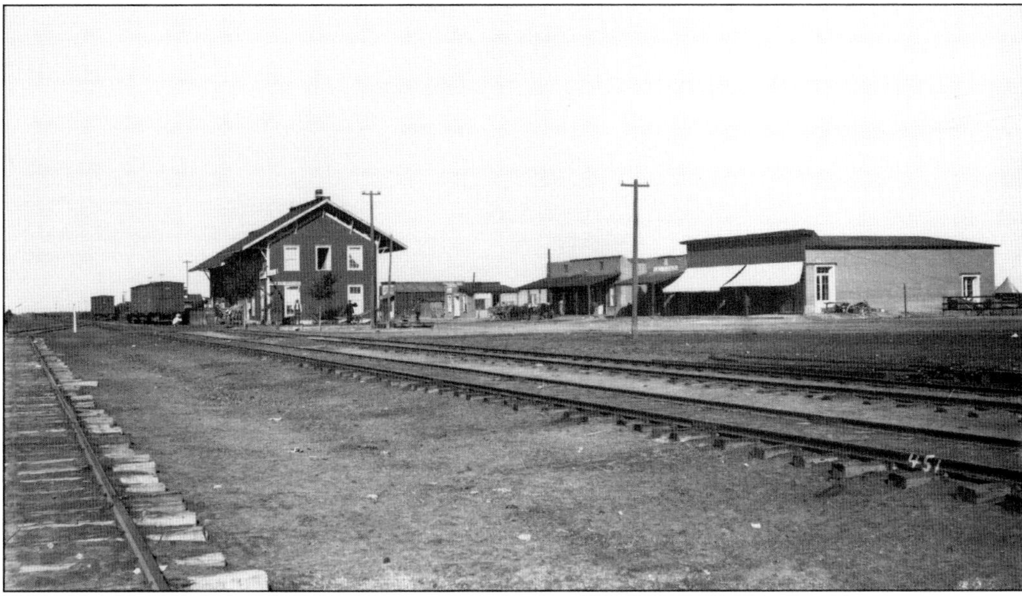

By 1886, when this photograph was taken, a business district was growing up on the north side of Main Street across from the Southern Pacific railroad depot. The depot originally had been the Yuma station, but when the railroad continued east, the old Yuma station was dismantled, transported to Terminus (Casa Grande), and reconstructed.

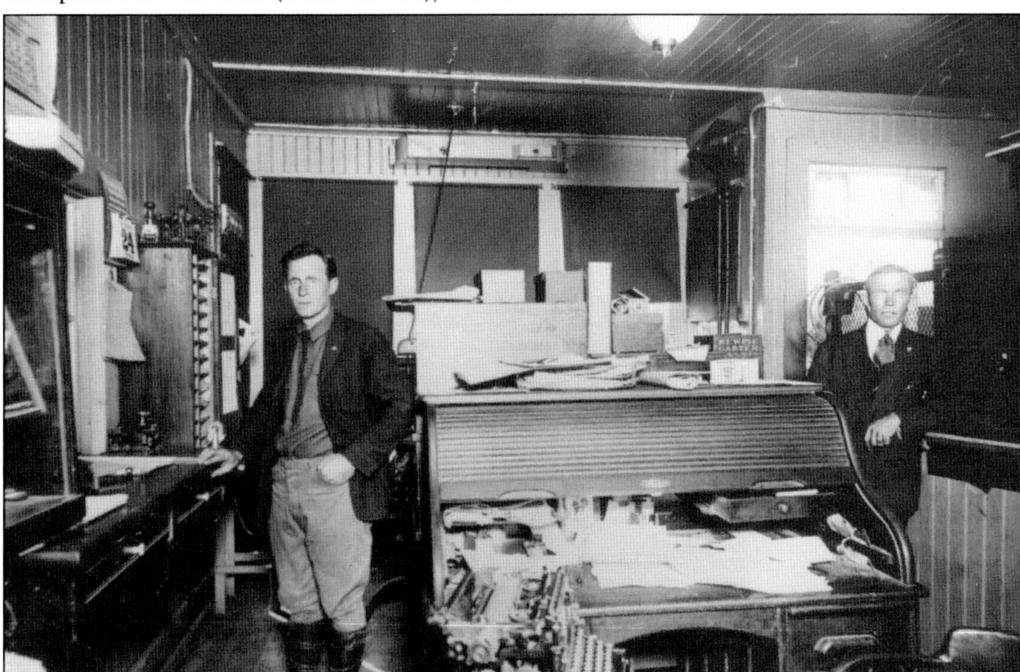

This is the interior of the first Southern Pacific railroad office in Casa Grande as it looked in 1909. Arthur Elliot is on the right and Paul Hobby is on the left. Elliot, who was born August 28, 1883, is often cited as the first Anglo born in Casa Grande. He followed in his father's footsteps and became a telegrapher for the Southern Pacific Railroad before becoming the Casa Grande station manager.

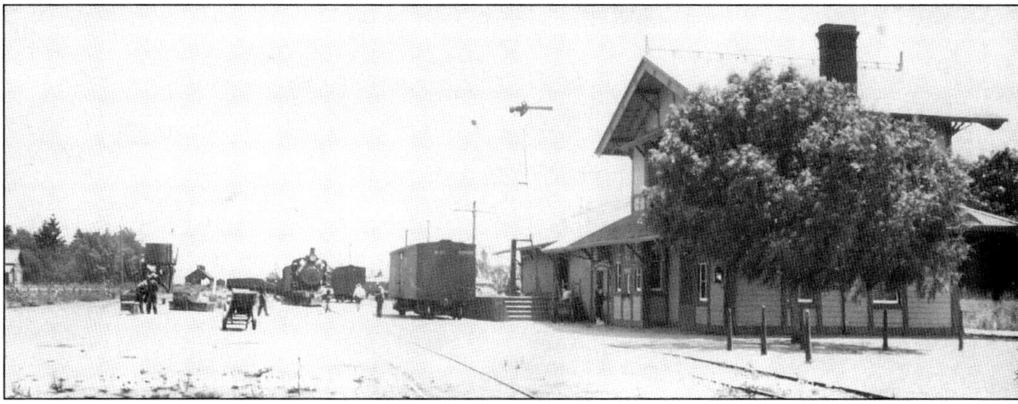

By 1908, the Southern Pacific railroad depot, which housed the family of the stationmaster, had acquired a second-floor balcony. The train station was one of the more substantial structures in town. Often, men and boys gathered hoping to get work unloading the freight being delivered for the mines and farmers in the area. Others gathered to meet family and friends who would be arriving on the next train. It also served as a good meeting place for the folks who had nothing more urgent to do than wait for the big noisy steam locomotives to roll into town. The newfangled truck in the photograph below was probably one of the few in town in 1913, the year this picture was taken.

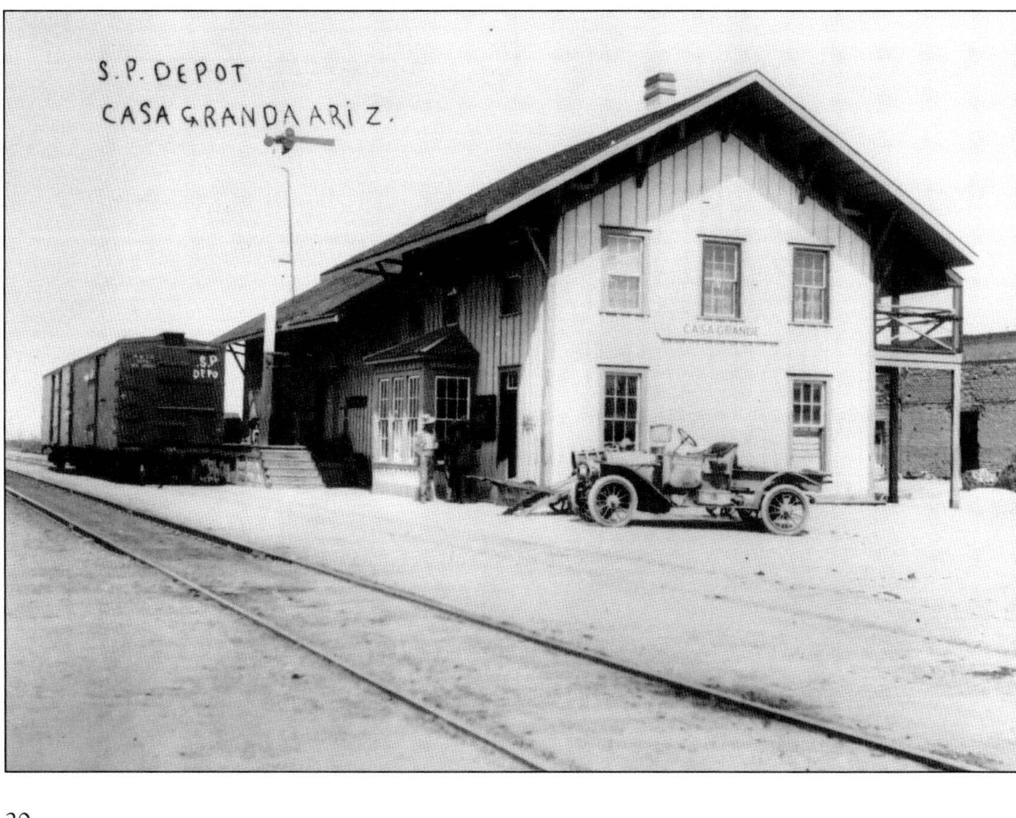

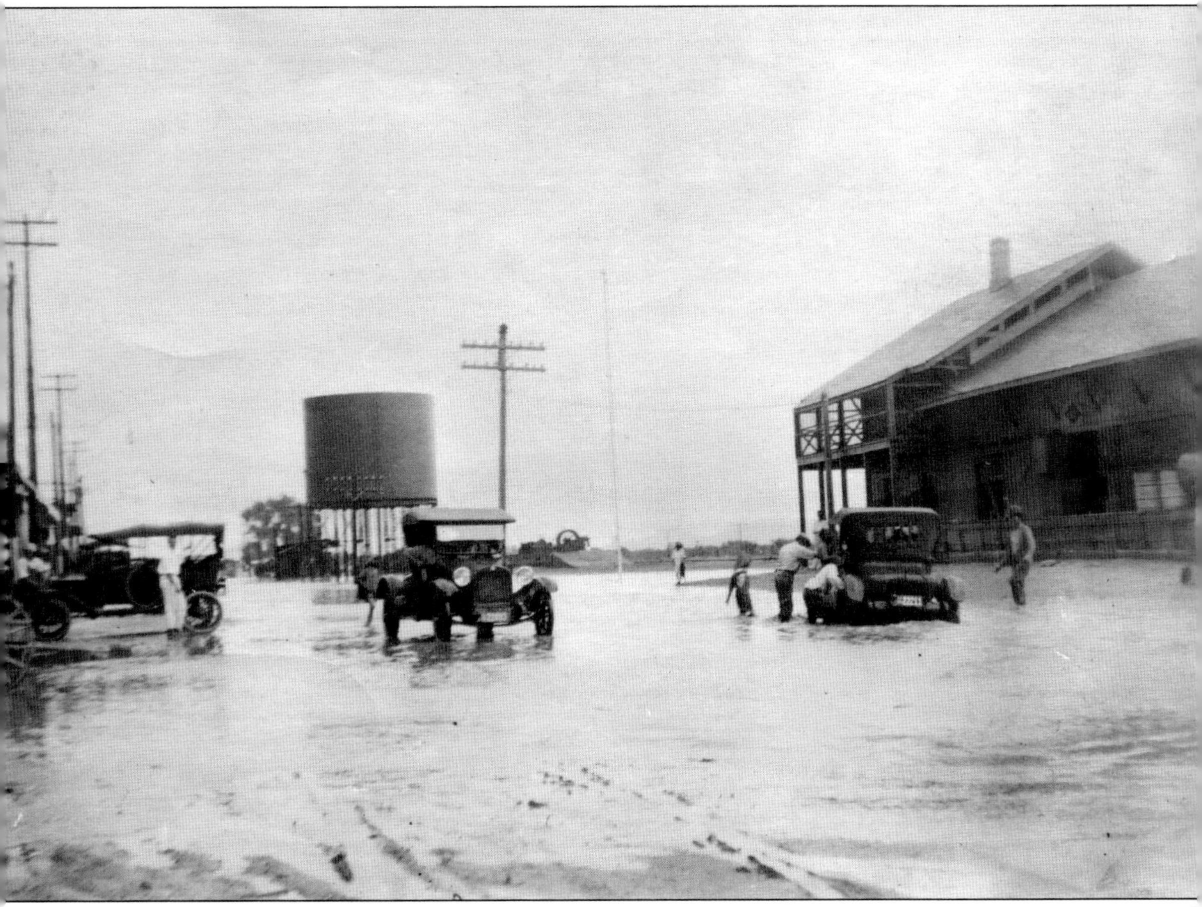

In 1917, local residents awoke to a rare occurrence in Arizona: water, water everywhere, even on Main Street in Casa Grande. This photograph depicts an image rarely seen in a desert town. Excessive water is generally not an issue in desert towns; in fact, too much water is definitely an uncommon, unexpected, and unwelcome occurrence. The railroad depot and water tower are prominent features amidst the water that is the scarce lifeblood of the desert, except when it becomes too much and rare floods occur. A flooded Main Street no doubt claimed many automobiles on this day. Here, men are assisting one unlucky driver and his stranded Model-T Ford in front of the Southern Pacific Railroad depot. Heavy rain covered the railroad tracks and streets of the city, leaving ruts and stalled cars in its wake. Ironically, an irrigation control device can be seen in the background.

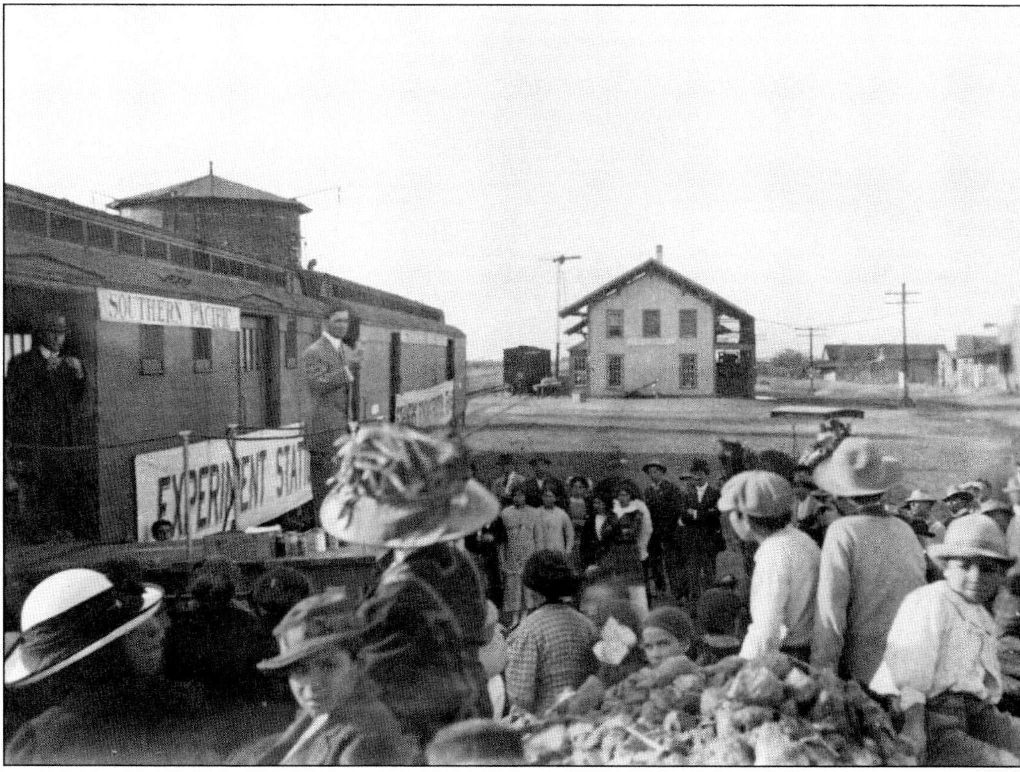

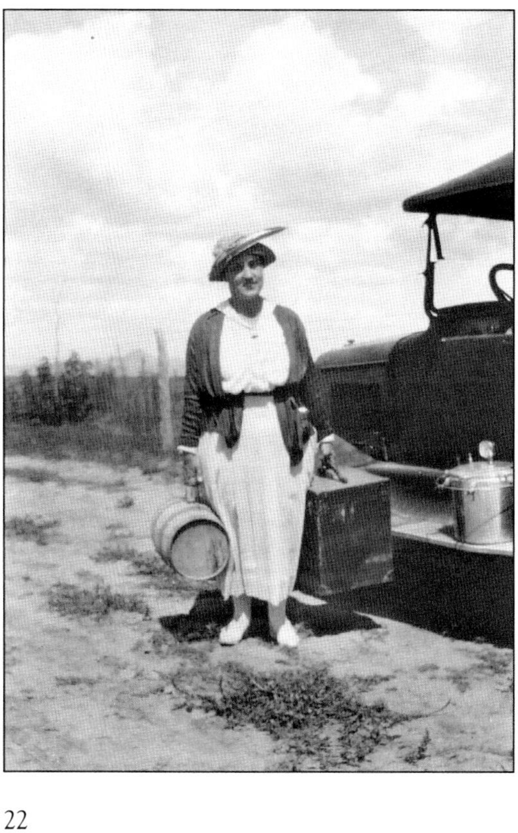

Agriculture and home demonstration agents often traveled by train to rural communities to teach new farming and homemaking techniques. Their arrival in the small towns scattered throughout Arizona in the early 1900s was generally considered a major event and usually drew a large, diverse, and festive crowd. Casa Grande was no exception, as seen in this photograph.

In 1917, Flossie Barmes was the first University of Arizona, traveling, home-demonstration agent in Arizona. Hauling all her own equipment, she often traveled by train to the rural communities of the state. She taught women how to can food, bathe children, make clothes, and pickle olives, among many other helpful hints to make life easier.

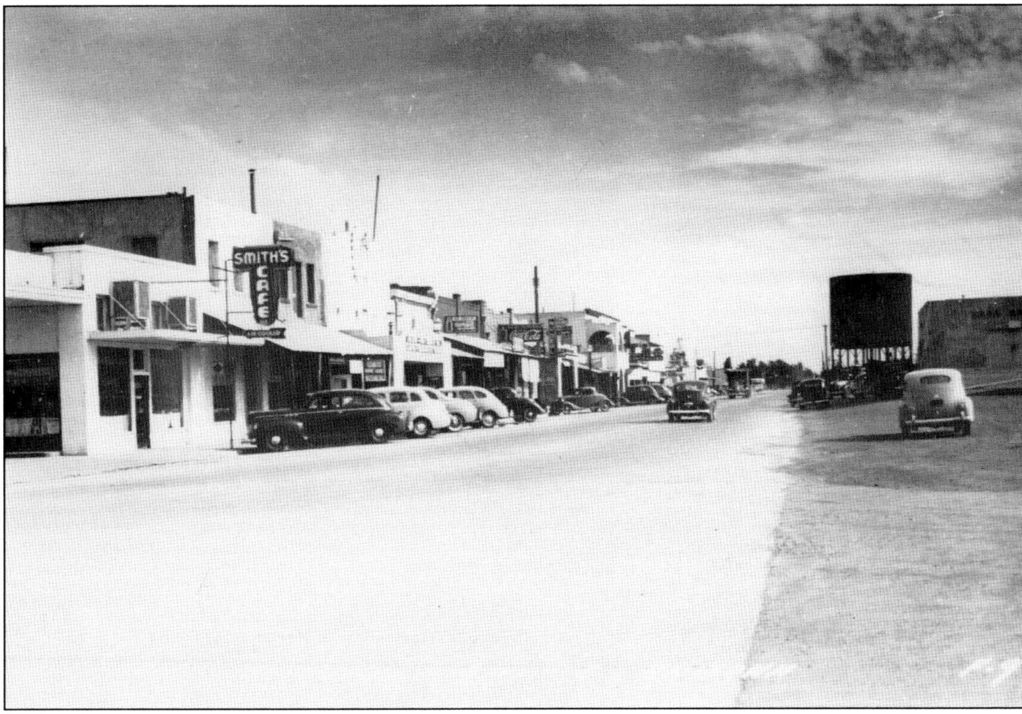

Looking east on Main Street around 1939, it is clear that Casa Grande had grown; however, this photograph is most interesting for what is not in the picture. Although the water tower remains, the Southern Pacific train depot is missing. It was destroyed in a fire in 1937 and had not yet been replaced.

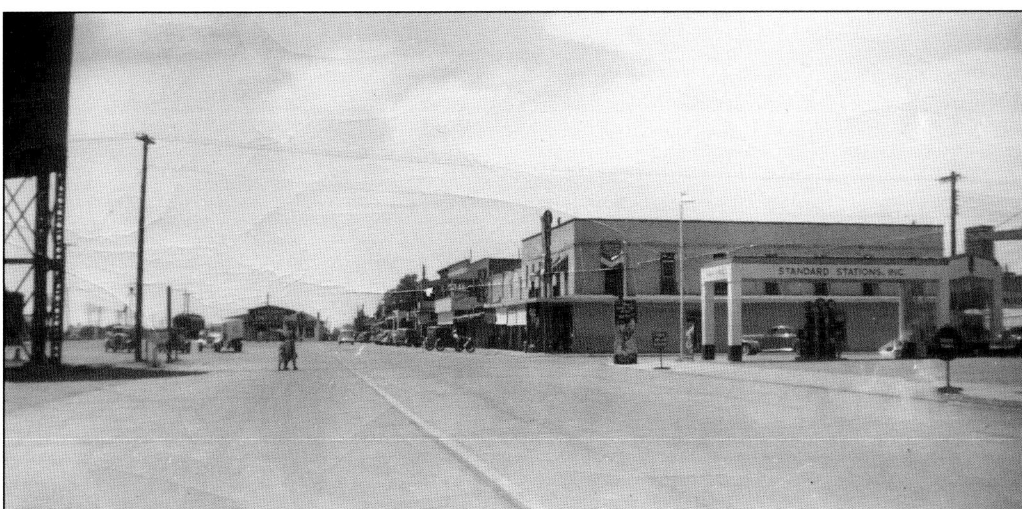

Looking west, the absence of the train depot is striking, but the addition of new businesses along Main Street provides evidence of a growing community. The Standard Oil service station on the right and a lumberyard at the far end of Main Street are just a couple of new enterprises joining the existing commercial endeavors located near the railroad.

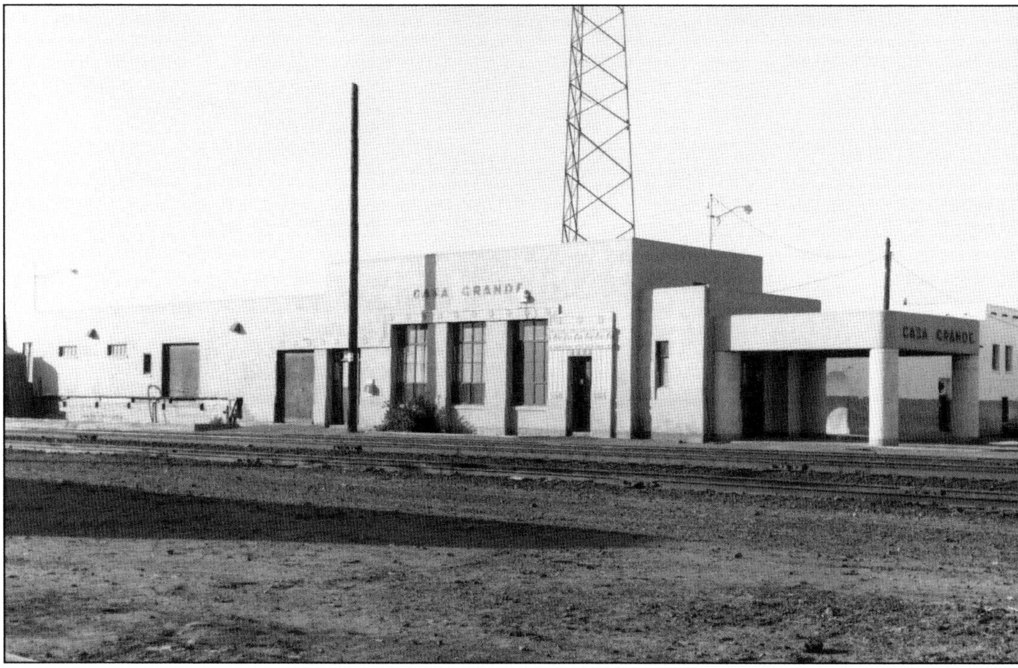

Built in 1939 and dedicated with great fanfare in 1940, the new Pueblo Deco–style Southern Pacific railroad depot became one of the best-known structures in Casa Grande. It burned beyond repair in 2009 and was razed. The town is currently without a train depot and is likely to remain so for the foreseeable future. In the c. 1950 photograph below, the interior of the new train depot displays the decorative elements of Pueblo Deco–style designs along the ceiling and around the counter. Pictured are J.B. Brown, Mr. Kilcrease, Art Elliot Sr. (back to the camera), Esta Bayless, A.S. "Pappy" Guinn, and on the right, Marie Guinn and Anne Don.

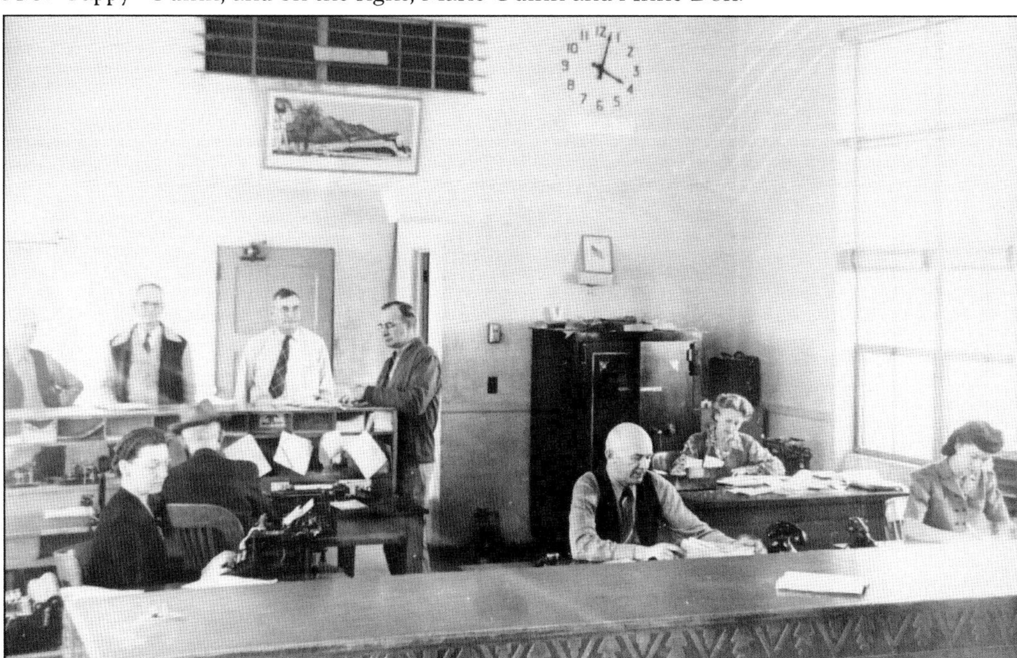

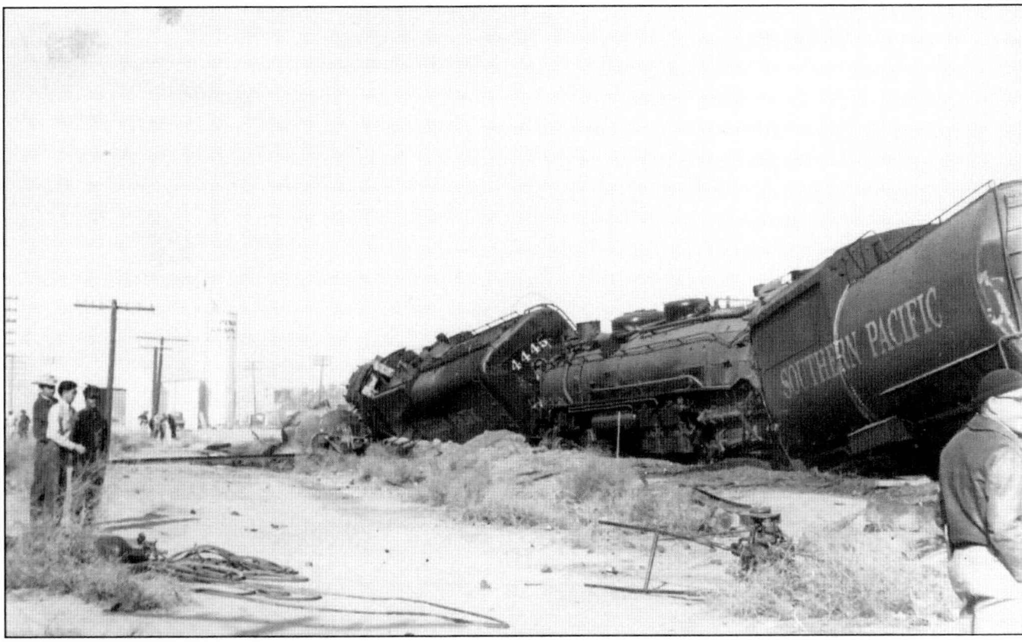

At 8:55 p.m. on December 19, 1953, a loud noise signaled the collision of three steam engines with a kerosene-loaded tanker car that had mistakenly been left on the main Southern Pacific track along Main Street. Fortunately, no one was seriously injured, and the $50,000 worth of damage was restricted to the railroad cars and rails. Massive equipment was brought to town, and additional railroad workers joined locals to remove the damaged railroad cars. Below, the badly damaged engine is being lifted back on to the track. Three days after the accident, full rail service was restored.

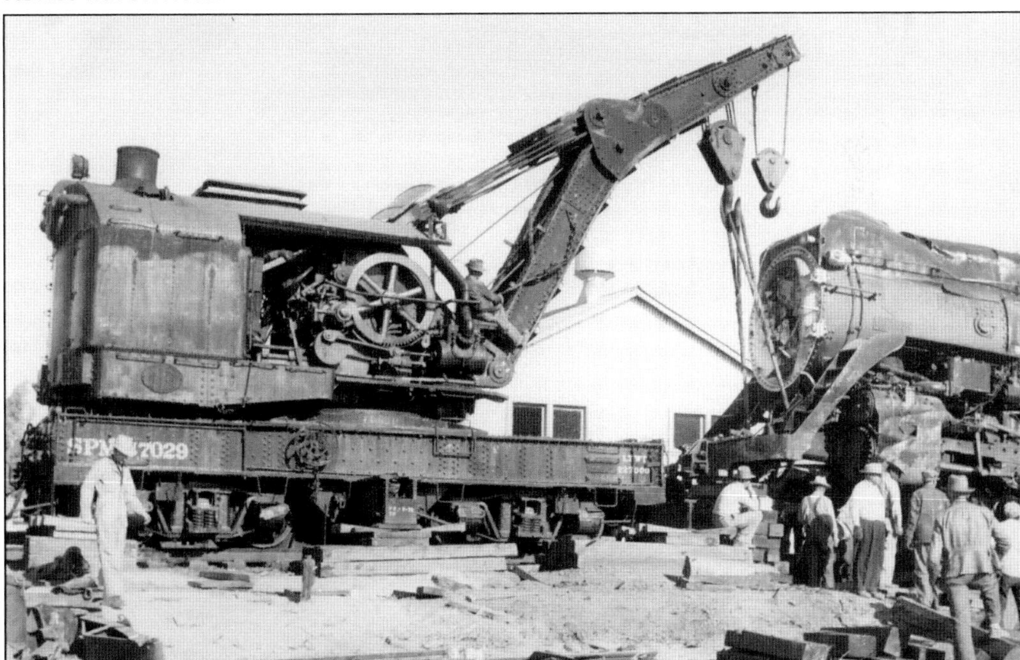

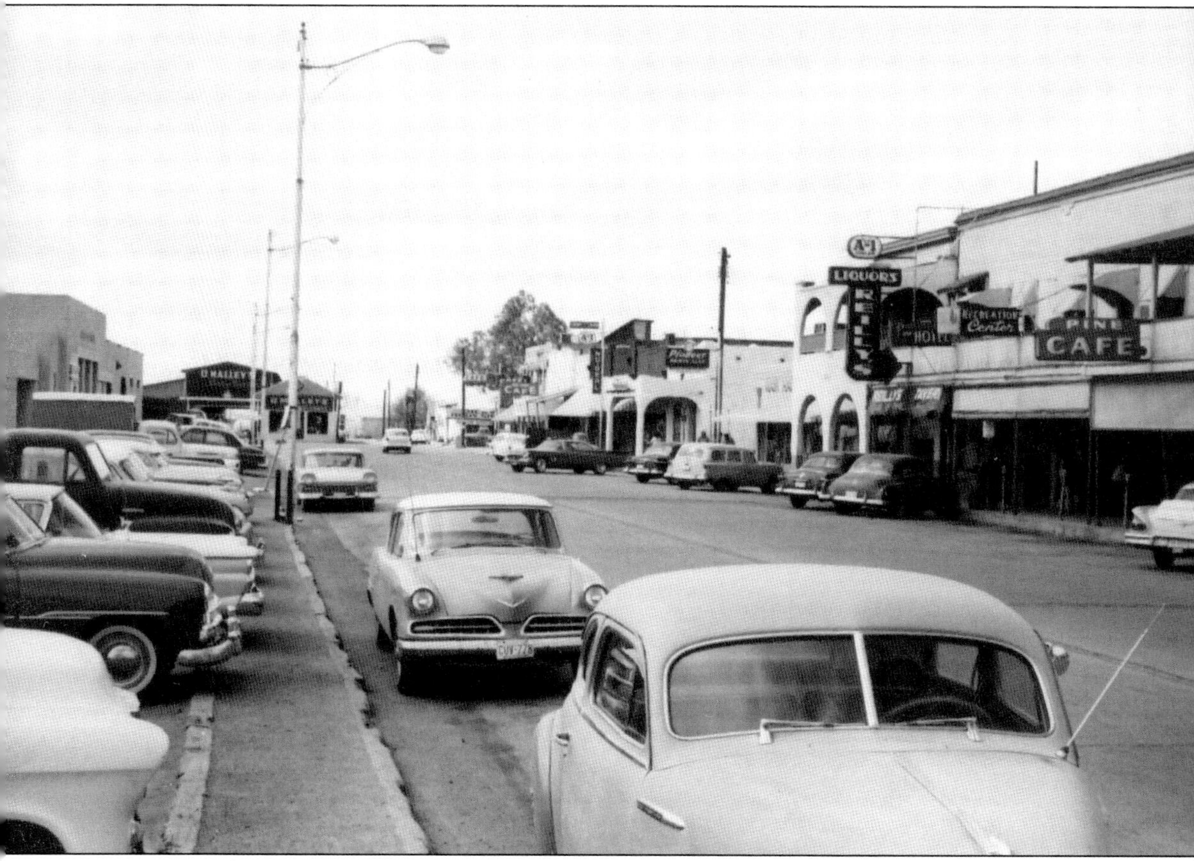

Ever since the railroad was constructed it has served as the most important trail to, through, and from Casa Grande. Early on, the centrally located train station hosted convenient passenger and freight service, both of which proved to be essential elements aiding the growth of Casa Grande. As seen here in the early 1960s, the Pueblo Deco–style railroad depot continued to be a motivating force for entrepreneurs to operate an ever-expanding variety of businesses along Main Street. Several blocks on either side of the Southern Pacific Railroad station contain hotels, cafés, bars, banks, drugstores, a lumberyard, and any number of other endeavors.

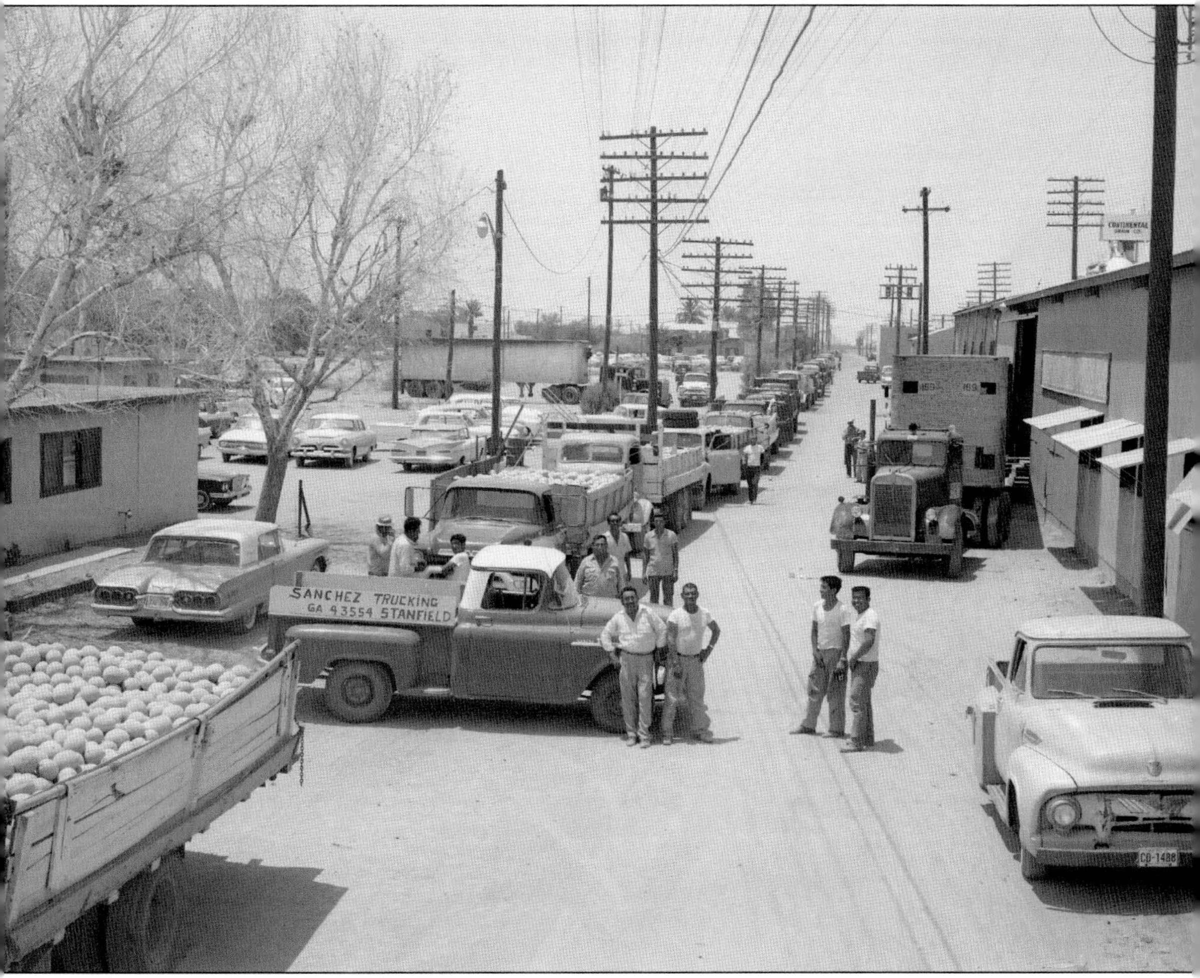

The opposite side of the railroad depot is equally busy. Here, area farmers gather at the melon and potato shipping sheds located along Main Avenue on the other side of the Southern Pacific railroad tracks.

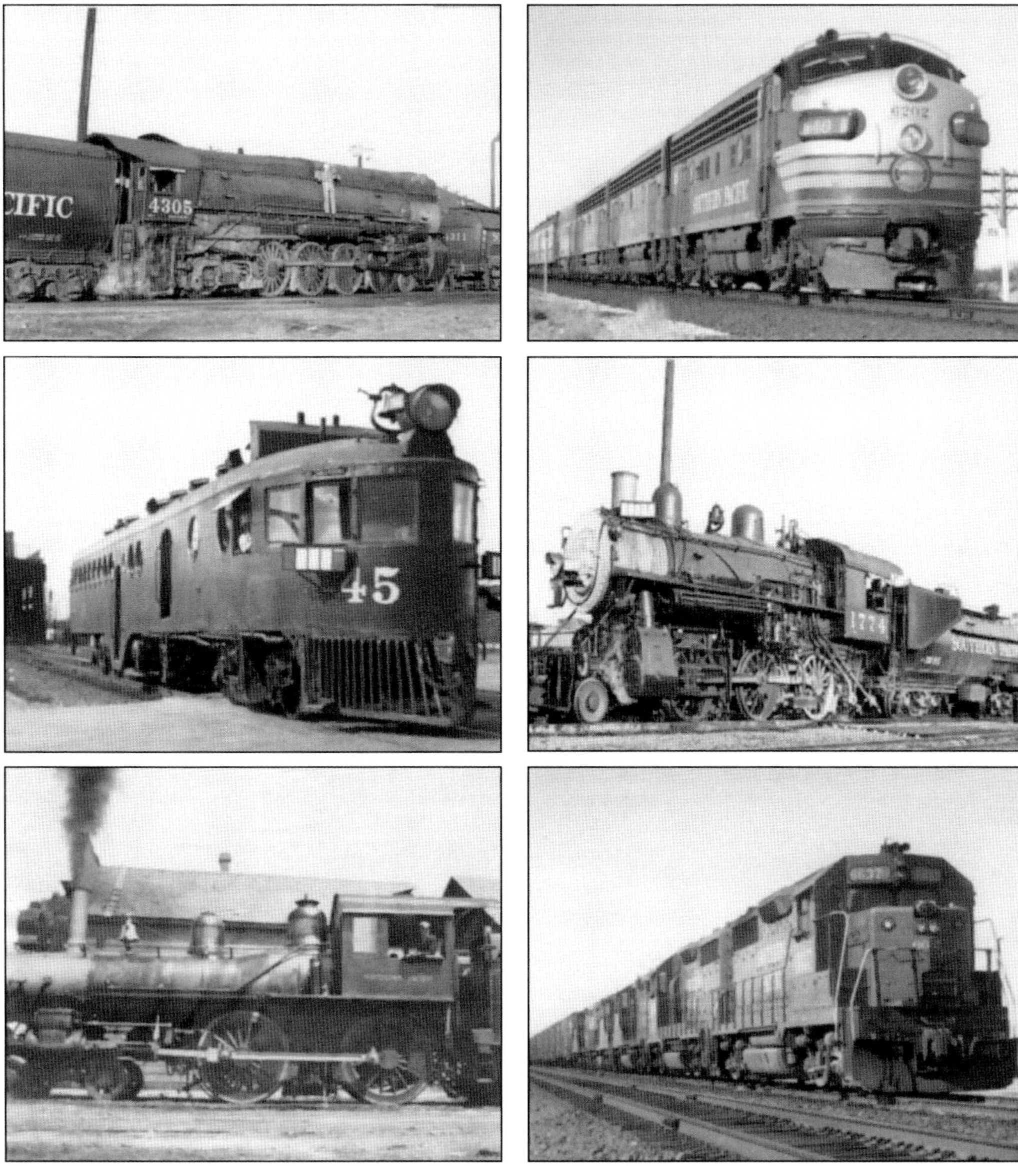

The transition from steam to diesel resulted in train engines that were not only more powerful, but vastly changed in appearance. For many train buffs, railroads—and especially railroad engines—continue to hold a special fascination. In 1946, the Southern Pacific Railroad ordered its first diesel freight locomotive, and by 1947, passenger locomotives were in service as well. The last steam locomotive was used in 1958, except for those maintained as tourist runs between small towns, mainly in the West. As rail travel decreased due to the advantages of air travel, freight transport became the primary mission for the nation's railroads. Following years of financial difficulties and drawn-out negotiations, the Southern Pacific Company merged with the Union Pacific Company in 1996. In 2009, even though the city no longer had a depot, the Union Pacific began expanding its freight service and adding additional tracks through Casa Grande.

Three

Hard Rock and Hard Times

The mountains surrounding Casa Grande provided a natural resource that contributed to the development of the town. Mines containing gold, silver, copper, and other valuable minerals were discovered and developed. Some were extremely productive, while others failed to produce as much as expected and soon closed. Many local residents were employed in the mines full-time, while individuals prospected for personal gain when they had the time.

By 1920, most area mines had closed or reduced their operations. Although the mines are no longer in operation, some of their colorful names remain as part of the historical record of the region. Among the more familiar names are the Reward Mine, Jack Rabbit, the Lakeshore, Christmas Gift Mine, Old Mammon, Turning Point, and Desert Queen.

During World War II, the need for industrial metals sparked a growth in mine activity; however, tests were to prove that the Reward Mine and other local mines did not have sufficient quantities of high-grade industrial metals. By the early 1960s, base metal prices rose, as did the technology required to detect and extract hidden mineral deposits. Following a short spurt of mining activity, largely of copper, prices again fell, and much of Arizona's copper production was shut down.

Many of the area mines are on Indian land, and in the past, individual tribes negotiated with large mining companies to search for substantial ore deposits. However, in the 1970s, when environmental impact studies were conducted around the Vekol Hills area, it was determined that it was part of a larger (undefined) cultural resource area and was eligible for inclusion in the National Register of Historic Places. This designation hindered further development. Since 1994, the Vekol Hills region and Reward Mine deposits remain undeveloped.

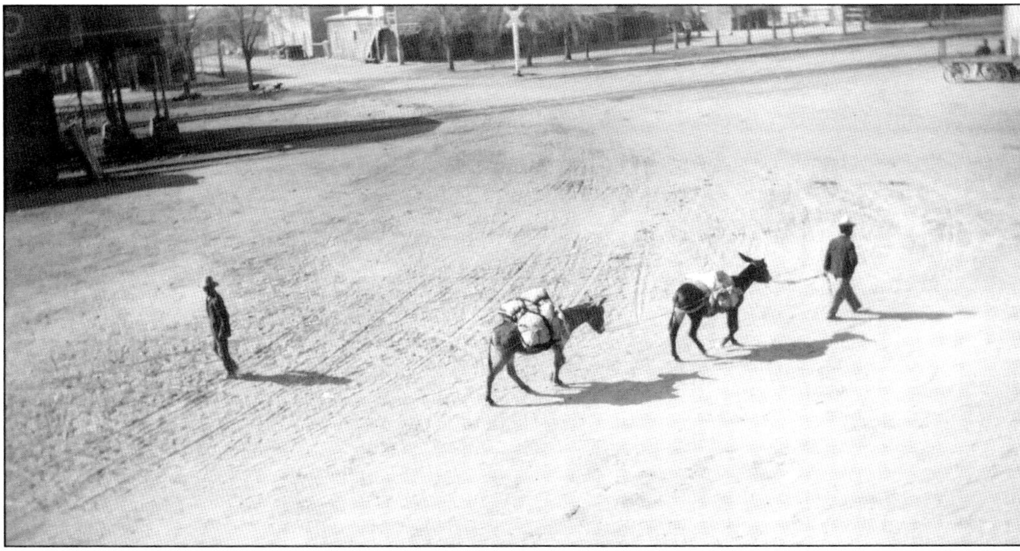

In addition to commercial mines, individual prospectors searched for gold and silver in the mountains surrounding Casa Grande. Around 1920, a lone prospector leads his pack animals laden with supplies and prospecting equipment down Main Street. The Casa Grande Hotel can be seen across the railroad tracks.

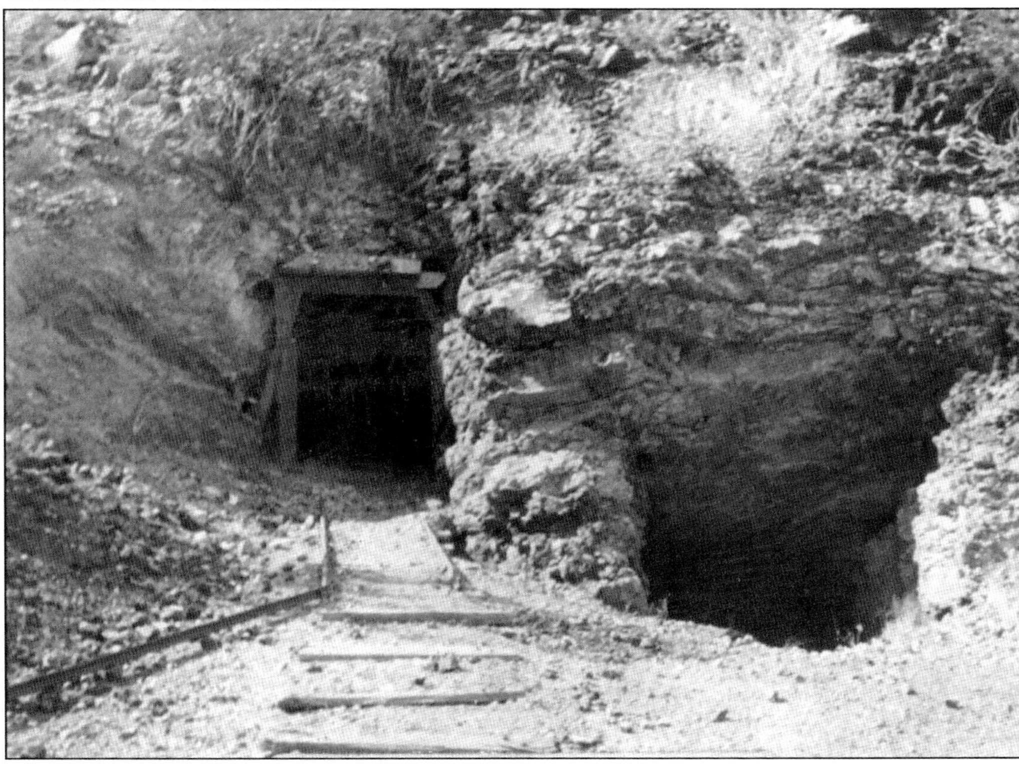

This is a mine adit, a nearly horizontal opening into a mountain side. Primitive tracks carried equipment, men, and ore to and from the interior of a mine. Hills in the mountains around the town were dotted with large and small adits, depending on whether it was a commercial enterprise or an individual undertaking.

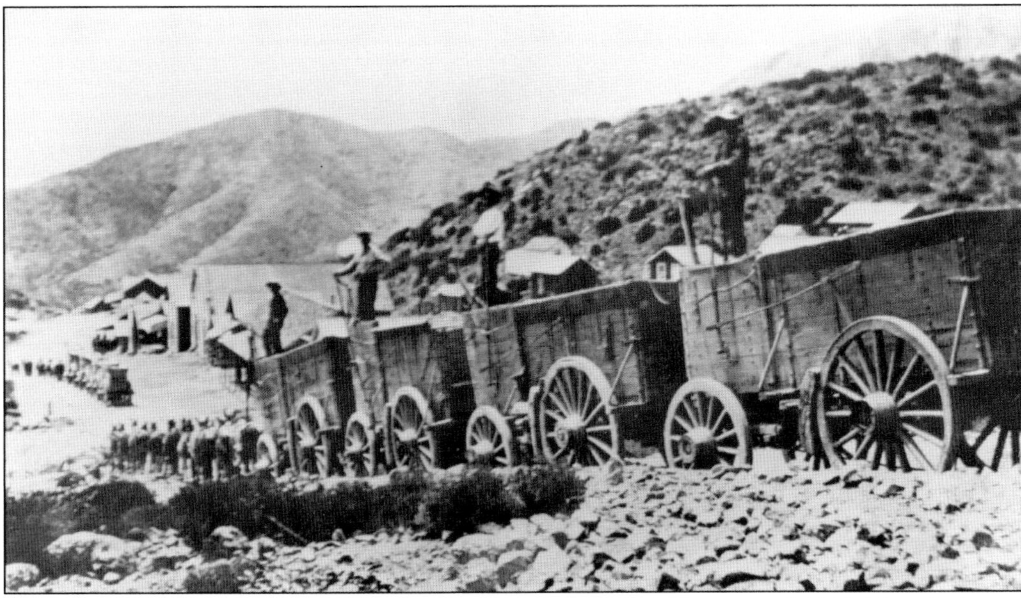

A typical ore hauling team is photographed at Silver King Mine around 1880 (above). An ore train descending a steep, rocky grade awaits its turn to enter the mill area. Each train consists of four heavy wagons pulled by 12 mules. Treacherous rocky mountain ascents and descents were made by the burros and their handlers several times a day. The ore was transported over well-worn trails to the railroad in Casa Grande for shipment. On the return trip, the wagons carried supplies for the mine as well as for the miners and their families. Note the small shacks behind the wagons on the grade where the miners and their families lived. Below, seemingly unattended burros are carrying supplies up the trail, and fully loaded ore wagons are heading in the other direction, possibly to the railroad in Casa Grande.

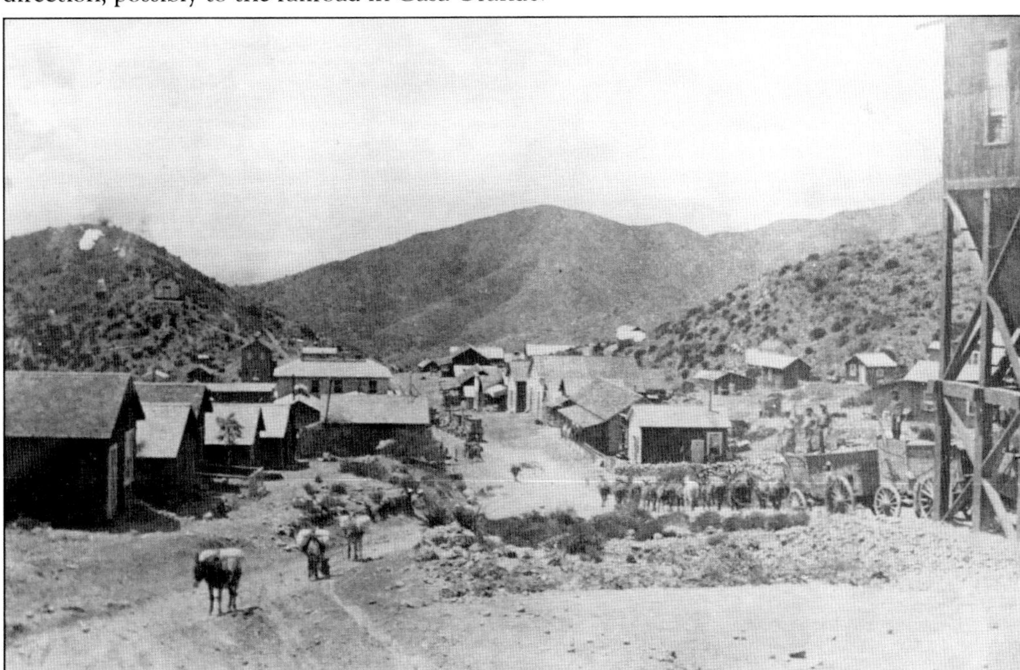

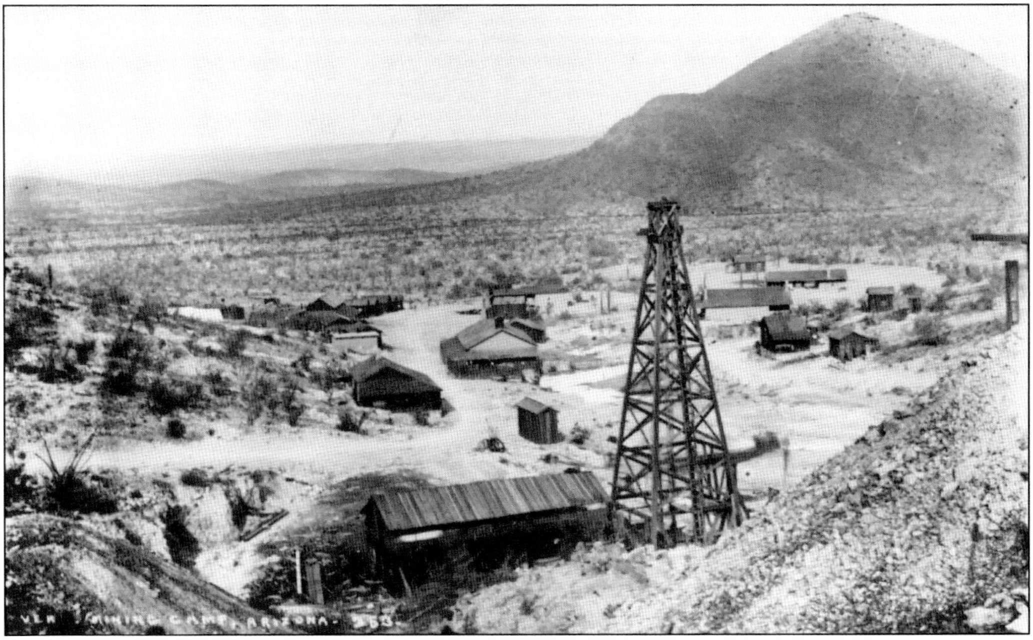

Mines dotted the foothills of small mountains throughout south-central Arizona. Vekol Mine was larger than most others in the region but was typical of mining towns of the period. Around 1890, Vekol was one of the thriving communities of Pinal County. Some 40 to 50 families lived there. The community was made up mainly of tin shacks and tents for housing, although a few more substantial frame homes were also built. Also present were a school and buildings for mine operations, including carpenter and blacksmith shops and an assay office. Many of the mining towns had a company store. Interestingly, the town of Vekol had no church, and perhaps even more interestingly, it had no saloon. Some of the company towns would occasionally have payday dances with an orchestra. It is not known for certain if Vekol was one of them.

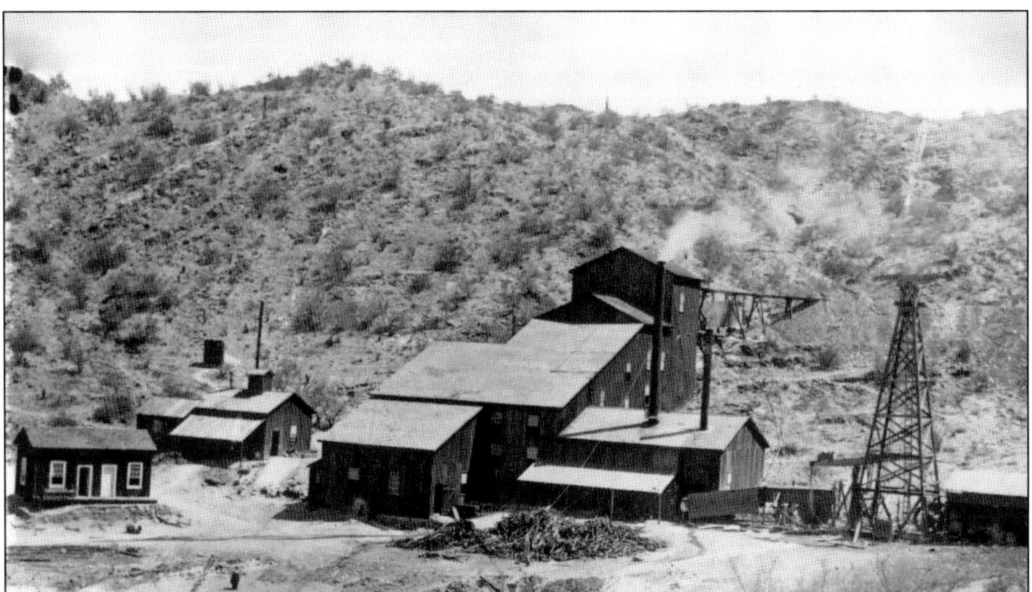

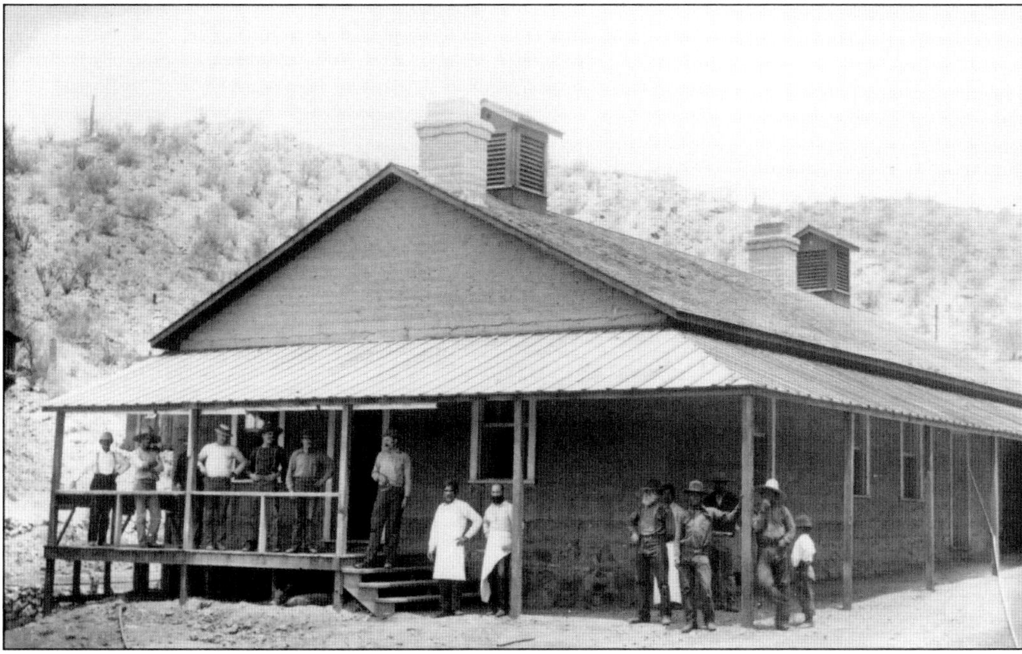

A bunkhouse was a common component of a mining enterprise. A popular meeting place for unmarried miners or those whose families lived elsewhere, the bunkhouse often served as the cook shack as well as a place to relax and sleep. Some cooks and miners pose on the porch of the Vekol Mine bunkhouse in 1900.

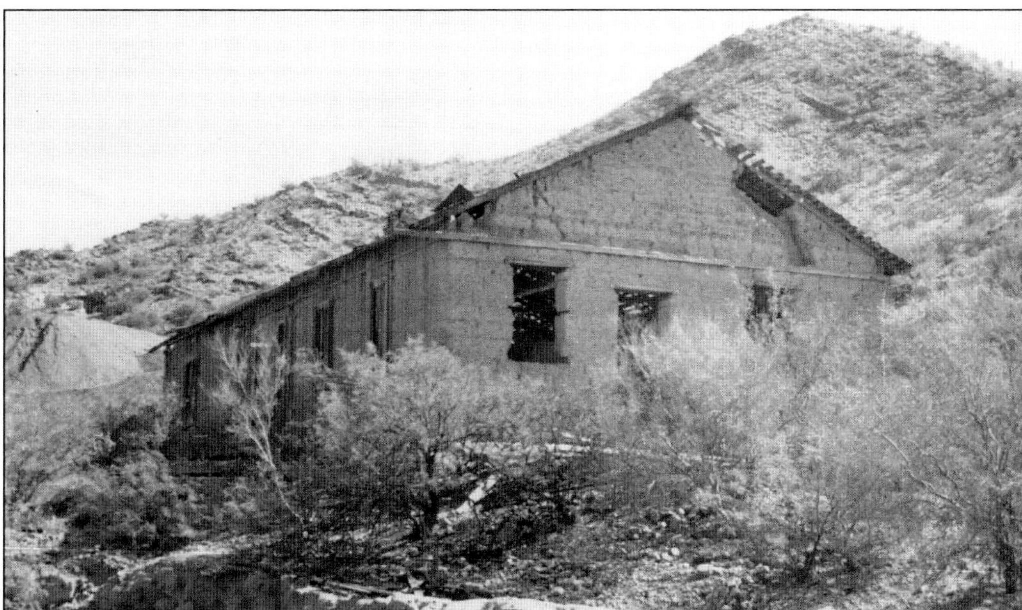

The story of the Vekol Mine is probably somewhat typical of mines throughout the southwest. In 1879, a Papago Indian showed John D. Walker a silver deposit in the mountains. In 1880, John Walker named the mine Vekol, which is Papago for "grandmother." Walker and his brother developed the mine, which proved to be exceptionally lucrative, producing 525,030 ounces of silver between 1885 and 1889. An abandoned assay office is left to attest to the mines success.

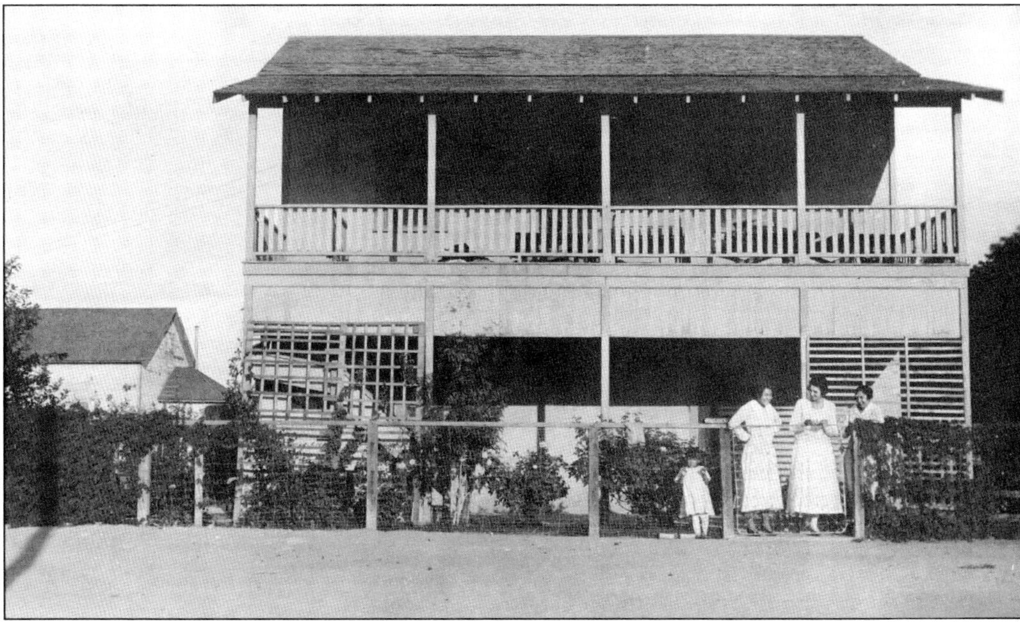

Unfortunately, the success of the Vekol Mine was short-lived, and John Walker fell upon hard times. Because his marriage to a nonwhite woman was illegal, his Papago daughter was denied a claim on his estate, which was valued at $1.5 million. It is believed that Walker died in a California hospital for the insane in 1894. Shortly after his death, the silver market fell and the mine was shut down. Around 1880, John Walker built and lived in this house at 210 South Washington Street in Casa Grande (above). Subsequently, the Armenta family purchased the Walker house. Pictured from left to right are Sara Armenta Bussari, Lupe Armenta, Virginia Kellner, and Rose Armenta Sullivan. The Walker-Armenta house as it stood in 1975 is shown below. Exact records are unavailable, but it is known that the house was demolished shortly after 1991.

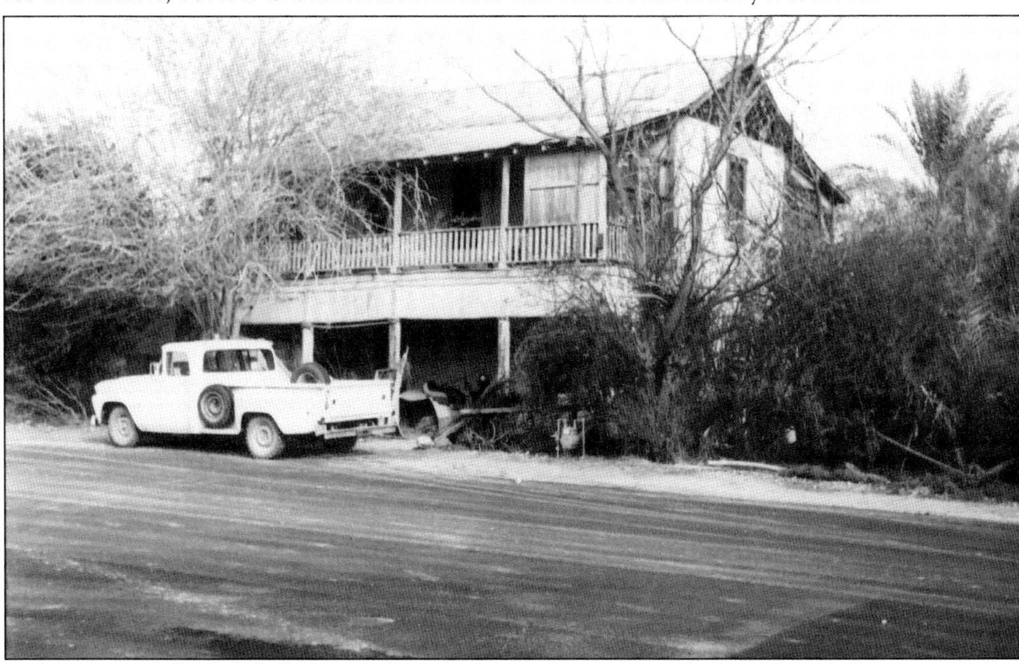

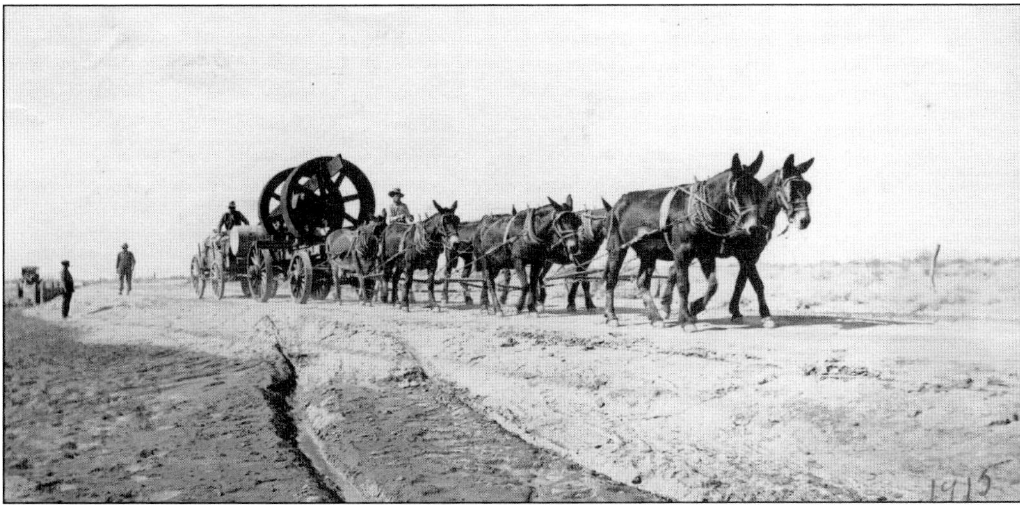

Prior to the arrival of the railroad, mule-drawn wagons were the primary mode of transport. Many of the trails that crisscrossed the area began as routes for transporting mine supplies and extracted ore. Here, in 1915, mining equipment is being carried from the railroad depot in Casa Grande to the Jack Rabbit Mine about 12 miles south of the city. On the return trip, ore would be carried to the city for shipment to a processing plant via the railroad. Brothers Charlie and Walt Nelson are pictured.

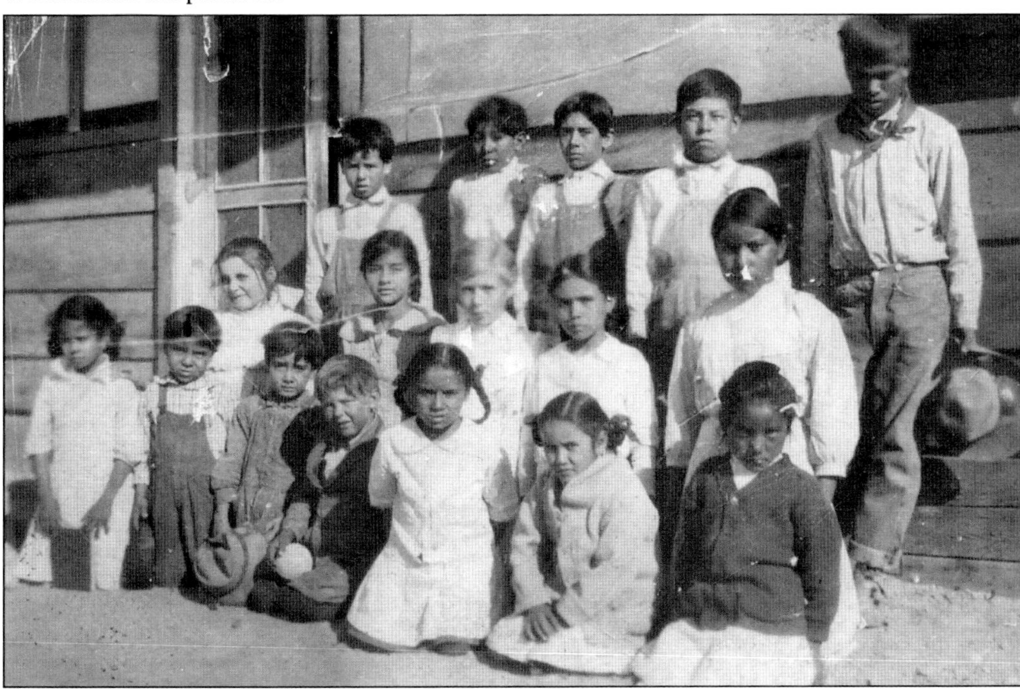

Often entire families lived in mining towns, generally known as company towns. Some formed complete communities, including schools. In 1916, these students lived at the Jack Rabbit Mine and attended the Jack Rabbit School located there. Among the students (but in no known order) are Fred Andrade, "Beto" Armenta, Felix Antone, Sara Andrade, Ila Pyeatt, Marcia Antone, Lupe Armenta, Salvadore Andrade, Myler Pyeatt, Rossura Armenta, Mercedes Armenta Lopez, and Iona Armenta.

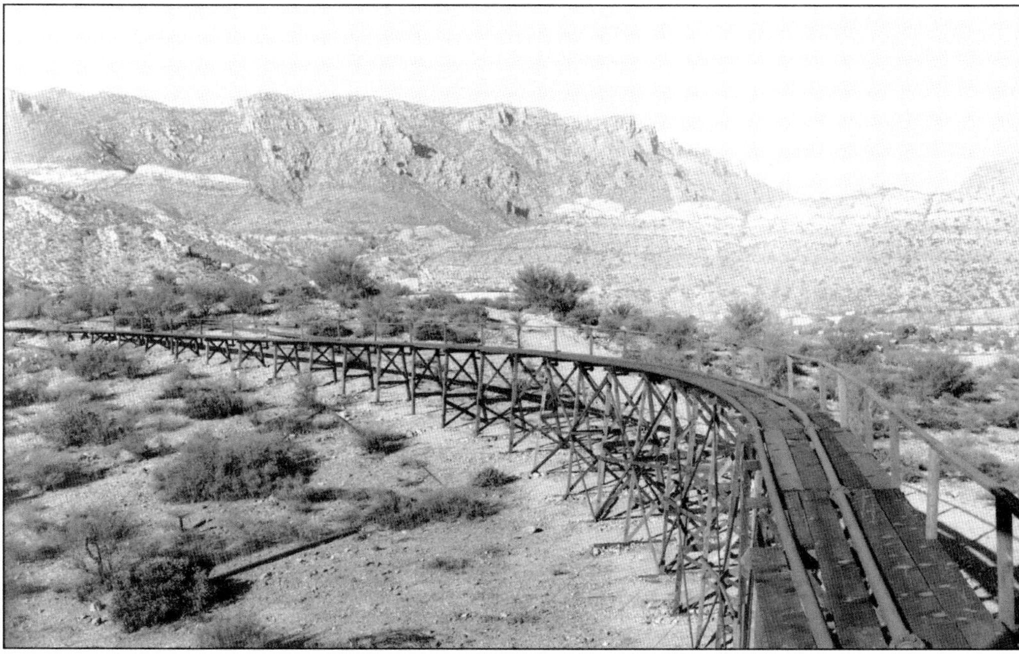

Magma Mine, located in northeastern Pinal County, was a large copper mine that also produced smaller quantities of other minerals. Ore-laden wagons traveled along a graded track (above) that extended across the desert from the mine to a processing plant or to a point of transport. The loaded ore wagons were driven from the mine along what appears to be an electrically-powered, trolley-like line (above). In 1949, large mechanized equipment was being used for a variety of activities; however, much of the day-to-day work still required hard physical labor, as shown by men hand-loading an ore cart (below).

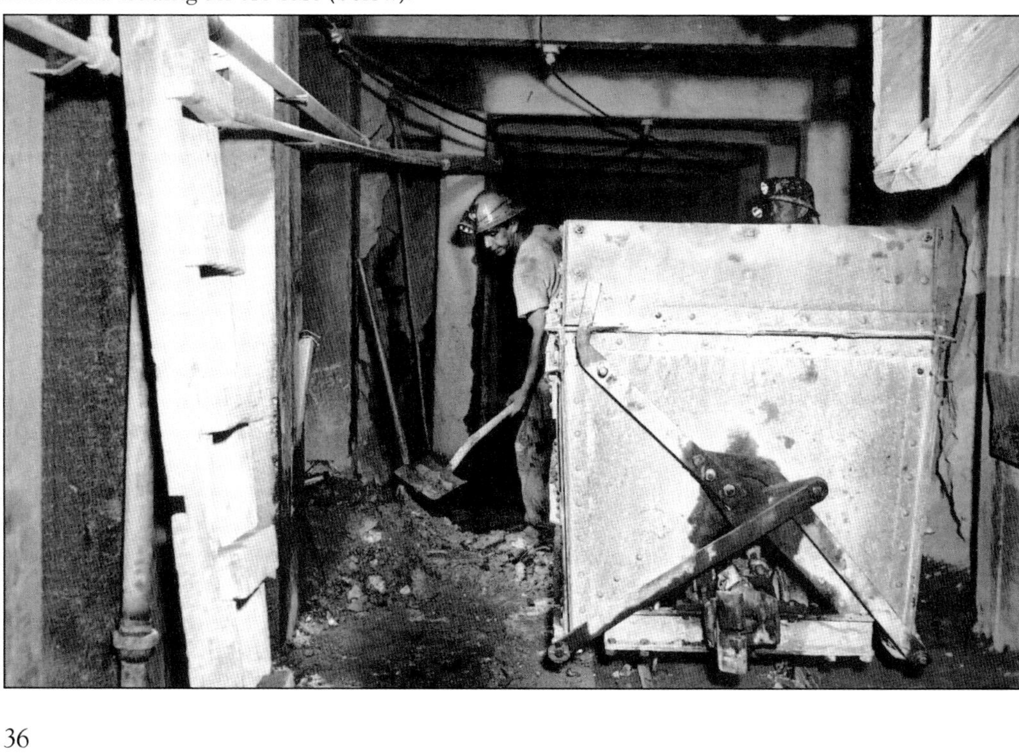

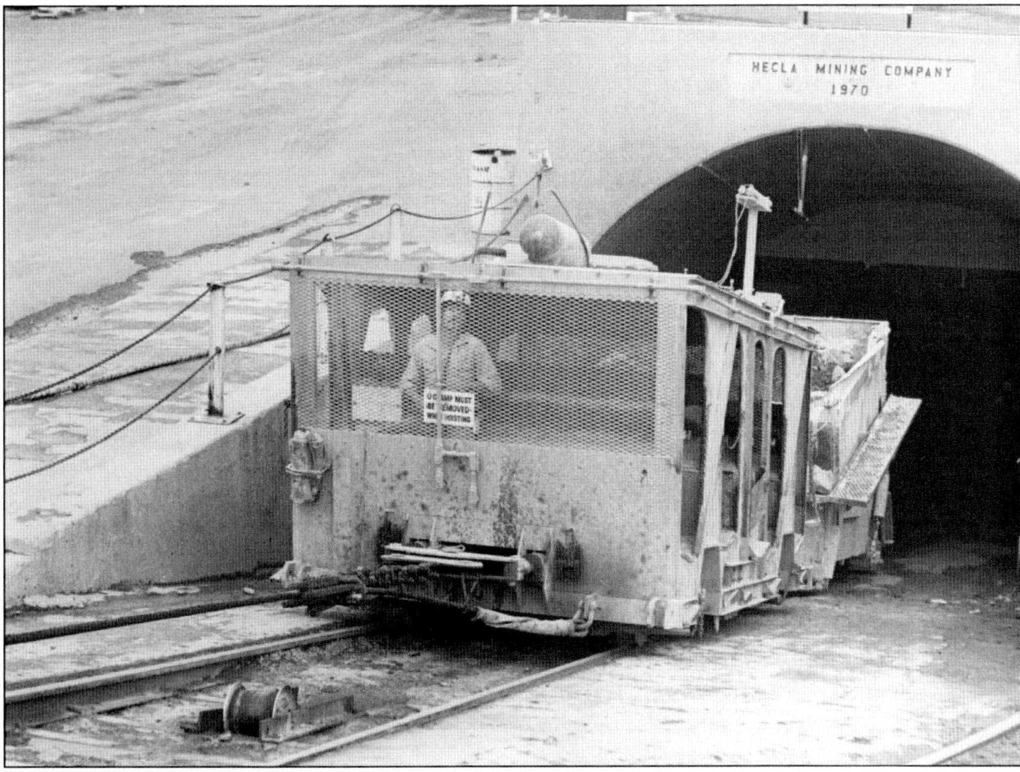

By 1970, mining operations almost exclusively used heavy, mechanized equipment to harvest the various minerals that were buried in the ground throughout the region. The Lakeshore Mine was located southeast of Casa Grande on the Tohono O'Odham Reservation. The large copper mine, which was purchased for development by Hecla Mines of Idaho in 1967, proved to be a costly undertaking. By 1977, when the mine closed due to falling copper prices, Lakeshore had cost Hecla $96 million. On the right, Rick Blackburn is pictured in the changing room of the Hecla Lakeshore Mine in April 1977, just before mining operations ceased.

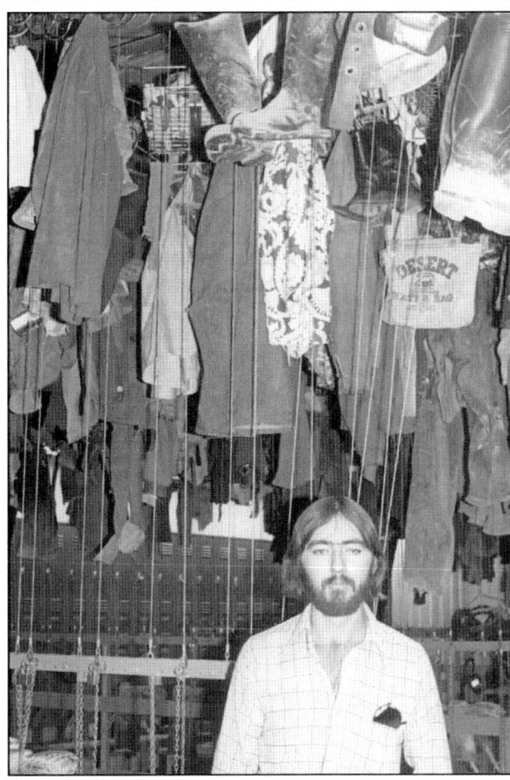

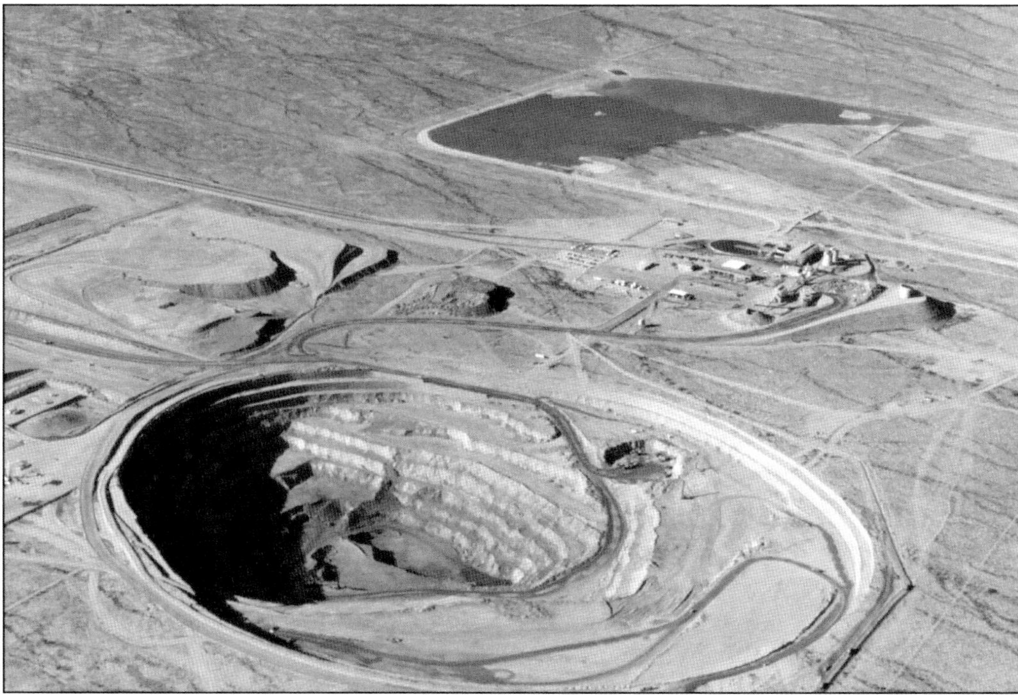

One of the last active mines in the area was the ASARCO Mine, located just west of the city. These aerial views show the Sacaton unit of the ASARCO open pit copper mining operation as it existed in 1973. It has been an inactive mine since 1984. Later, ASARCO, in conjunction with the US Bureau of Mines, began an experimental operation utilizing new mining technology at another site seven miles away. Federal funding was eliminated in 1997, and although work continued for a brief time, it too was shut down. Currently no mines are in operation in the Casa Grande area.

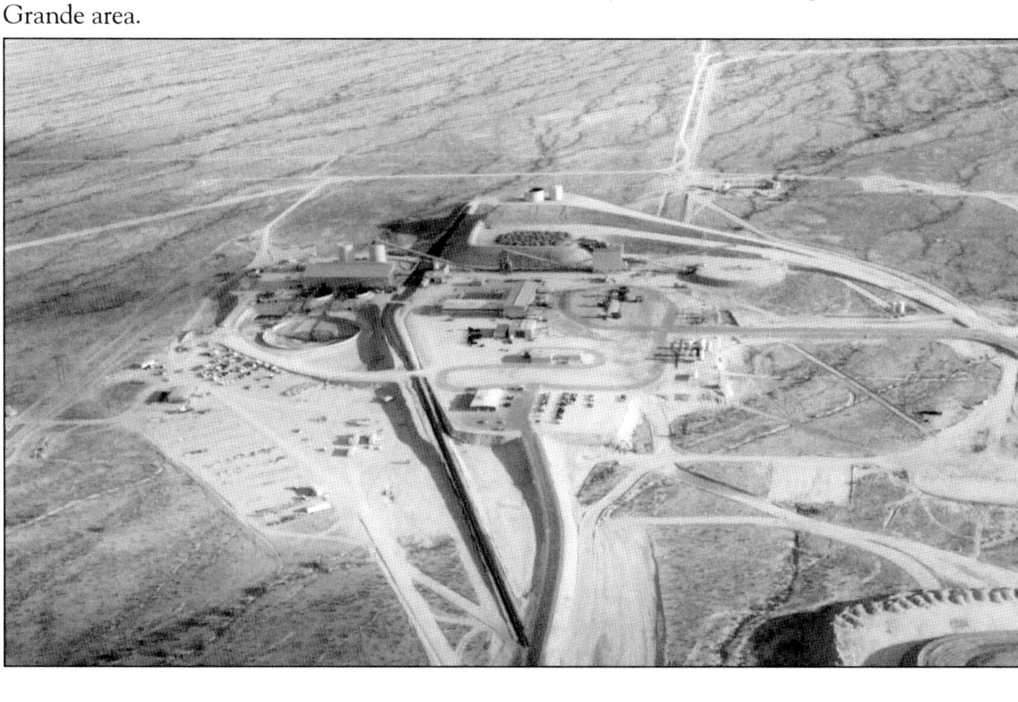

Four

ADD WATER AND STIR

Under the terms of the 1877 Arid Desert Land Act, an individual could purchase up to one section (640 acres) of land for 25¢ an acre, provided they irrigated a portion of it within three years. If they were able to do so, they could get full title to the acreage for an additional $1 per acre. This act encouraged many ambitious individuals to move west and try their luck at becoming land-owning farmers. Some had been successful farmers in other parts of the country, while others were first-timers drawn by the dream of owning their own land. All were ultimately challenged in their attempts to acquire enough water to irrigate the land, and many were forced to give up. A few farmers were able to grow enough food for their families, and some of the more fortunate were able to irrigate enough land to grow crops for stock animals as well as a money-making endeavor.

One of the first crops to be grown successfully and profitably was cotton. When World War I began, additional fields were dedicated to cotton because of military need. By the time World War II began, the Army Quartermaster Corps had a procurement list for more than 11,000 cotton products; thus, cotton became the most important crop grown in the area.

Later, many cotton fields were converted to growing alfalfa and corn, both of which were sold to the feed lots that had sprung up around the city. Although for a time many cotton fields, as well as fields dedicated to other crops, had been sold to housing development companies, the recent economic downturn has resulted in some land being reverted to agriculture. Nevertheless, the rural, agricultural heritage of the area continues to change in spite of efforts to retain the small-town feel that has been Casa Grande's signature through the years.

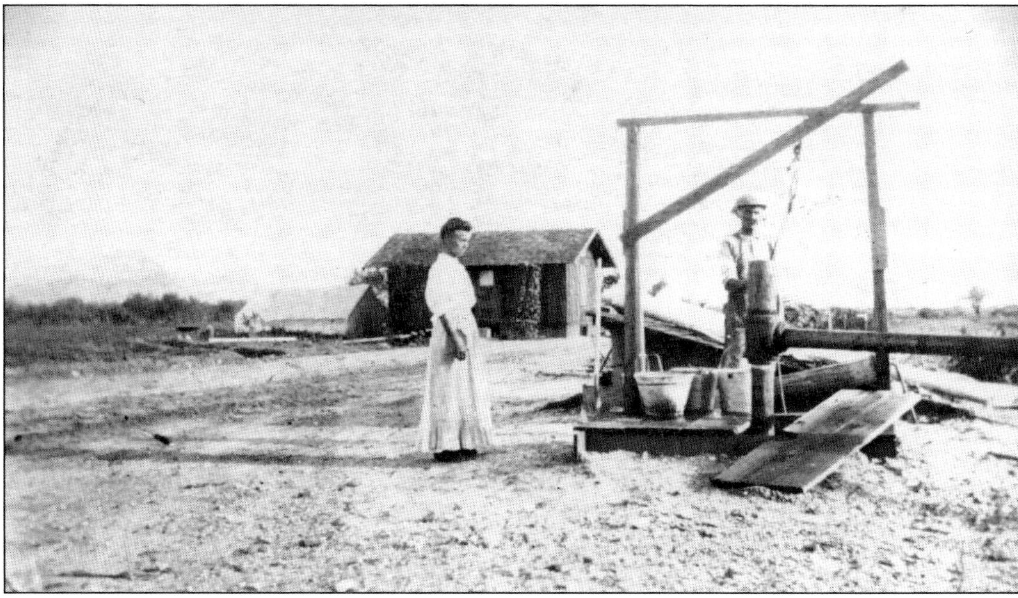

Homesteading in the desert was a challenge, and the acquisition of water was of primary importance. Although this is the Will Sherrill 1910 homestead (above), it is typical of most farm operations during this period. Will and his wife are shown attending to the irrigation system on their property located east of Casa Grande. Although living conditions may have been rustic and difficult, there was still a time for Jeanne Sherrill to dress up in her Sunday best (below). Note the handmade cart as well as the household utensils around the door, on the table, and hung on the wall. Around 1912, the Sherrill family apparently was doing well, based on the presence of a rarity in the community—a new automobile in the front yard.

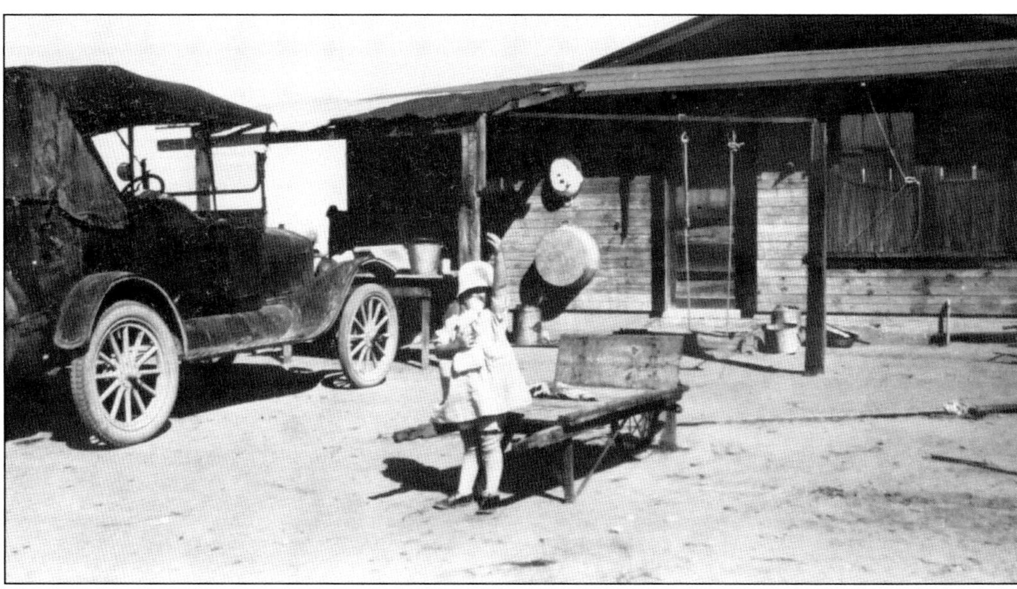

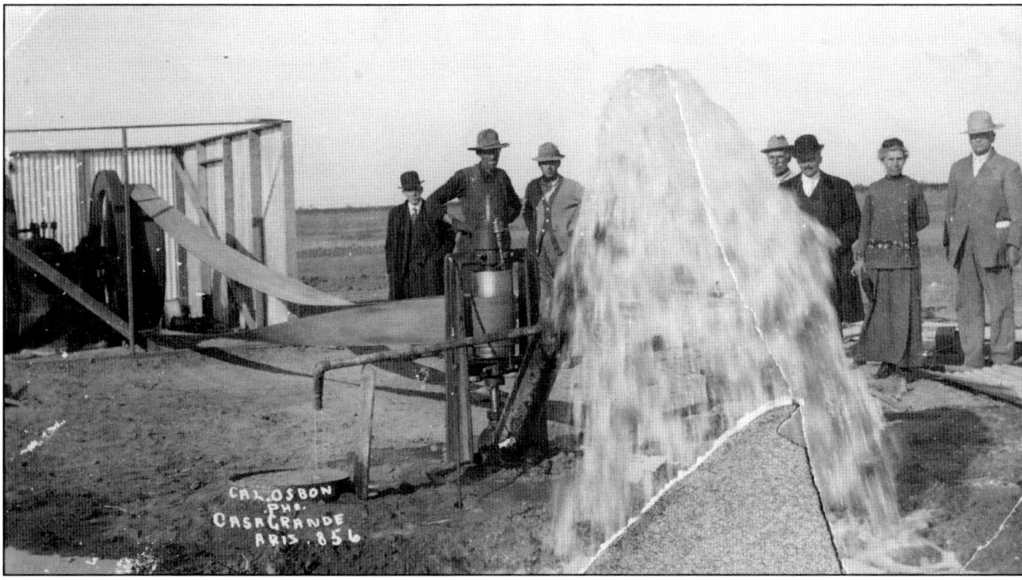

Running water was an unusual sight in the desert, and when a new well was dug and water for irrigation became available, it was an event to be welcomed and appreciated. This c. 1913 gushing well (above) was observed by a small celebratory crowd, including a woman attired in what appears to be a fine dress and hat. Most of the men are decked out in a shirt, tie, and suit. Note that the working mechanism is sheltered, but the observers are not. By around 1920, as acreage ownership grew and the need for water increased, well-drilling rigs (right) were a common sight throughout Pinal County. This particular rig belonged to J.B. Junkins. Ernest Cates is waving his hat as he fearlessly sits on top of the rig.

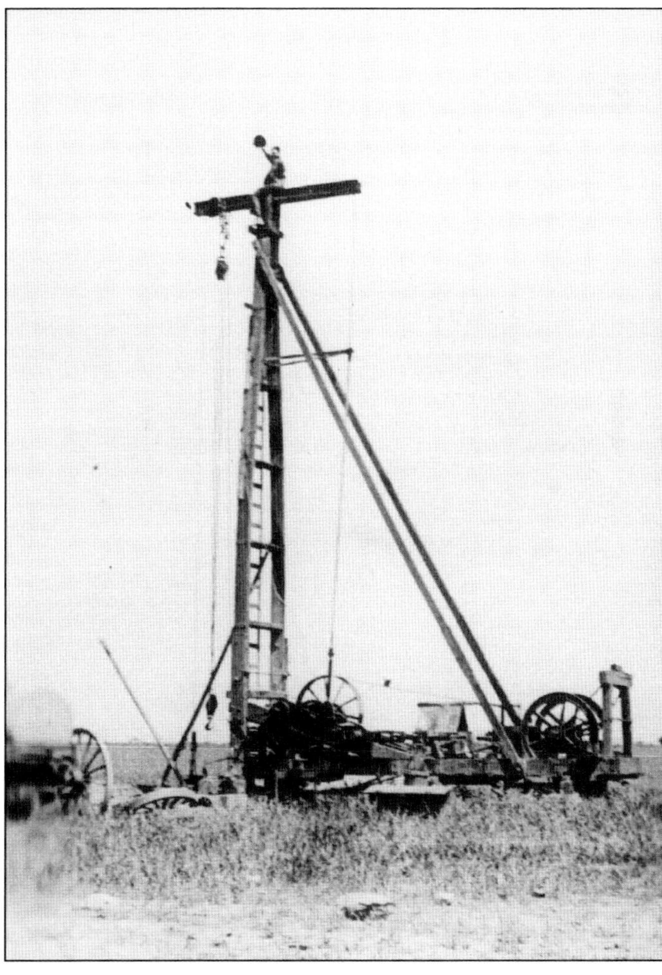

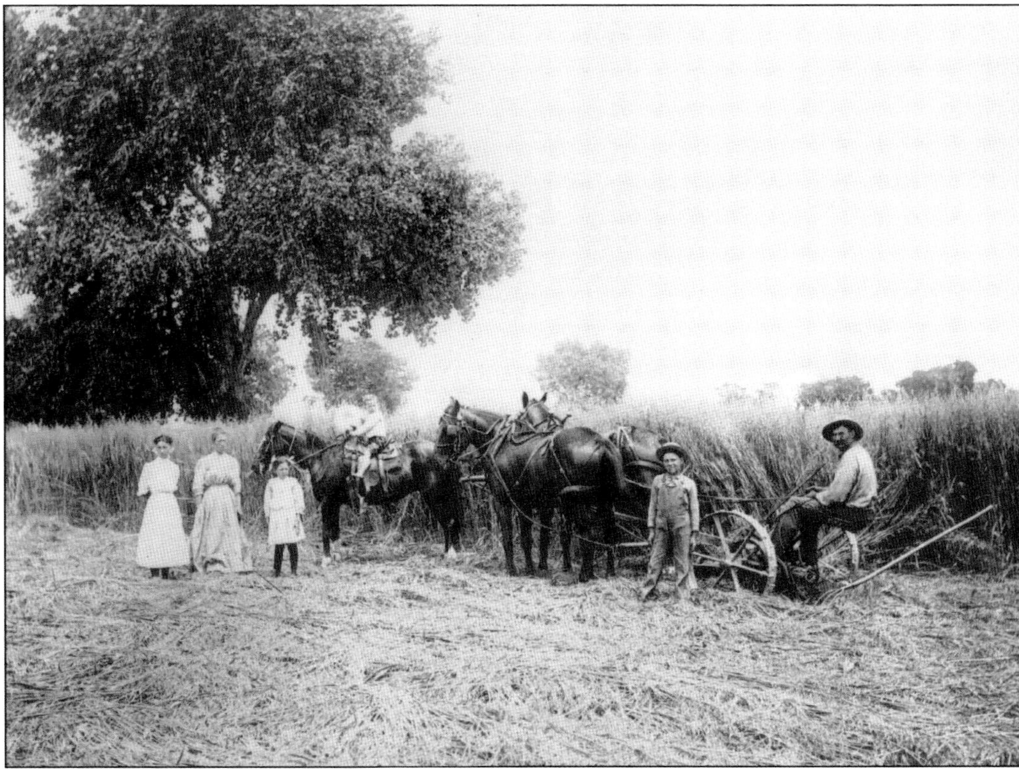

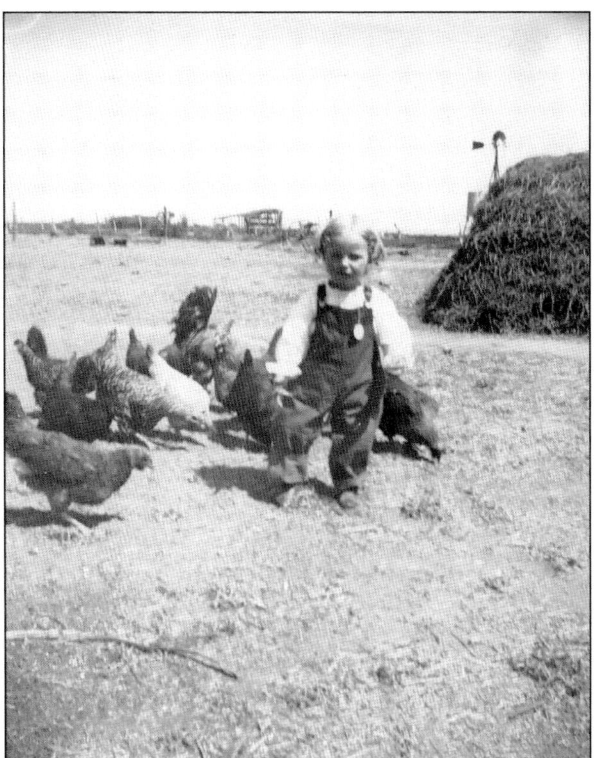

This two-horse team mower (above) has a precarious perch that serves as a seat for the driver, which likely made for a long day "in the saddle." The pitchfork behind the rig was probably used by the young man in overalls. Although entire families often worked the fields, this appears to be a visit by the women of the family, possibly to bring lunch and water to their hard-working men. Even the smallest family member was expected to help around the farm. In the photograph on the left, three-year-old Lucille Weaver feeds the chickens on her family's homestead located about five miles east of Casa Grande.

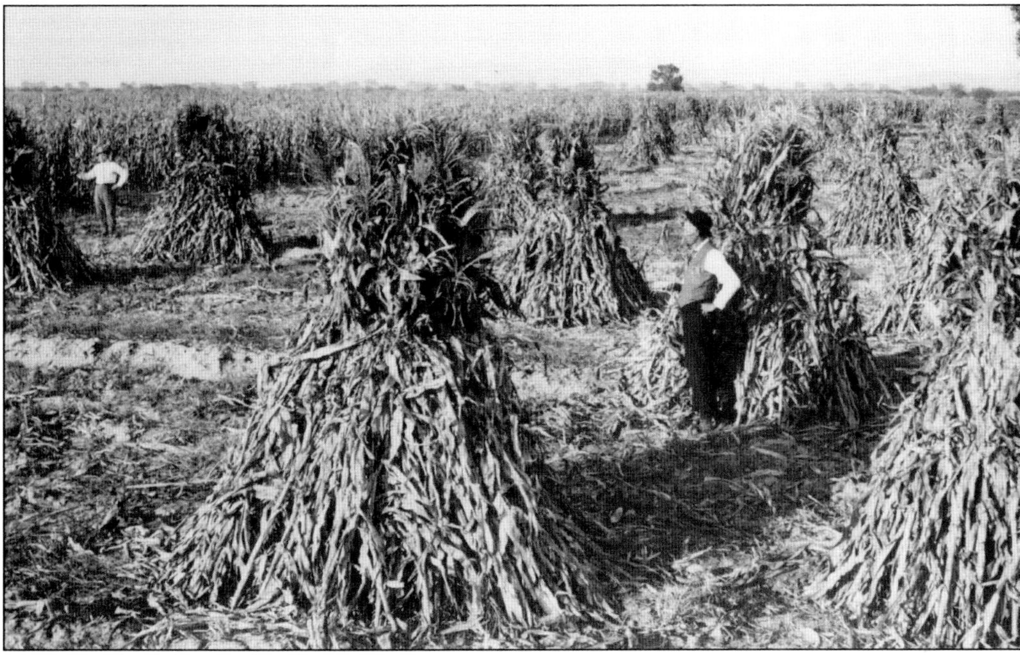

Various crops were grown in and around Casa Grande in the early 1900s. Corn was always a prime crop, and many fields were dedicated to growing it for fodder as well as for family use. Although these two men are standing in a field of shocked corn at the Sacaton Cooperative Agricultural Station, alfalfa was the first crop grown at the experimental station.

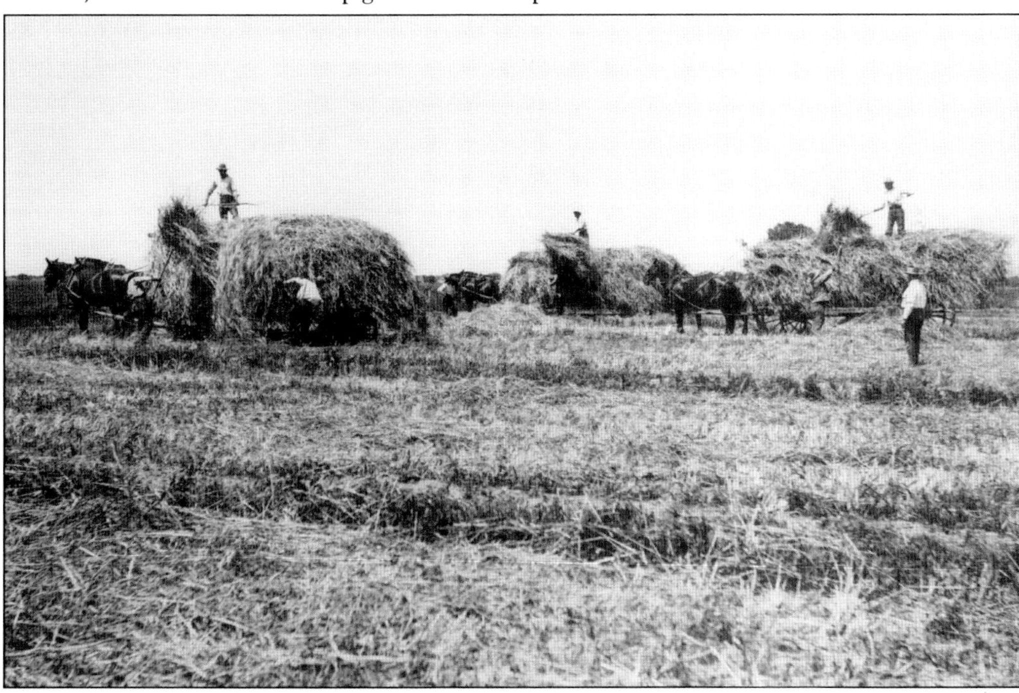

The thankless task of gathering hay in the hot desert sun is pursued by field hands who work as a team. Some of the men are tossing the cut hay to the man on top of the wagon, and he spreads it evenly as the two-horse teams wait patiently for the orders to move on.

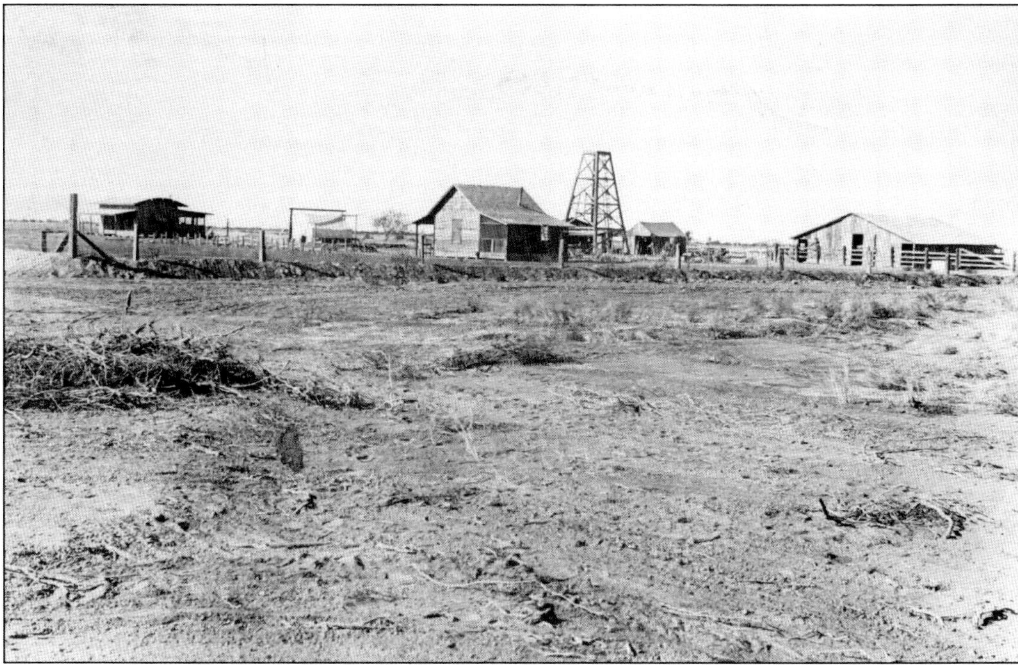

Just as a city grew in the midst of the Arizona desert, so too did ranches sprout and prosper. The Trekell family arrived in the area in the early 1900s and became prominent land owners. Seen above around 1917 is their ranch, with the house being one of the smaller buildings on the property. Also visible is the all-important well and a variety of outbuildings. On Armistice Day 1918, several children sit on a truck decorated with the American flag (below). Behind them is a large barn. Today, a replica of that barn sits on the museum grounds and serves as a meeting place for local events such as the Old Timers' Picnic and museum fundraising parties. One of the main streets in town is named for the Trekells.

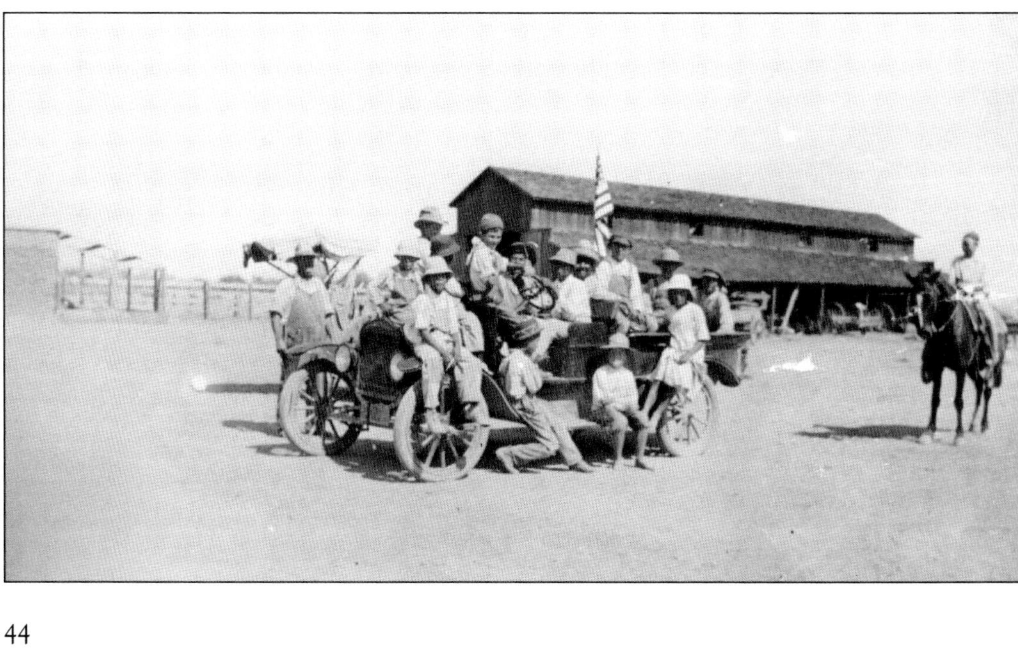

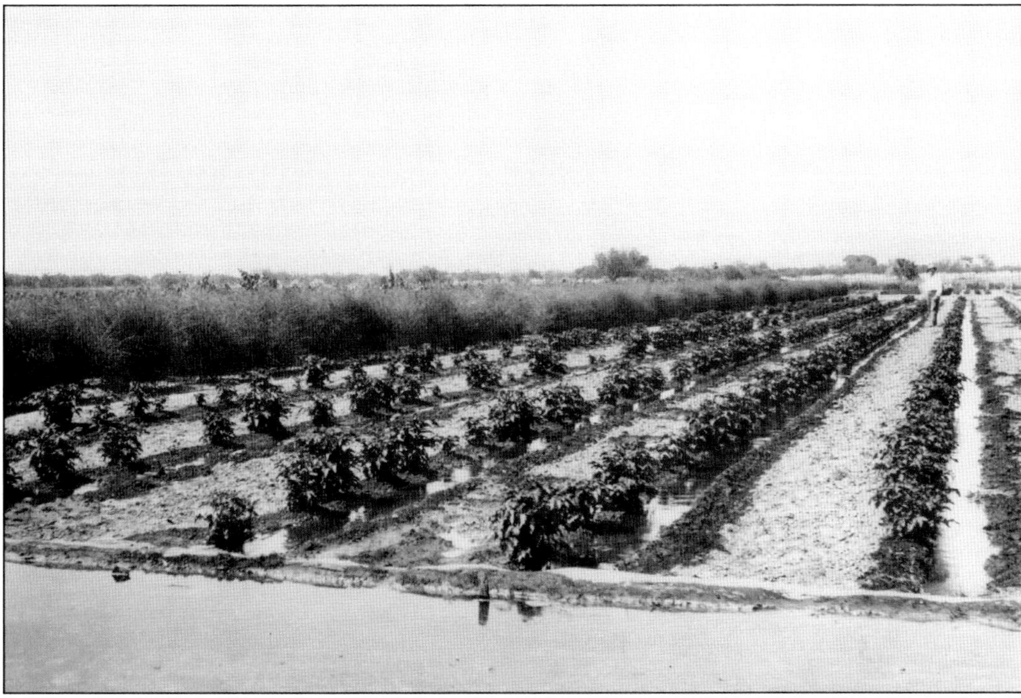

By 1914, the difficult task of acquiring sufficient amounts of irrigation water had abated somewhat, and cotton was on its way to becoming a major cash crop for the farmers of the Casa Grande Valley. The flooded cotton field above depicts the preferred method for watering the crop at the time. Another unidentified crop is adjacent to the cotton field. In 1919, when the photograph below was taken, long-staple cotton was already an important commercial crop for cotton growers in the Casa Grande Valley. Workers are fluffing and spreading the cotton to sun dry prior to its being sent for processing to an on-site mill or packed for shipment to a gin.

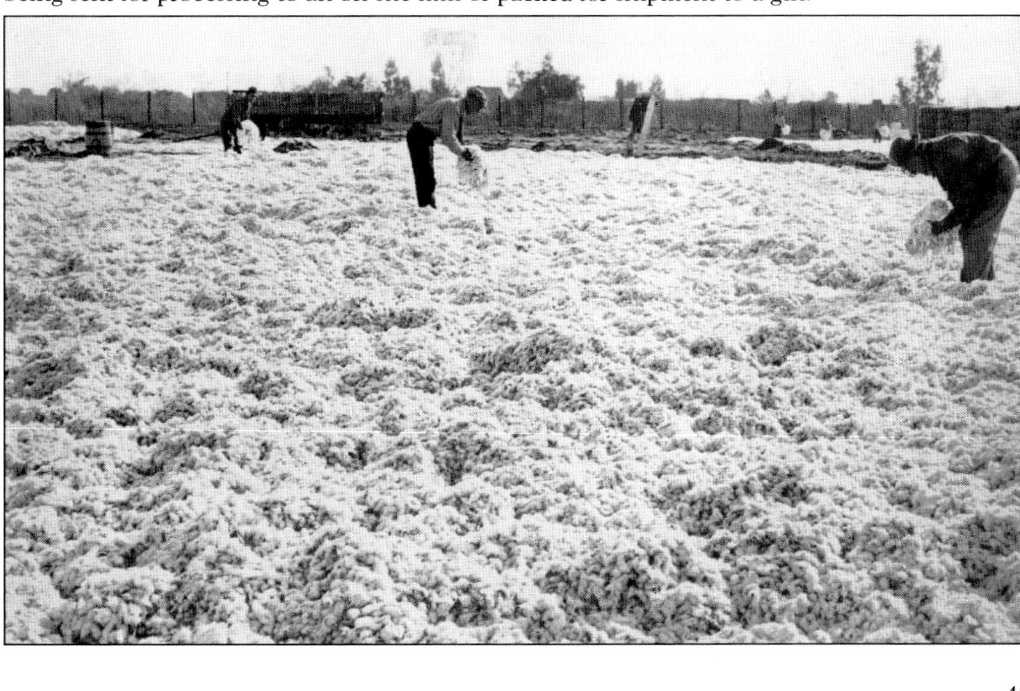

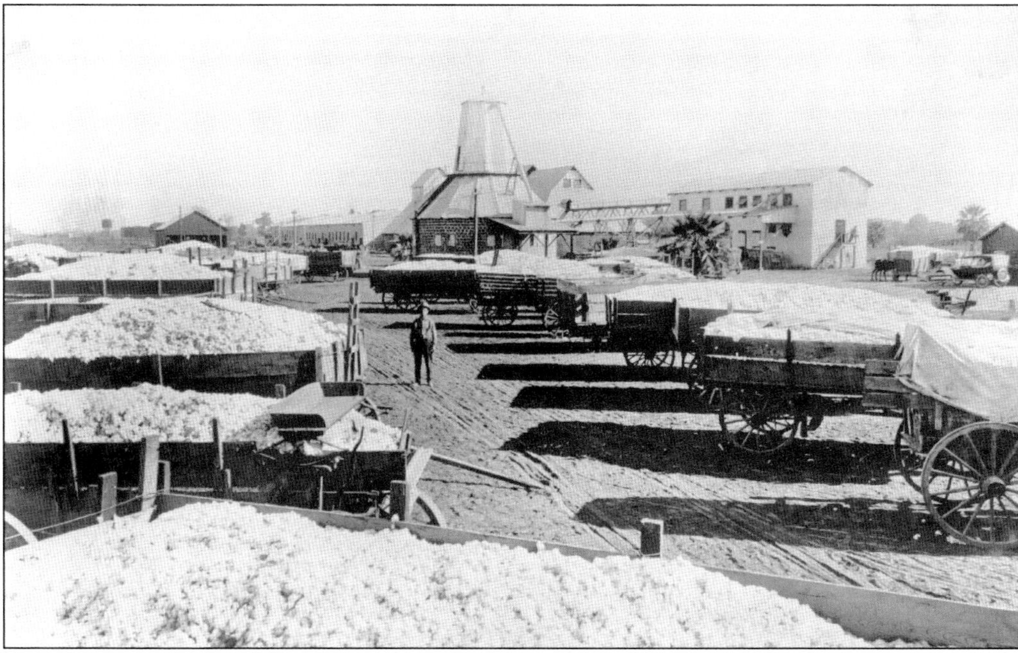

Occasionally, a gin was owned by the same individual that grew the cotton, but more often growers sent their cotton away for processing. Many gin yards accepted cotton from the majority of growers who did not operate their own gin. The facility above appears to be capable of handling a large quantity of cotton. The yard is full of wagons waiting to unload their cotton for processing. The interior of a cotton gin (below) did not provide a pleasant work environment. Crowded conditions, dust, heat, and poor ventilation were accepted as normal. Some farmers supplemented their income by working the gins after their cotton had been harvested.

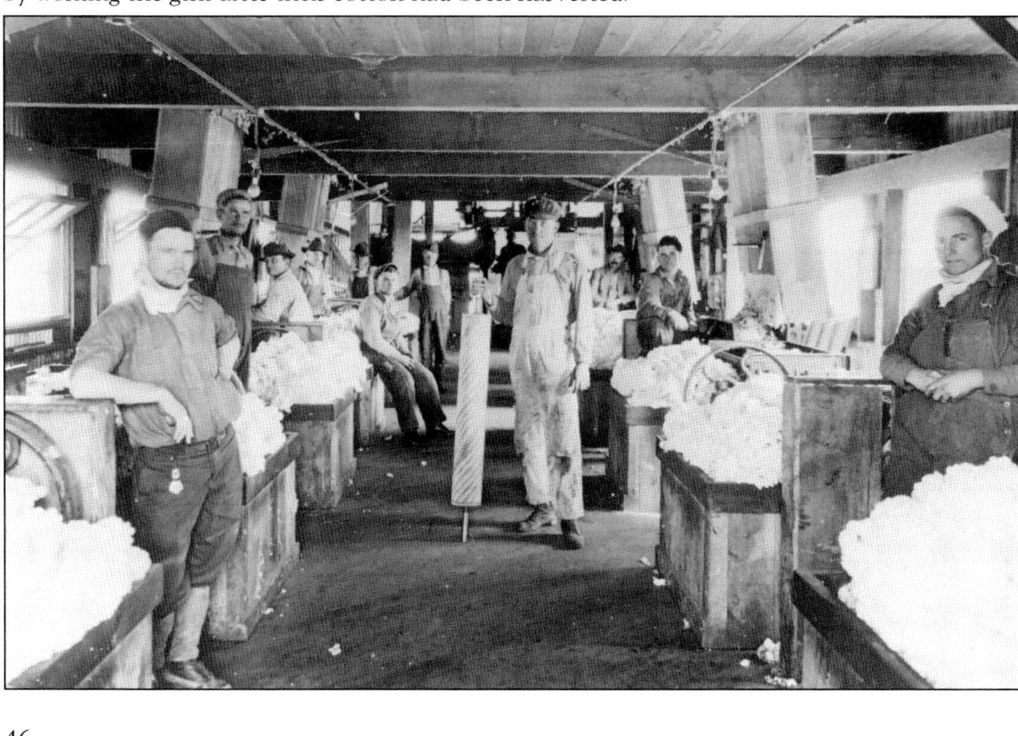

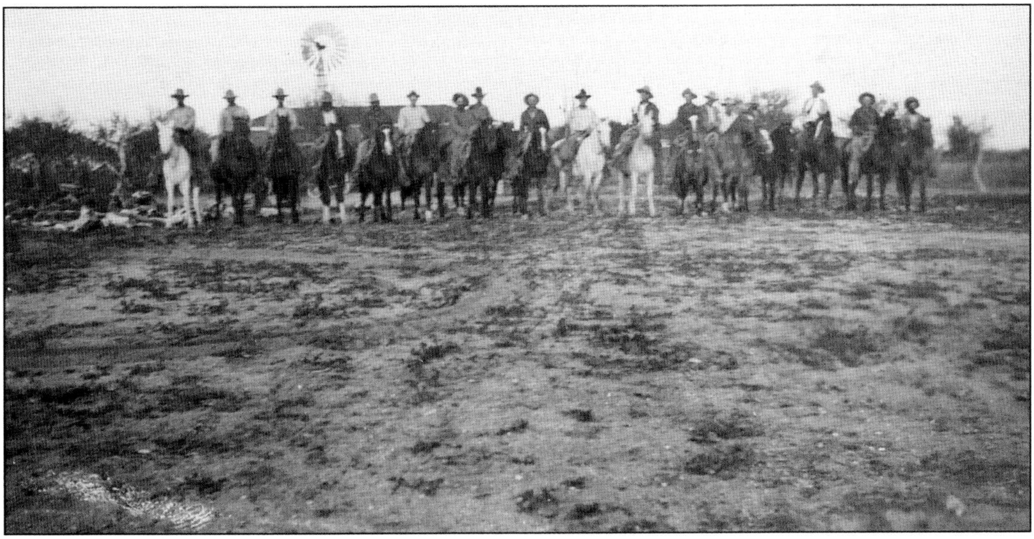

Even though cotton was king, the raising of livestock provided an increasingly important contribution to the growth of Casa Grande. The c. 1920 photograph above shows the last pool or chuck wagon event in Casa Grande before the implementation of the Herd Law. The Herd Law dictated that cattlemen were now obligated to restrain their stock by herding them rather than letting them range freely. In addition, the cattle had to be branded, and the brands had to be registered. In the early 1920s, the first Brahma cattle arrived in Arizona. It was an exciting day in Casa Grande as the strange-looking cattle arrived via the Southern Pacific Railroad. Shown below, they are being temporarily held in the stock pens at the railroad yard.

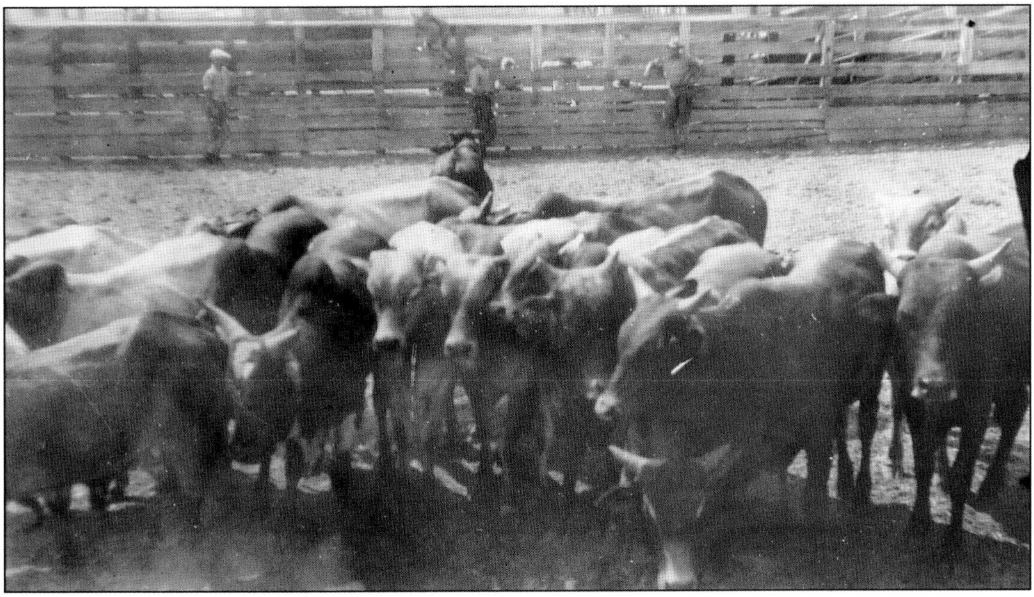

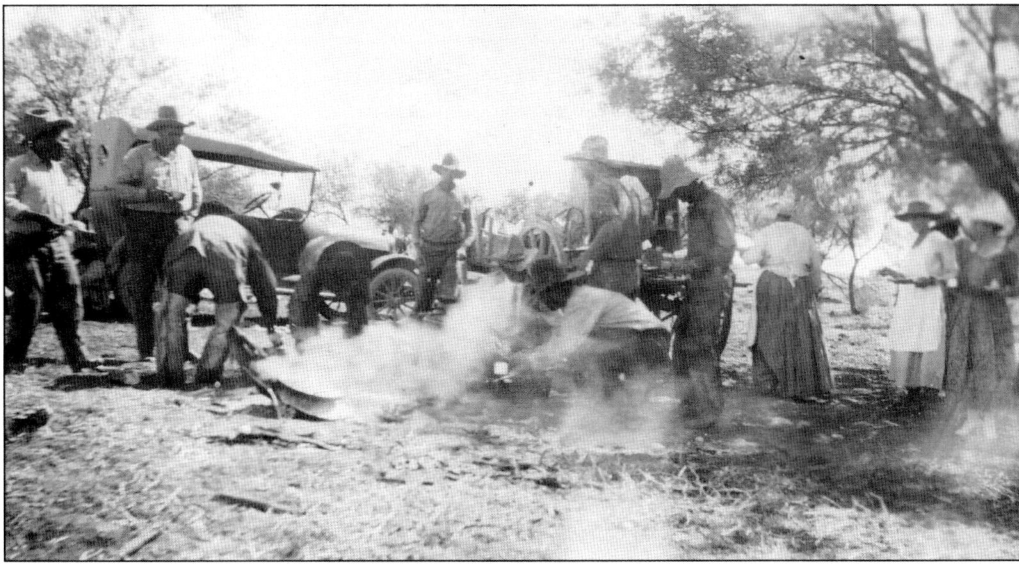

With the passing of the Herd Law and the arrival of Brahma cattle, the working cowboy became an even more essential element of ranching activities in the area. Here, visitors are helping themselves to a campfire cookout while the cowboys are still out working. The roundup wagon is at the Schultz Ranch across the road from Curry Ranch around 1923.

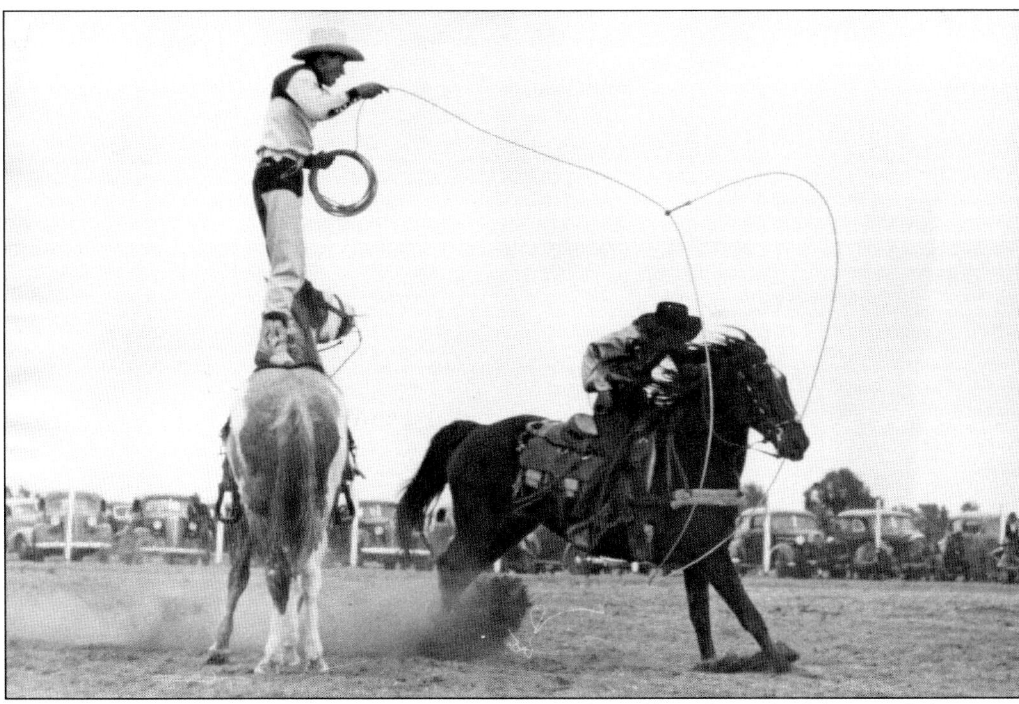

Once a cowboy always a cowboy, it seems. Even on their days off, cowboys plied their trade by testing their skills at local rodeos set up in arenas or even empty fields. It did not take long for a crowd to gather to witness bronc and bull riding, roping, and trick roping and riding, as seen here.

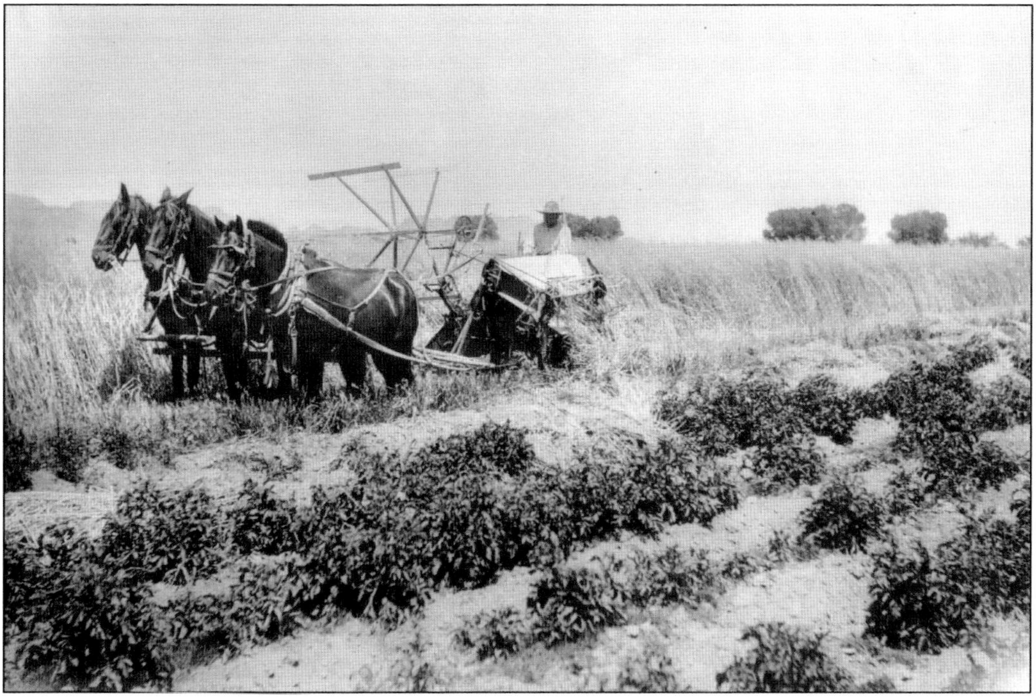

While cotton was the dominant commercial crop, another crop that thrived in the Casa Grande area was oats. It was an important cash crop because if a farmer harvested more than he could use himself, the excess oats could be sold to local ranchers for stock feed. A three-horse team is pulling a six-foot McCormick binder, also known as a reaper, which mowed and baled the crop in one operation (above). Although mechanical farming devices were becoming available, mechanically-driven farming equipment was in the early stages of development. Most cultivating, planting, and harvesting was still done by horse- or mule-drawn teams. A row of two-horse teams and drivers are waiting for the signal from the supervisor on horseback to begin preparation of a cotton field (below).

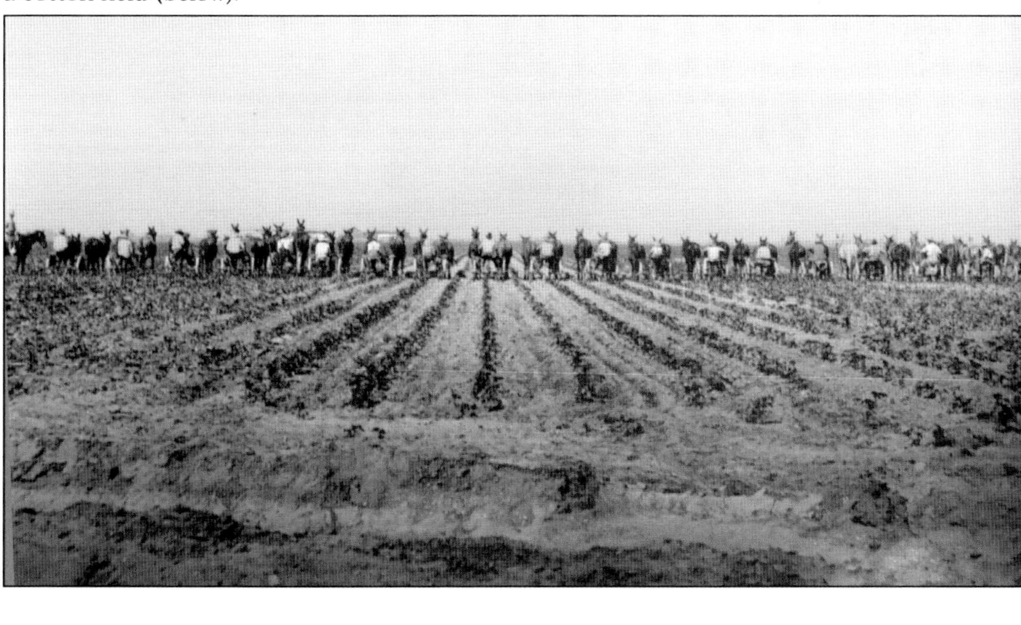

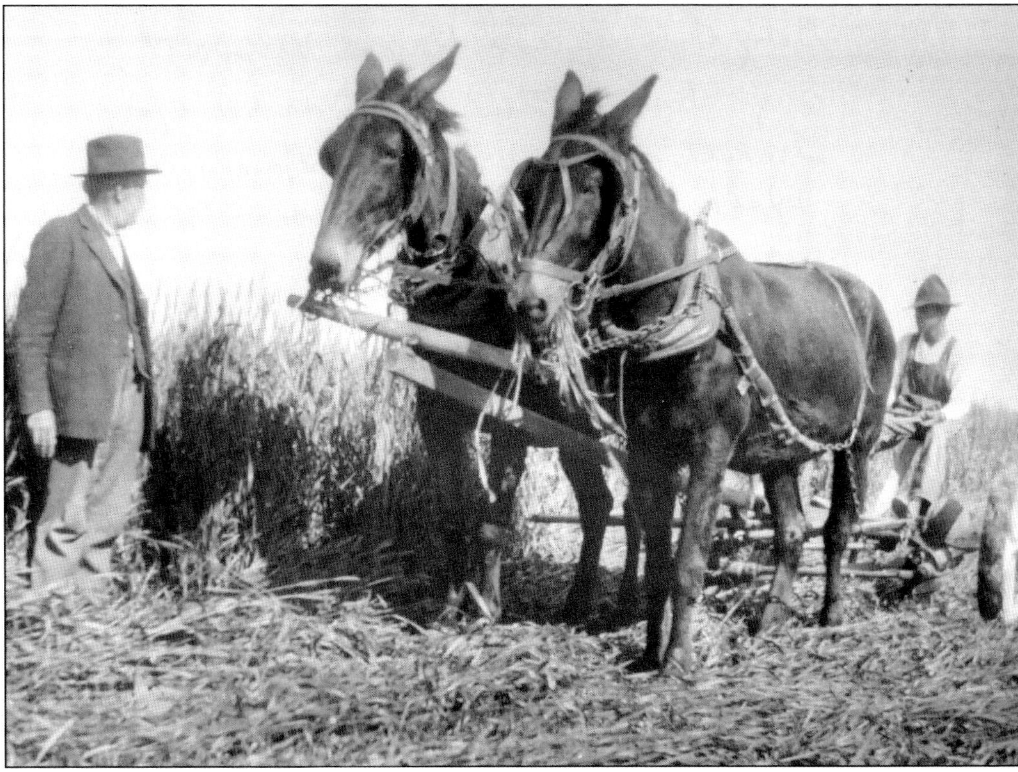

Today, the northwest corner of Trekell Road and Florence Boulevard contains a credit union backed by a strip mall and houses at one of the busiest intersections of the city, but around 1924 it was planted with cane. A horse-drawn mower driven by Guy Gilbert is cutting a cane crop as David Hellworth looks on.

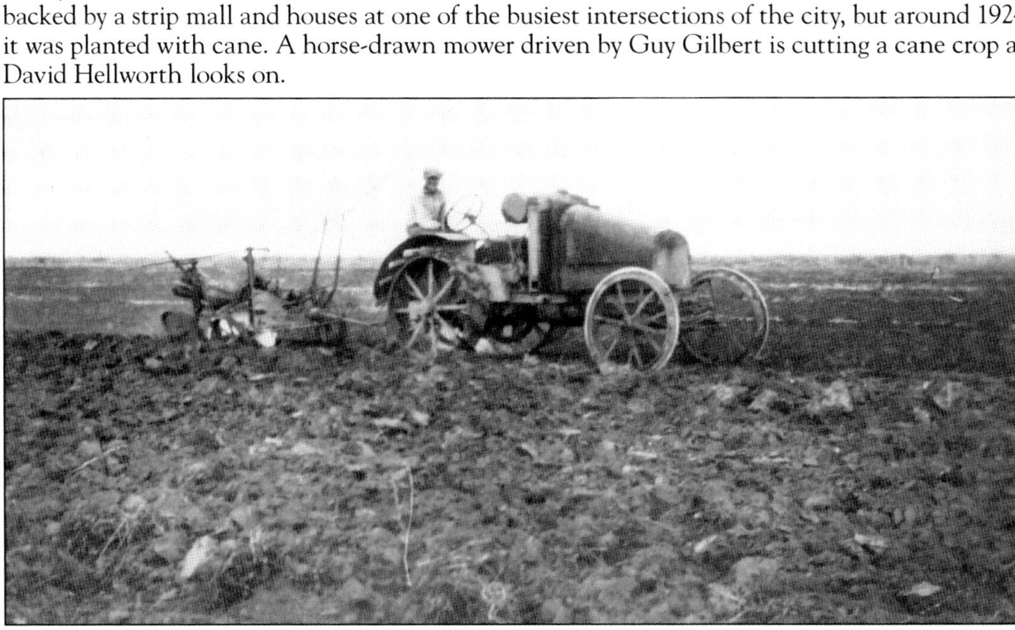

On the Steele farm, Paul Keeling sits on an early mechanized tractor pulling a plow, a vast improvement over horse-drawn plows. The Steele farm was one of several that sprouted up in the early 1900s. Keeling eventually acquired acreage of his own and became a successful farmer and important member of the community.

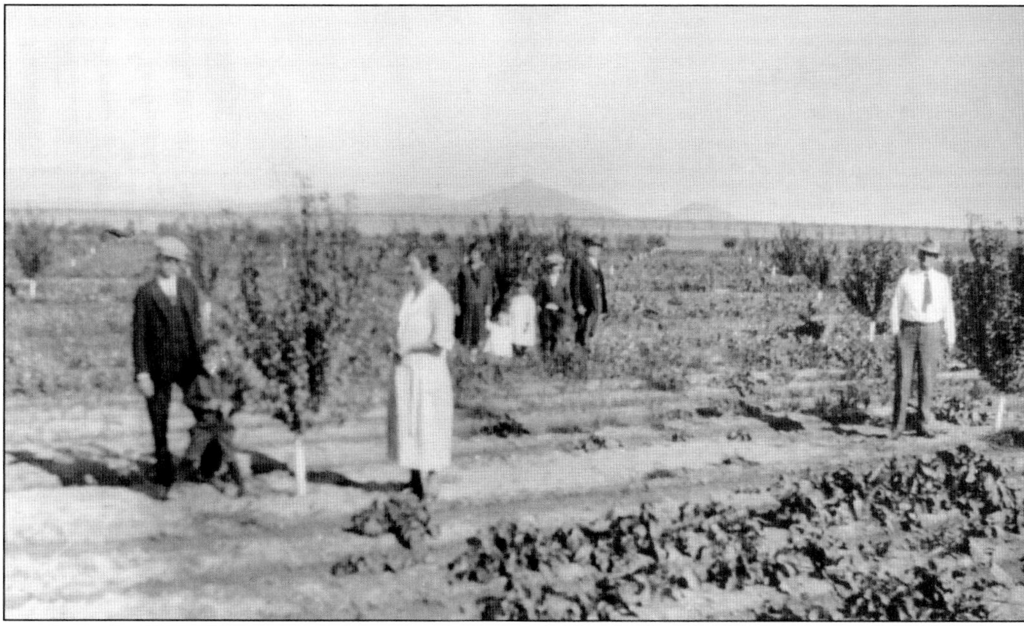

Arizona's climate is conducive to the growing of citrus, and in 1924, a young fruit orchard is visited by members of the Gilbert family at their ranch on Florence Boulevard just east of Trekell Road. Those present include Guy and George Gilbert, Cabrilla Hellworth Gilbert, Frances Gilbert Fawcett, Parke Gilbert, David Hellworth, and Frank Gilbert. The Gilberts were so prominent a family that today a city street bears their name.

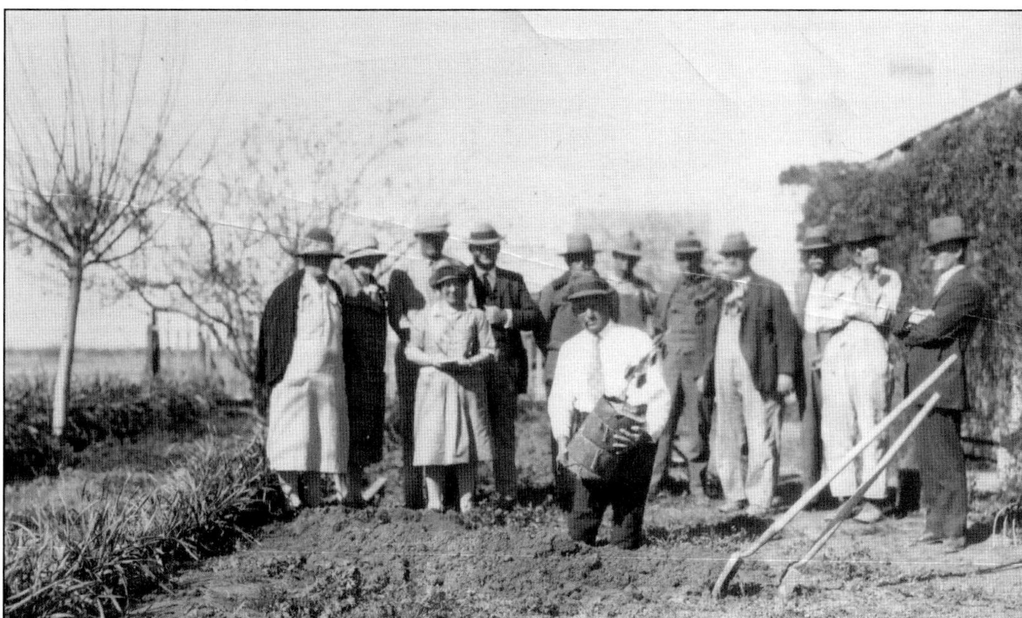

J.E. McClain of Tempe is demonstrating the planting of citrus trees at the Amandus Peters home. Among those attending the demonstration, only a few are identified. In no particular order are May Forbach, Edna Peters, Gertrude Hager, and Gordon McMurray. McMurray Boulevard is named for the McMurray family.

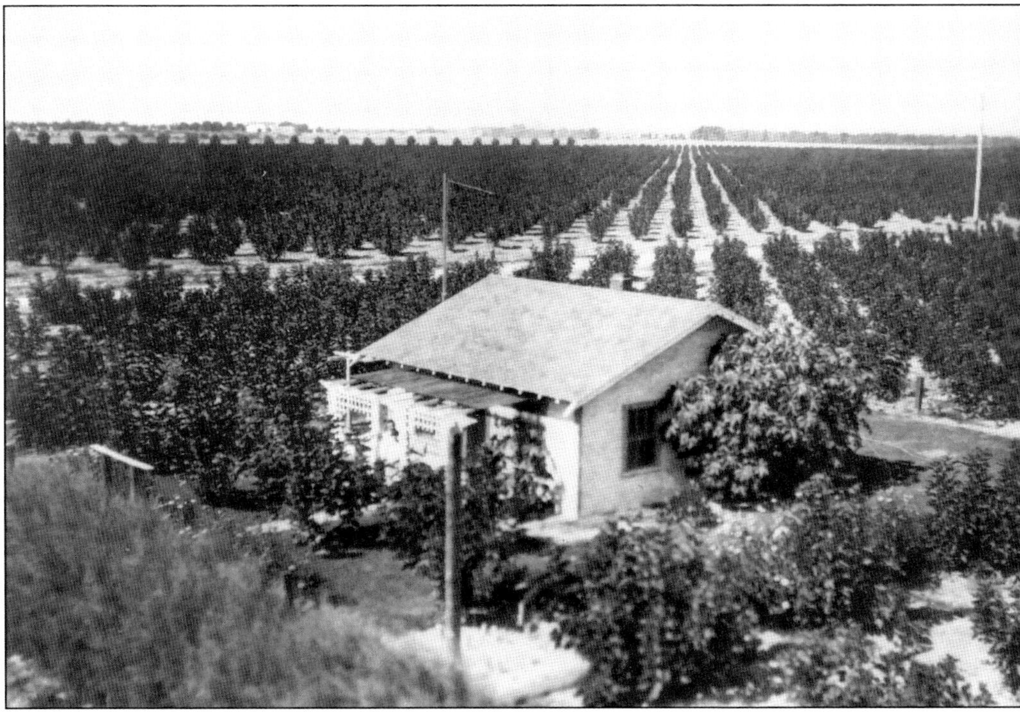

In 1926, George Sellers and Henry Moeller purchased 880 acres of land for the purpose of establishing a five-to-ten-acre lot housing subdivision (above). The acreage was intended for use as a fig-growing enterprise that would make the buyer independent as a fig grower. Kadota fig stock was planted in 1927, and a cannery (below) was built in 1929. More than 60 people purchased land in the project. Due to the hot desert winds and sand storms that damaged the fragile fruit, the stock market crash of 1929, and the lack of expected water flow, coupled with the fractured nature of the plots conspired to create the ultimate failure of the venture. By 1935, the fig farm lands were converted to other crops. The only reminder of this ill-fated endeavor exists in a few place names, such as Kadota Street and Avenue A.

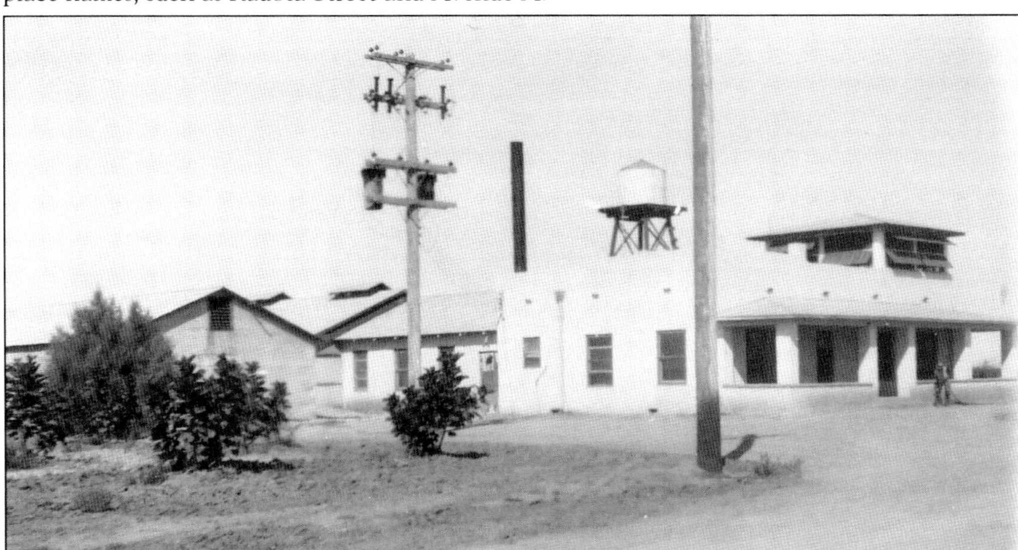

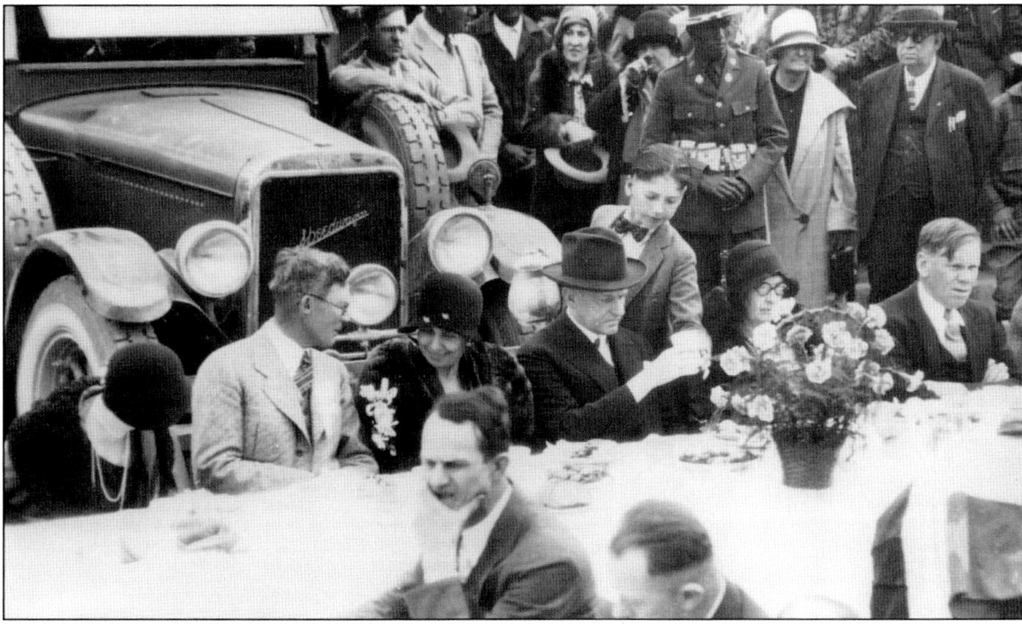

With the continuing expansion of agriculture as an important economic growth factor for Casa Grande and environs, water once again became of major concern. In an effort to alleviate the irrigation needs of farmers, Coolidge Dam was built to impound water from the Gila River. On March 30, 1930, Pres. Calvin Coolidge (above in the black hat) was present for the dedication of the dam that was named after him. Will Rogers, renowned social commentator and wit, was among the many dignitaries who attended the dedication. The dam, seen below filled with spectators on the day of dedication, was considered a modern marvel and of critical importance to the irrigation needs of the farming community. Although the dam is located many miles from Casa Grande, local farmers benefited from knowing that flooding of the river was now controlled and irrigation water would be available in the San Carlos Reservoir.

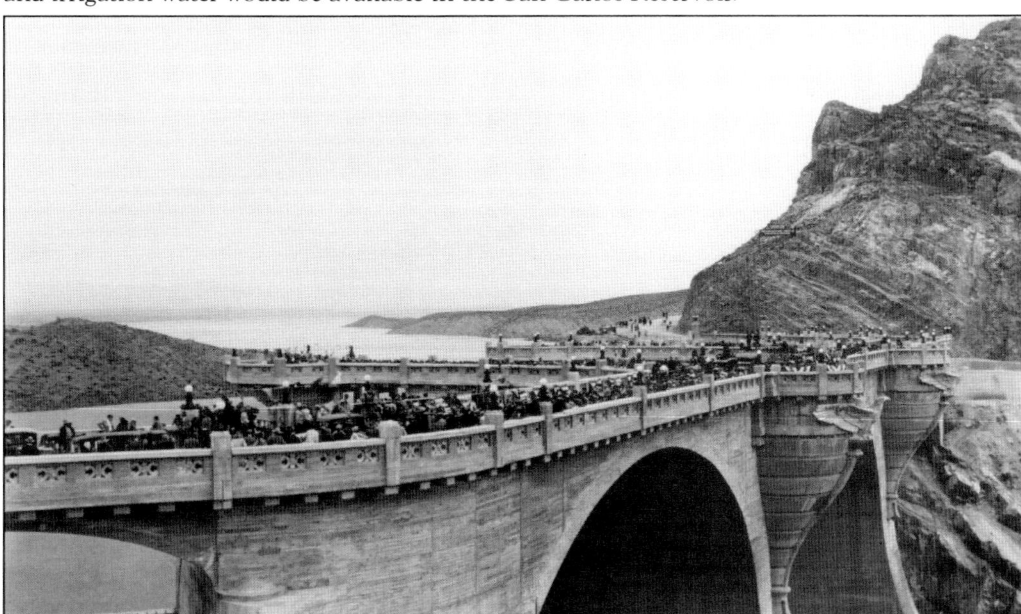

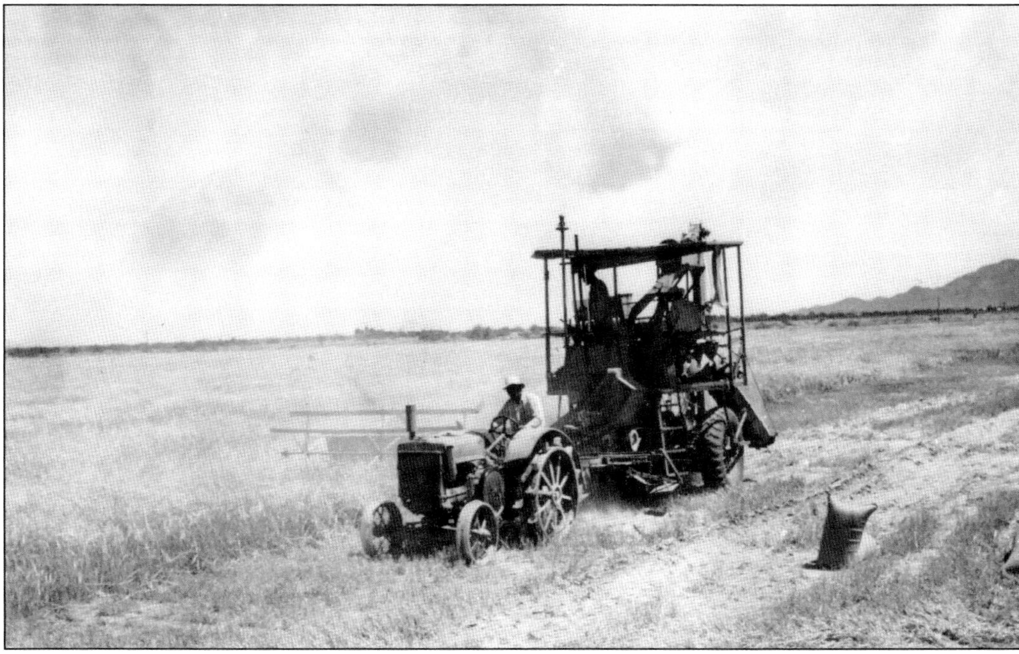

By 1942, farm equipment was motor-driven and more sophisticated. This photograph shows a John Deere combine and a Model D 1937 tractor working in tandem on the Gilbert Ranch outside of the city. Parke Gilbert is on the John Deere tractor and Guy Gilbert is on the combine, a huge improvement over the horse-drawn equipment that Guy had used in years past.

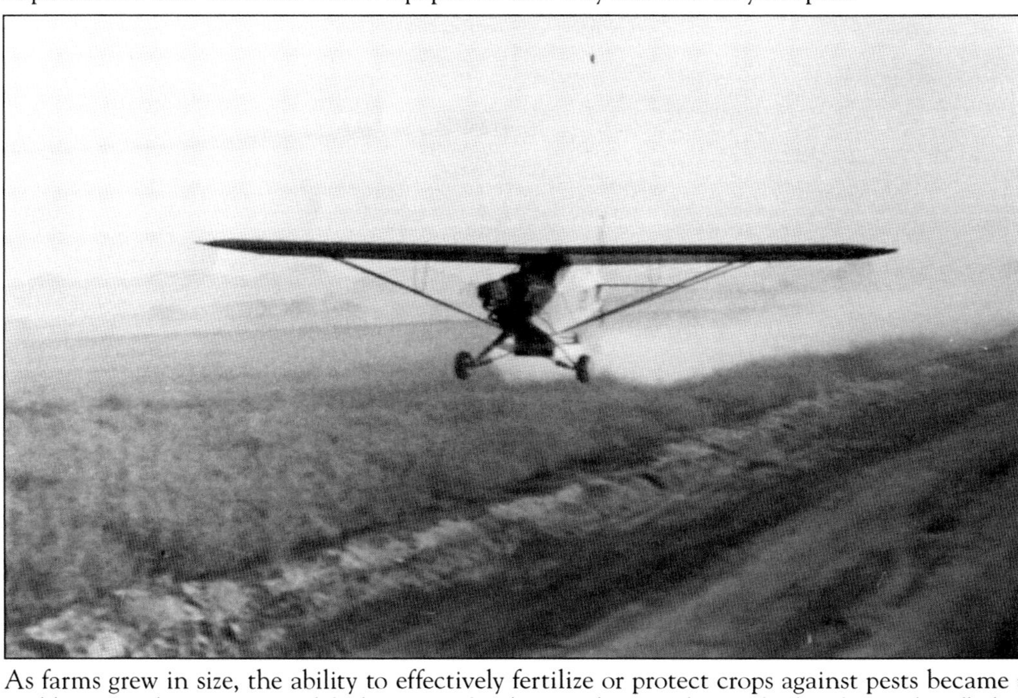

As farms grew in size, the ability to effectively fertilize or protect crops against pests became a problem. Airplanes were modified to carry fertilizer and pesticides, and pilots learned to fly low over the large fields dusting crops. George Gomez's CUB crop-dusting airplane is seen skimming a field near McMurray Boulevard in the 1950s.

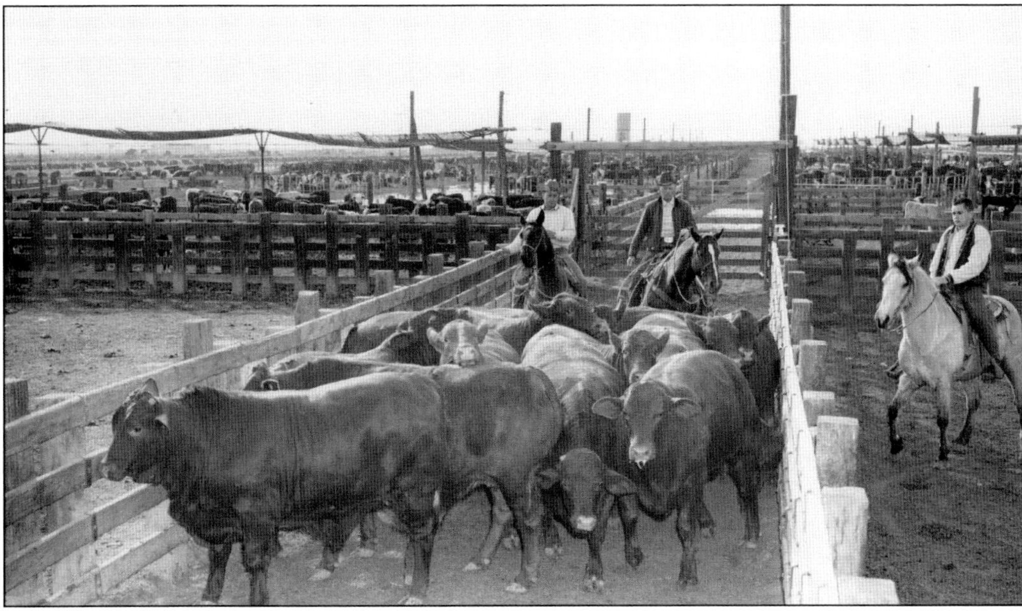

Even as farming continued to be the most prominent commercial enterprise in Pinal County, by the mid-1950s, the livestock industry was second only to cotton as an economic force. While cattle were free range to begin their lives, they ultimately were sent to feedlots for fattening prior to slaughter. The University of Arizona estimated that 35 to 40 feedlots were in operation in Pinal County during this time. One of the earliest and largest lots was owned by the Benedict family. The Benedict Feeding Company, located on the outskirts of the city, was known for innovative care and feeding of their charges. Sam Benedict (right), the patriarch of the enterprise, was continually studying ways to improve the feedlot industry, especially his lot. After almost 50 years in operation, the Benedicts sold their family business in 2004.

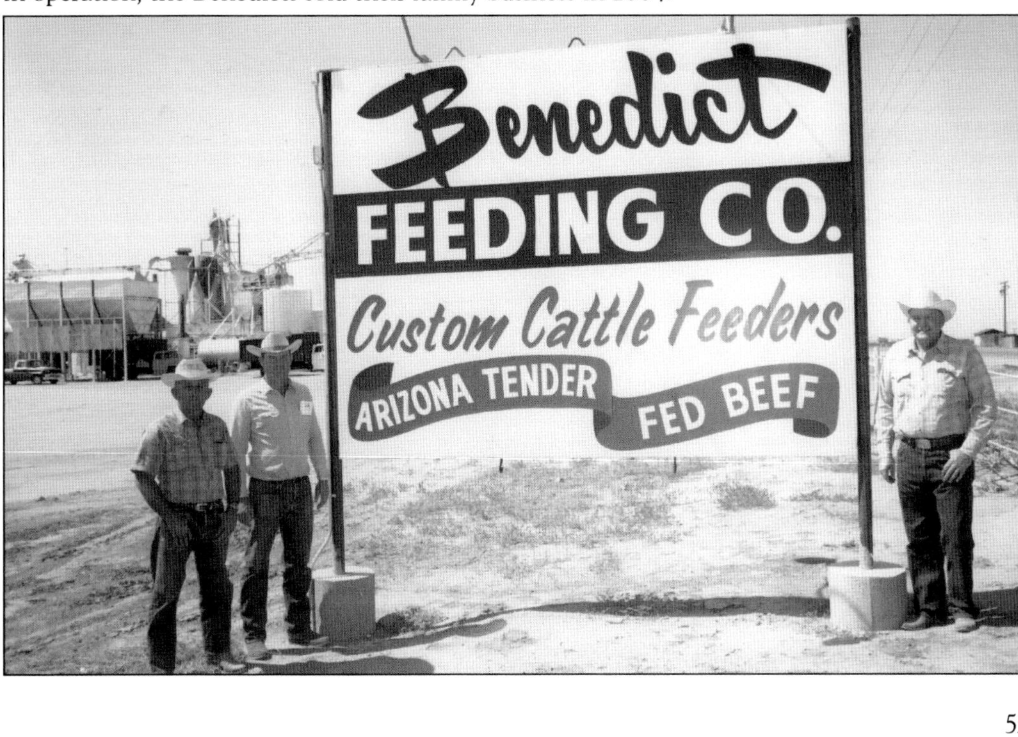

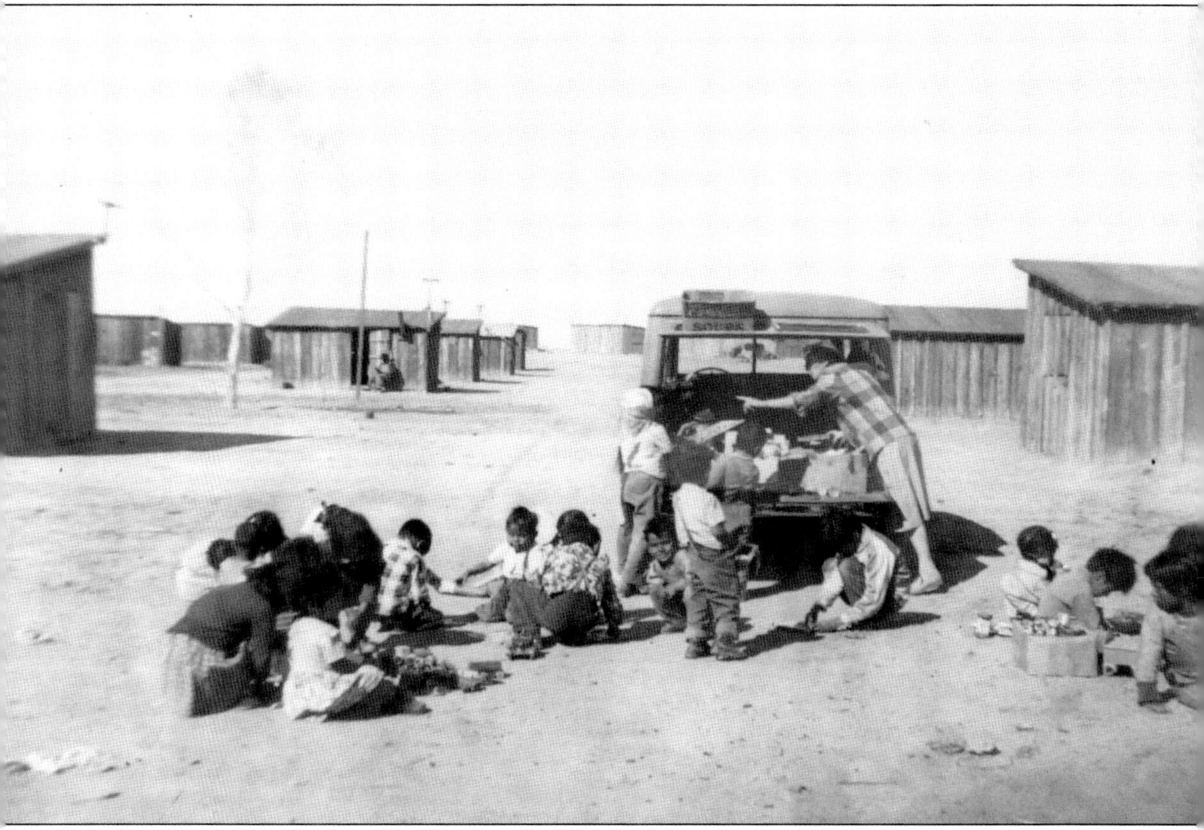

Early on, farm labor camps were established in several locations throughout Pinal County. Most of the laborers who lived in these camps were of African American or Mexican descent. This photograph of a typical camp shows several rows of wood-frame cabins, many of which lacked running water and indoor plumbing. It appears as though they did have electricity, based on the pole visible on the left and what appear to be television antennas on several of the cabins. The Estrada family lived in the second cabin beyond the pole on the left. Felix Estrada and his sister Yolanda are in the plaid and patterned shirts on the left. Pedro, the boy with one strap of his coveralls hanging down, is standing at the back of the truck. On the right are the Salinas twins. An unidentified person is unloading items from a vehicle to dispense to the children and their families. A sign on the back of the vehicle reads "Campbell Soups." By the 1960s, with the advent of mechanical picking machines, the number of camps began to decline.

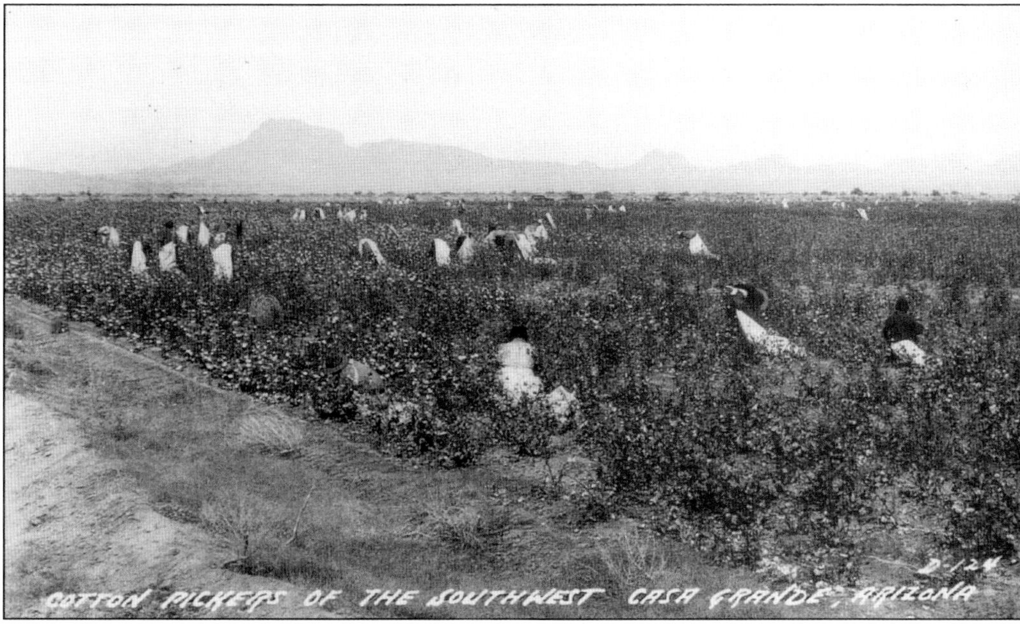

Migrant farm workers, including women and children, came from other states to pick cotton as well as other seasonal crops. Some families stayed and became members of the community, but most followed the weather and continued west to the next fields that were ready to be picked.

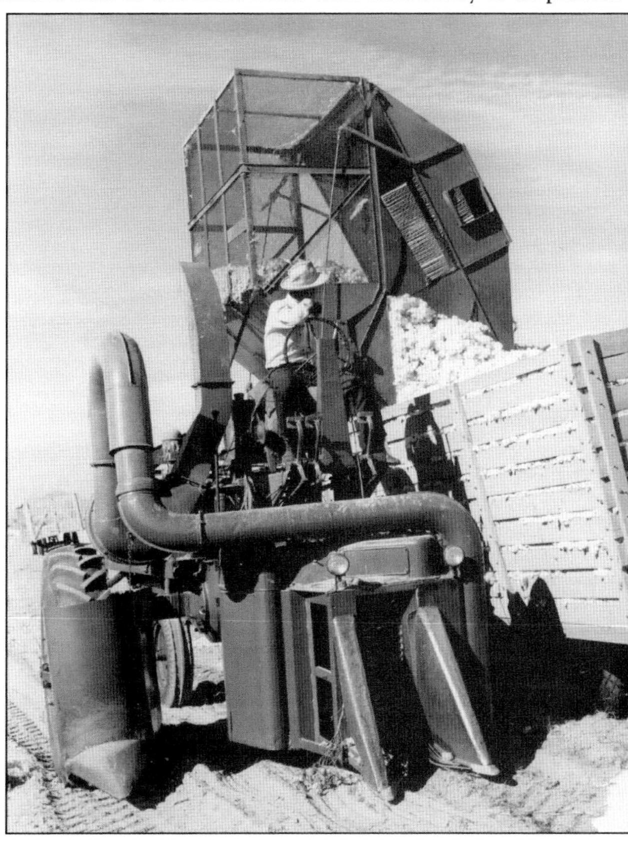

By the mid-1960s, even larger fields were dedicated to the raising of cotton, and mechanical cotton pickers had mostly replaced migrant cotton workers. This one-man operation allowed the cotton to be picked, rough sorted, and dumped into cotton trailers ready for shipment to a processing plant.

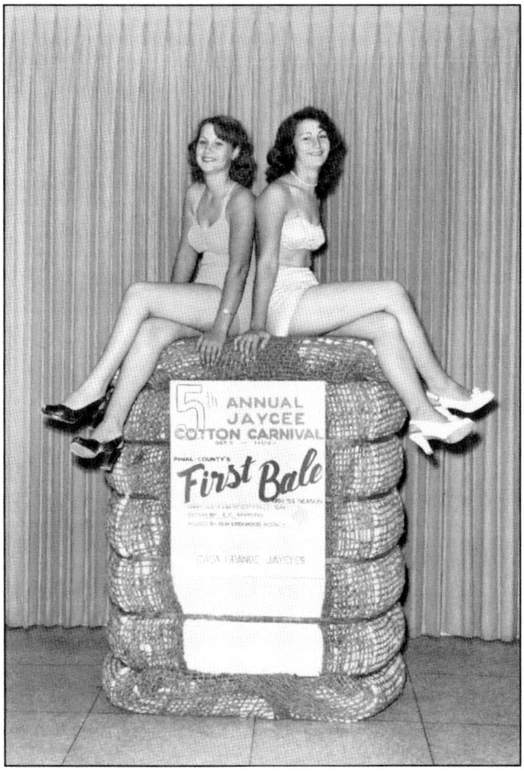

Ever since the end of World War II, cotton has been king in Pinal County. To celebrate the role of cotton as an economic force in Casa Grande, an annual cotton parade and carnival was held. Cora and Mary Tate are seated on the symbolic first bale of cotton produced in 1952.

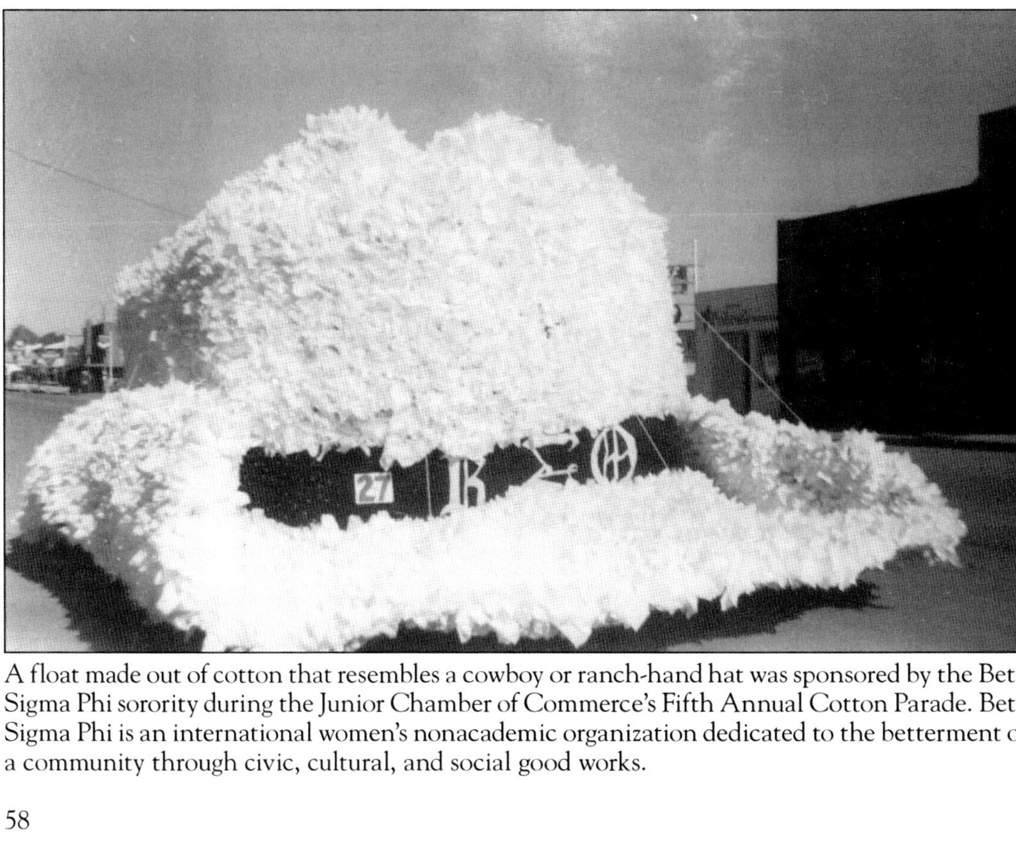

A float made out of cotton that resembles a cowboy or ranch-hand hat was sponsored by the Beta Sigma Phi sorority during the Junior Chamber of Commerce's Fifth Annual Cotton Parade. Beta Sigma Phi is an international women's nonacademic organization dedicated to the betterment of a community through civic, cultural, and social good works.

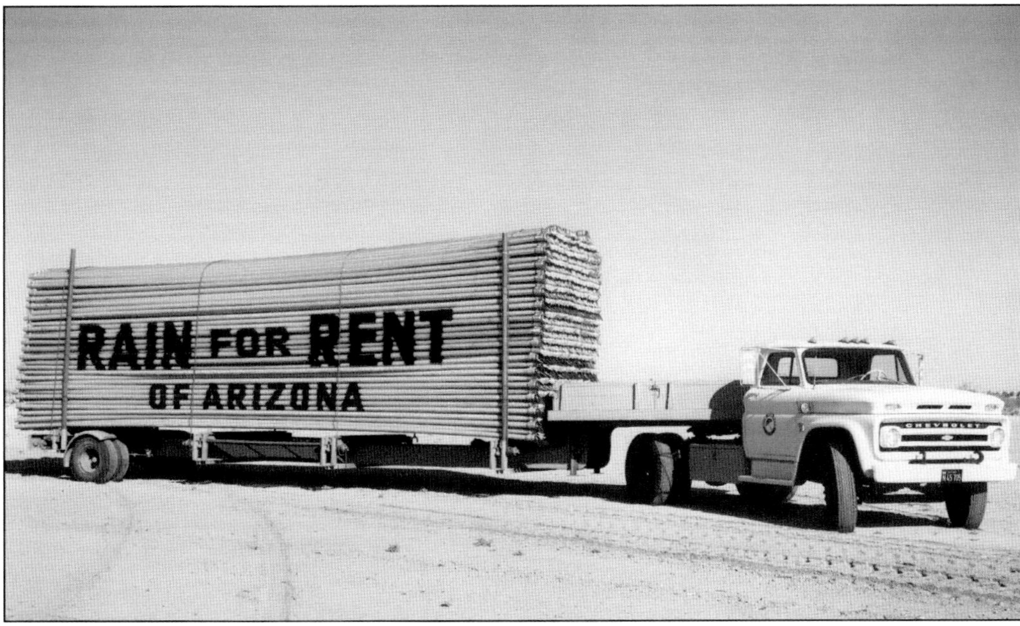

As agricultural endeavors continued to grow and establish the identity of Casa Grande as a farming community, irrigation was critical to sustaining a variety of crops. The lack of predictable quantities of rain led to the need for companies like Rain for Rent. Rain for Rent began in California as an oil field equipment company in 1934. It evolved into an irrigation equipment rental supply company with offices in 27 states, including four in Arizona as of 2010.

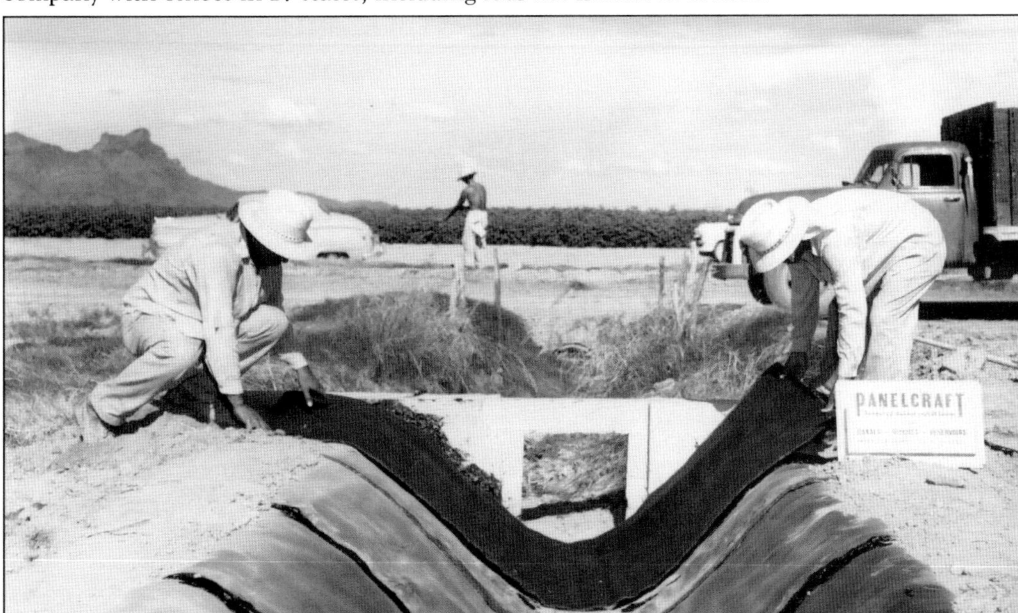

In other efforts to water their fields, farmers dug irrigation ditches and constructed canals and reservoirs. These earthen devices were subject to erosion and seepage. Several companies created concrete forms and asphalt sheets that were easily installed to prevent that from happening. Fullerform concrete from the Bentson Concrete Company and Panelcraft asphalt sheets from the Arizona Salvage Company were two of the more commonly used products.

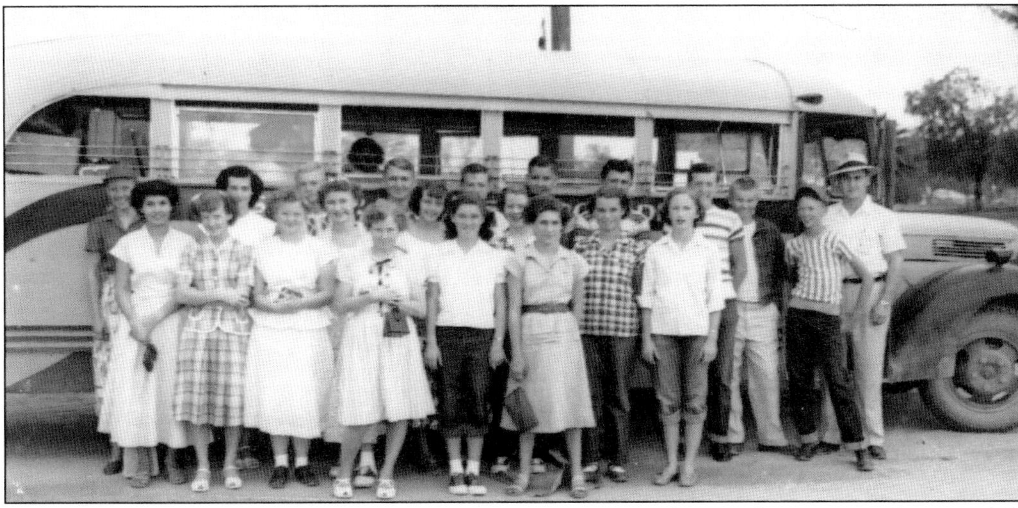

Because of the importance of agriculture and ranching in and around Casa Grande, 4-H clubs have always played an important role in the community. Many young people have followed in their family's footsteps and continue to participate in farming pursuits, such as the raising of crops, animal husbandry, canning, and sewing, among other endeavors. The group of boys and girls above is headed for the 4-H Roundup in Tucson in 1950. In the 1964 photograph below, Peter R. Van Dernoot, a *Reader's Digest* representative, is presenting awards to a group of 4-H Club members at an 11-Mile Corner ceremony. To this day, many students, as well as descendants of early farmers, participate in school programs and 4-H clubs as they keep the tradition of the community alive.

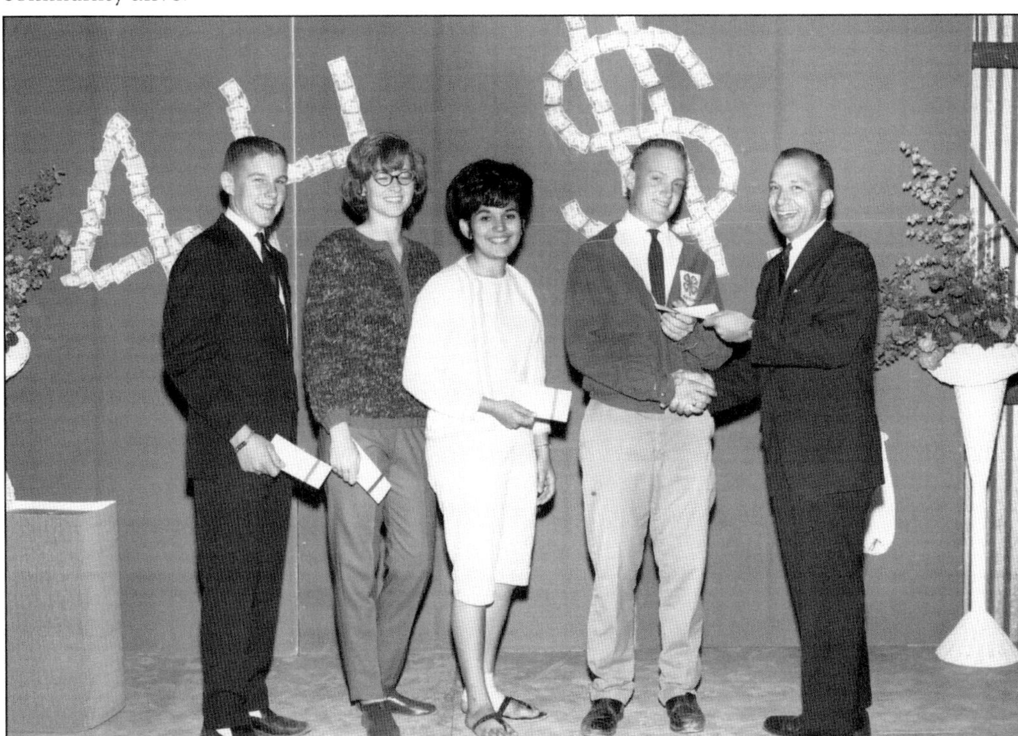

Five

Becoming a Town

As soon as a group of people, no matter the size, decides they are ready to become a viable, vibrant entity, that is the moment when the idea of a city begins to become a reality. Neighborhoods, businesses, schools, churches, newspapers, and various public services then determine the size and effectiveness of that city. Casa Grande became that community soon after the railroad stopped in the Arizona desert in 1879. Although only two stores and a hotel existed at that time, within the next few years the town had grown, and successful entrepreneurs were contributing to the needs of the community.

The Casa Grande townsite was not created until 1892, but that did not stop the citizens from viewing their community as a city. Among the first indicators that Casa Grande intended to become more than a stop on the railroad trail across the southern desert was the establishment of a school. In 1882, just three years after the town was named, the citizens of Casa Grande decided to build a structure that was to be used primarily as a school and secondarily as a public meeting place. By now, the town had 180 inhabitants, including at least 20 school-aged children. The three original businesses had expanded to include a boardinghouse, a restaurant, two blacksmith and wagon shops, and two saloons. By 1884, the population had grown to 500 residents and several more businesses had opened.

In addition to the businesses, private homes were being built near the railroad tracks. In 1880, John C. Loss built an adobe house at 107 West Main Street that stood until 1989. Early on, most of the houses and businesses were built of adobe, although as more folks moved west and brought their ideas of home with them, many houses were being constructed of wood.

During the early 1900s and into the late 1930s, Casa Grande continued to grow, even as it was largely abandoning its reputation as a railroad and mining town and becoming better known as an agricultural center.

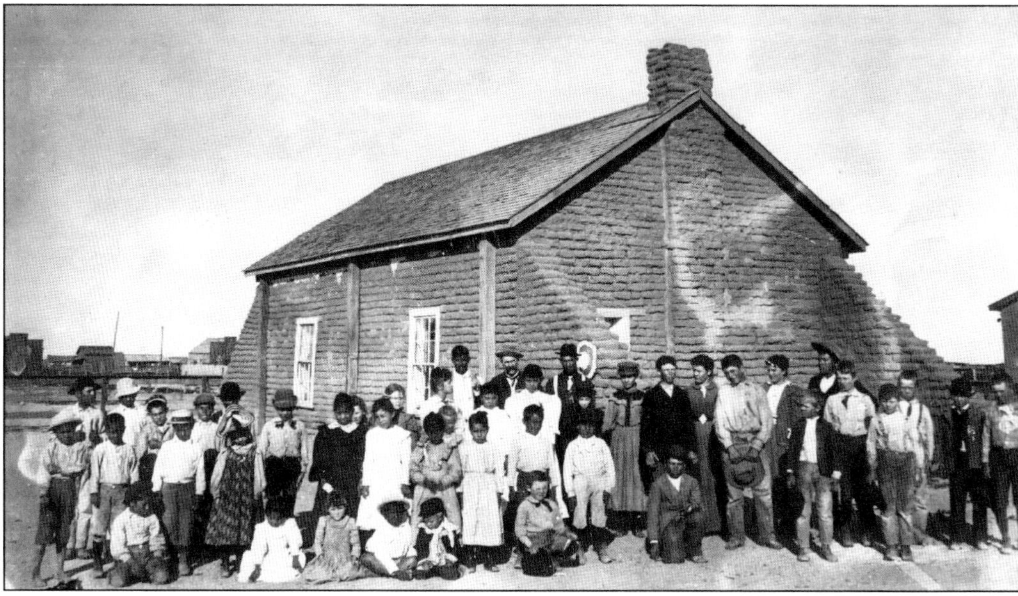

The establishment of schools is often a sign that a city views itself as a community. As early as about 1895, the education of children living in Casa Grande was considered of primary importance. A class of Anglo and Hispanic students of all ages stands next to their one-room adobe school located west of the Southern Pacific Railroad tracks (above). Downtown Main Street can be seen in the background. The wood building below was the second school constructed in Casa Grande. William J. Magaw, in the center back, was the teacher for all grades in 1911, when this photograph was taken. The children appear to be a mix of Anglos and Hispanics. Girls seem to dominate the class. The building, which is in apparent need of repair, was located on Florence Street between Main Street and Second Avenue. That locale is now Elliot Park.

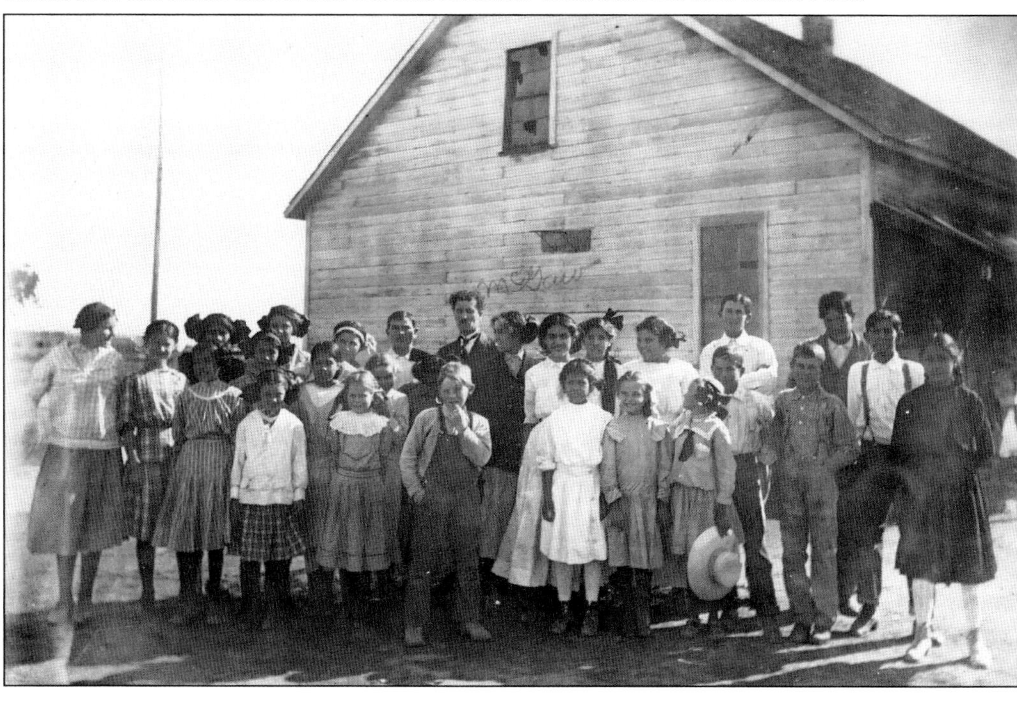

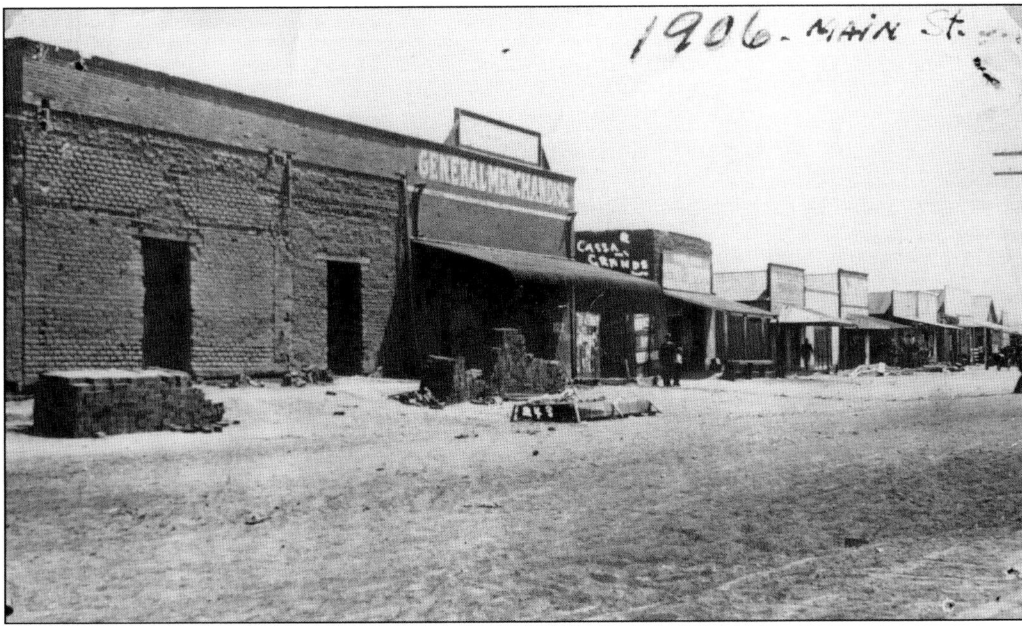

In 1906, some 27 years after the founding of Casa Grande, buildings lined Main Street. In 1965, Mrs. Ricardo "Dick" Vasquez identified several of the structures. From left to right, they are the Curriel home, a warehouse, Maldanado's General Merchandise, Cruz Trading Post, Tom Meehan's Saloon, Kratzka's Berlin Bakery, and the Peart and Armenta store. Lillian Peart, wife of T.R. Peart, had a café or coffee shop along here.

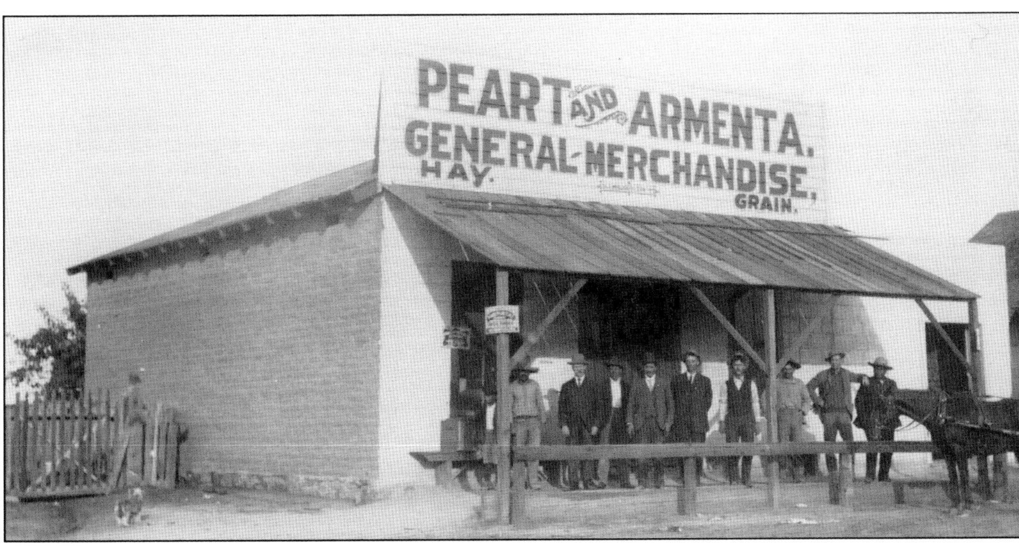

One of the early businesses in Casa Grande, the Peart and Armenta General Merchandise building exemplified the good working relationship between Anglo and Mexican businessmen and city residents in 1907. The store not only supplied farm and ranch items, but provided a meeting place for patrons to talk about important state and city issues as well as indulge in a little gossip.

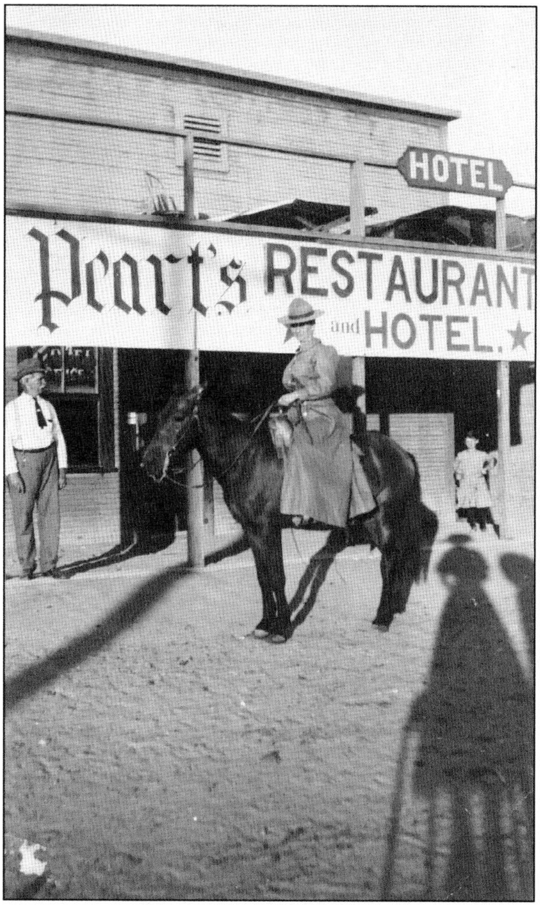

The Peart family arrived in Casa Grande in 1907 and quickly became known as successful entrepreneurs and civic leaders. This photograph, taken in 1910 or 1911, shows Lillian Peart (née Weaver) on horseback in front of the family restaurant and hotel on Main Street north of the railroad depot. Their daughter Alice Peart, on the right, was forever known locally as the girl who accidentally started a fire that burned down their house. T.R. Peart, on the left, served as mayor as well as on the city council and in other official capacities. In 1913, just one year after achieving statehood, Arizona's first governor arrived in Casa Grande after touring the region. Below, T.R. Peart is seated next to the driver, Dr. Randell. In the right rear seat is Gov. George W.P. Hunt. The other two gentlemen are unidentified.

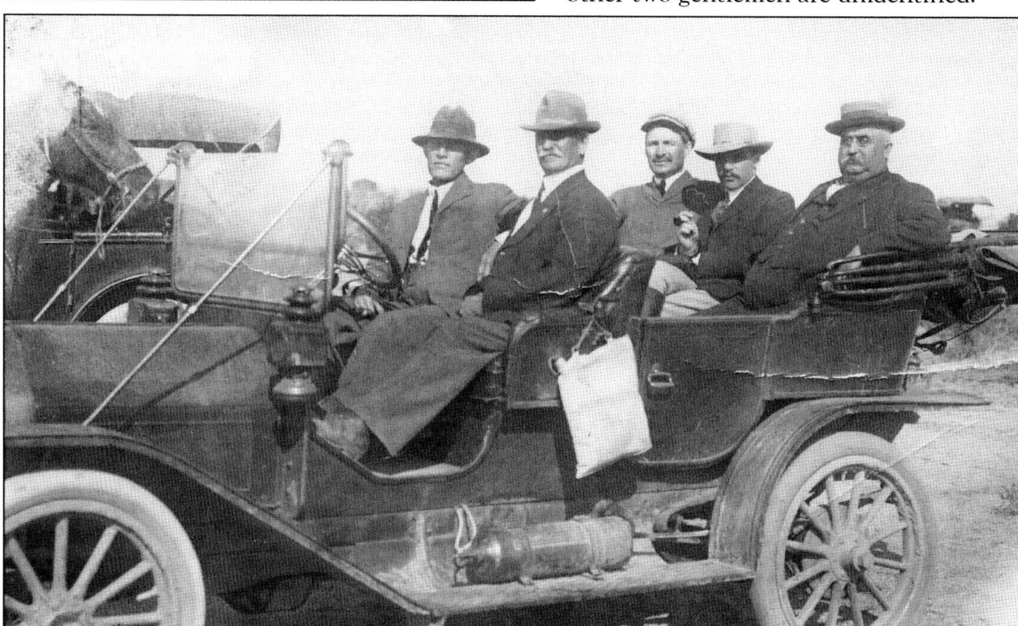

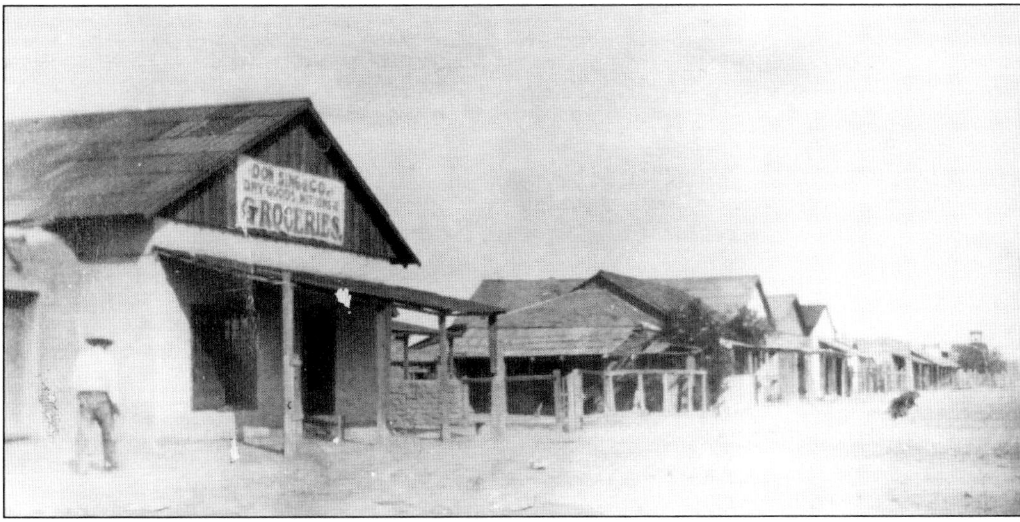

The story of Chinese immigrants in Arizona is only now becoming fully documented; however, in Casa Grande it is well known that the extended Don family played an important role in the early history and growth of the town. Their store, Don Market, was first opened by Don Sing in 1897. As early as 1910, it was already a landmark located at the corner of First and Florence Streets (above). This family-owned-and-operated store ensured that dry goods and groceries were readily available to the residents closest to the downtown area. When the store, still in the same location, closed in 1992, it was the oldest continuous business in Casa Grande. Pictured around 1920, from left to right, are Chin Oishau Don, Don June, their children Fay and Franklin, and the proprietor's brother Don Chun.

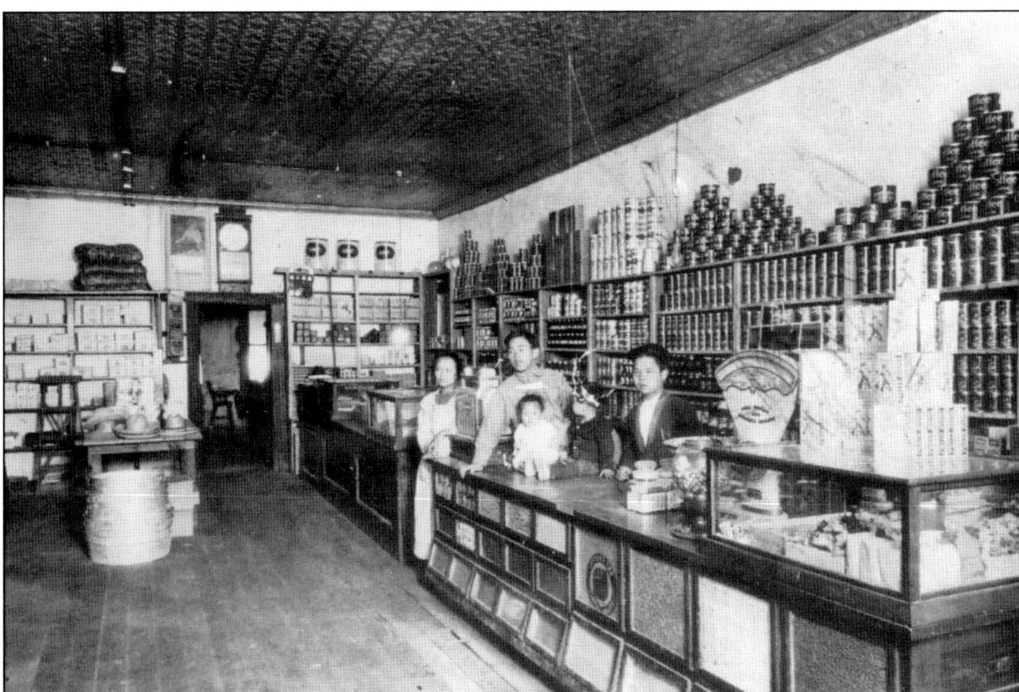

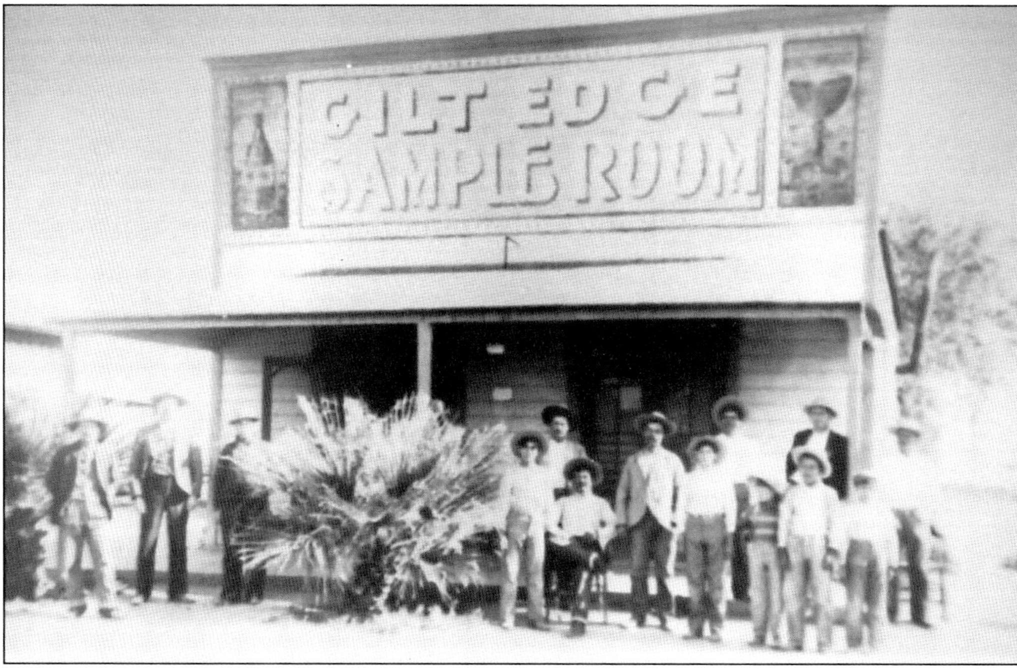

Although the name Gilt Edge Sample Room might create doubt as to the true nature of the building above, the decorations on each side of the sign clearly indicate that this was a saloon. Like most businesses in town, it was located on Main Street. Carlos Cruz and Ricardo "Dick" Vasquez are pictured (but are not specifically identified) in this c. 1913 photograph. Below, W.A. Lacey displays his business acumen. He makes it clear that he is the owner of what had been the Gilt Edge Sample Room by placing his name on the sign and changing the name to the Gilt Edge Saloon, which is how it was commonly known. Lacey apparently sold the building to Thomas Meehan. Unfortunately, shortly after he purchased the building it burned down in the April 28, 1914, fire that destroyed many Main Street businesses.

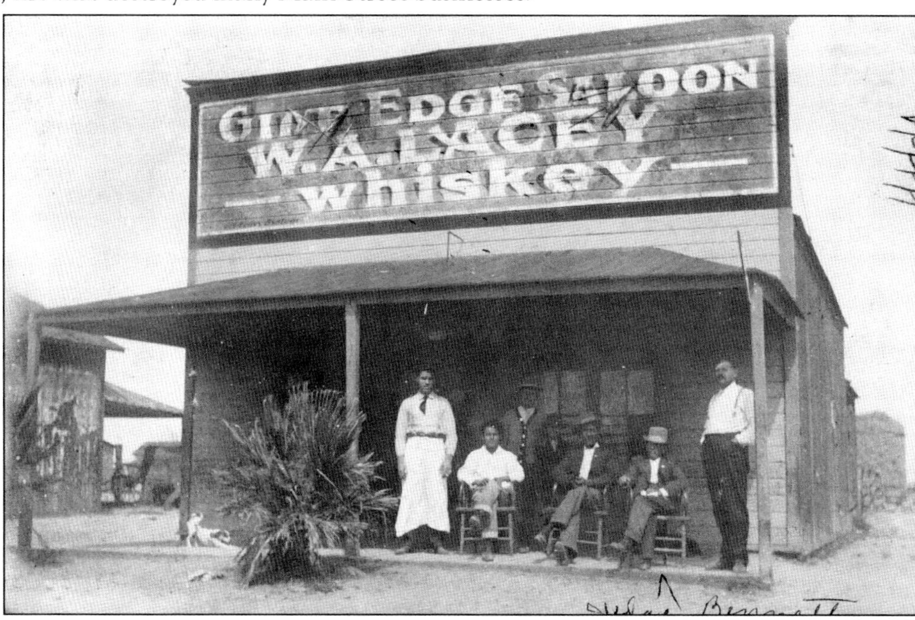

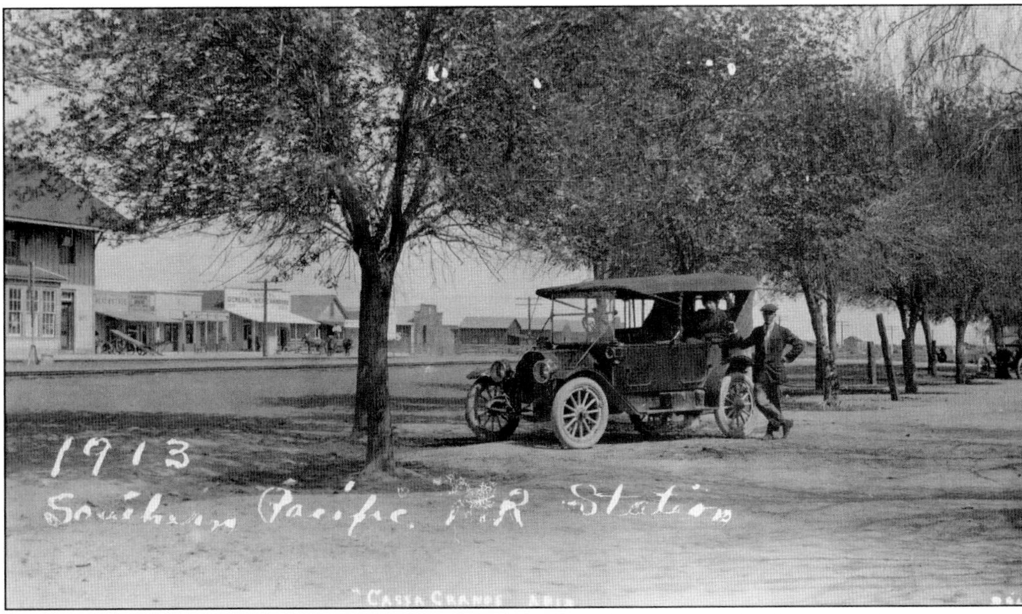

Automobiles were rare in Casa Grande in 1913, and this one, parked among the trees south of the Southern Pacific Railroad Station, must have garnered a lot of attention. The four-door Model-T Ford runabout cost $525 when purchased new. The jaunty pose of the man at the rear of the car seems to reflect pride of ownership. A well-dressed woman can be seen in the back of the four-seater.

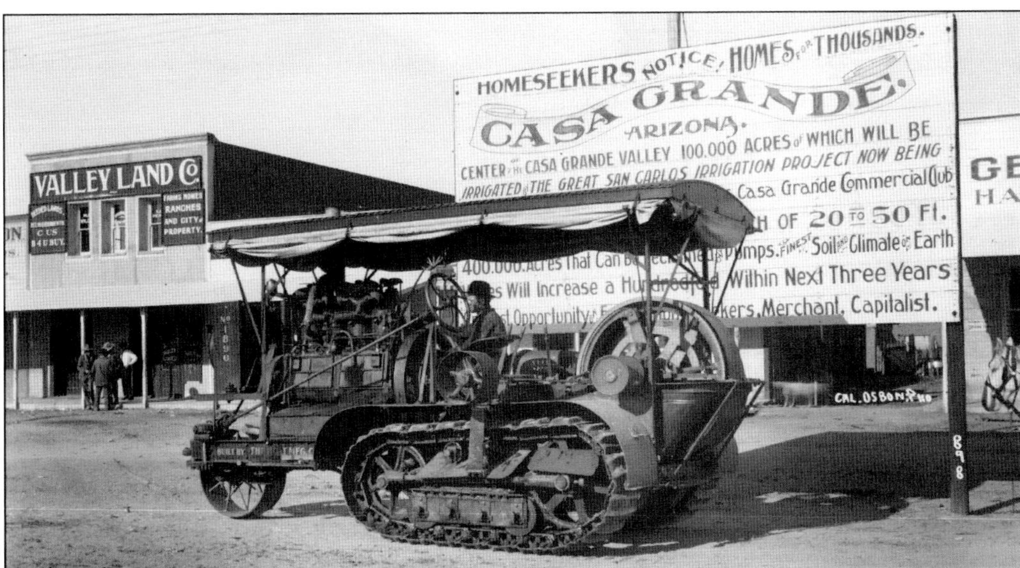

As Casa Grande was growing and many residents were doing well financially, land offices were touting the benefit of moving here. The Holt-Caterpillar tractor somewhat obscures the sign, but it is clear that land and water would soon be available for the capitalist and home seeker alike because of the pending San Carlos Irrigation Project. Perfect soil and climate, and now water availability, made this an opportunity not to be missed.

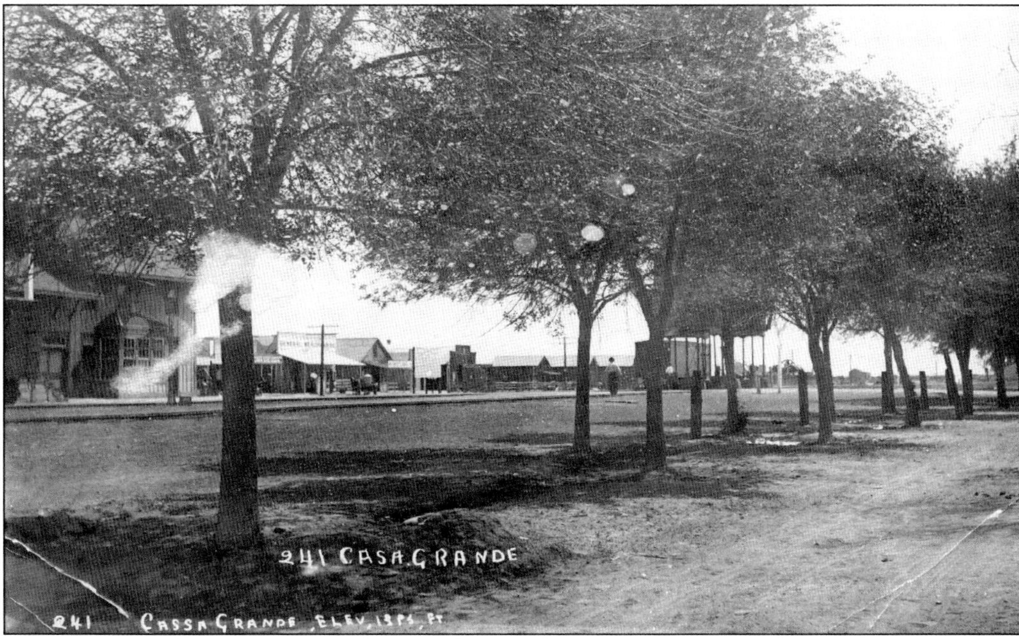

Perspective is everything, and these two photographs present an interesting contrast of downtown Casa Grande in 1913. It is important for the historical record that elements representing a city and its growth, such as the businesses that formed the economic center of the community, are photographed. It is equally important to record how people lived. Fortunately, during this time, around 1913, photographs of less commonly documented areas were taken and have survived. In the photograph above, taken from South Main Street, one can see the Southern Pacific Railroad tracks and Main Street. In the photograph below, taken from almost the same location on South Main Street behind the Southern Pacific Railroad depot and tracks, a tree-lined street and small, side-by-side, compact family homes are shown.

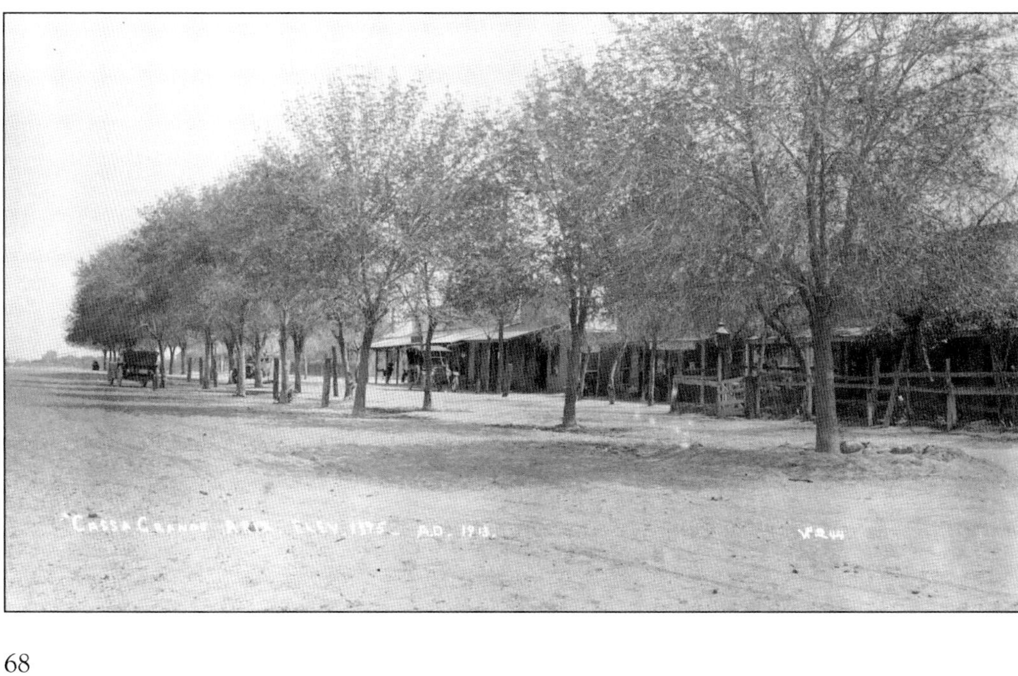

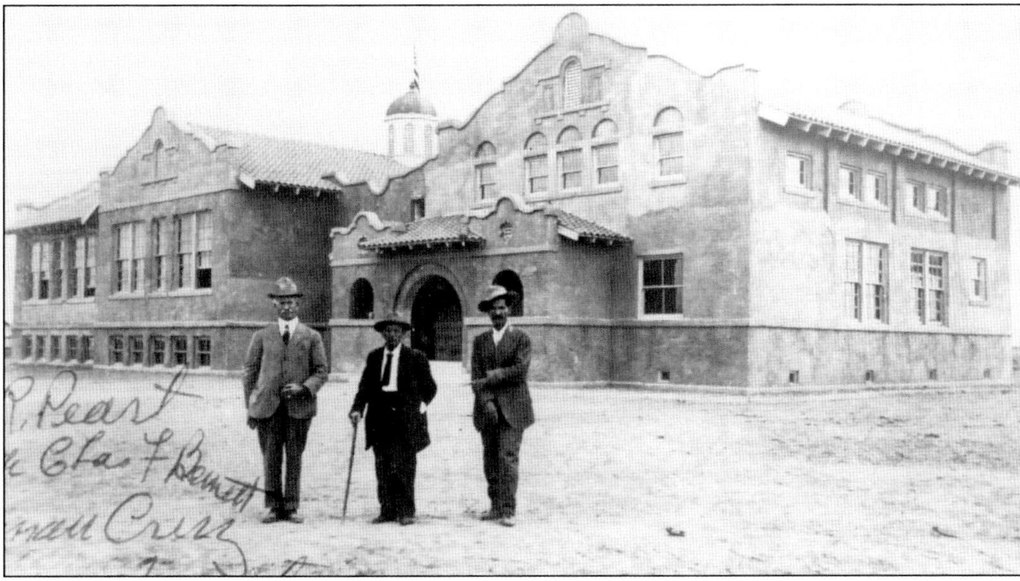

In 1914, a large, impressive building known as Central School was opened at the corner of Florence Boulevard and Sacaton Street. Pictured from left to right in front of the school are Ramon Cruz, Thomas R. Peart, and Judge Charles F. Bennett, who comprised the board of trustees that commissioned the building of the school. Construction began in August 1913, and the first classes were held in January 1914. A crowd of proud citizens dressed in their Sunday best attended the dedication (below). The building, which cost $21,000, was touted as a "hygenic" school because of the unusual aspect of having newfangled indoor plumbing. Locally referred to as the Northside School, for 60 years it housed both elementary and high school classes. In 1971, the building was declared unsafe and was ultimately torn down. The bell and cupola can be viewed at the historical society.

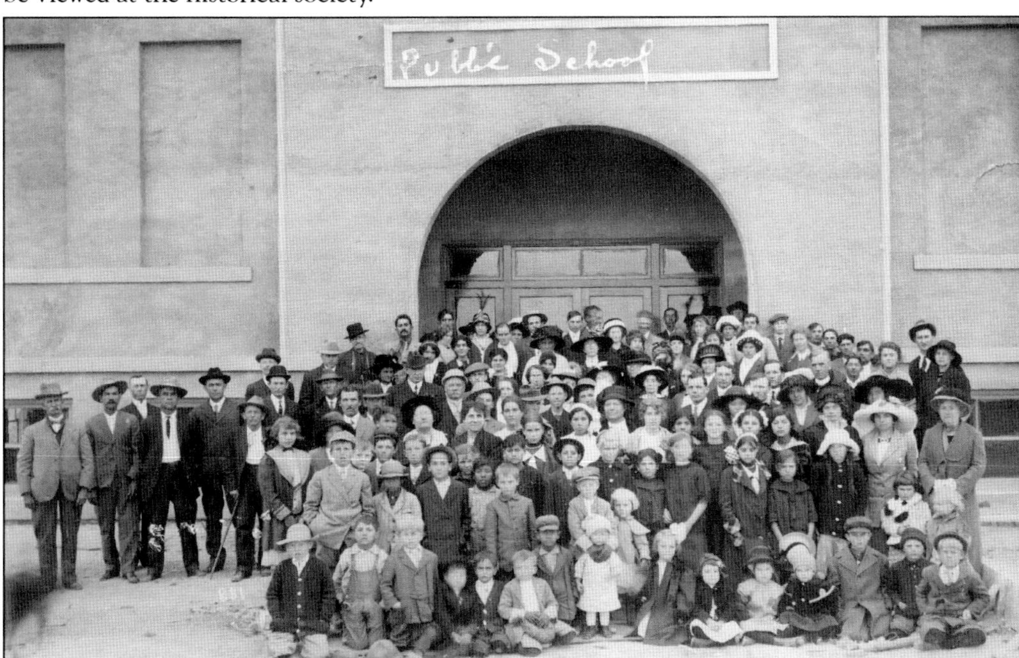

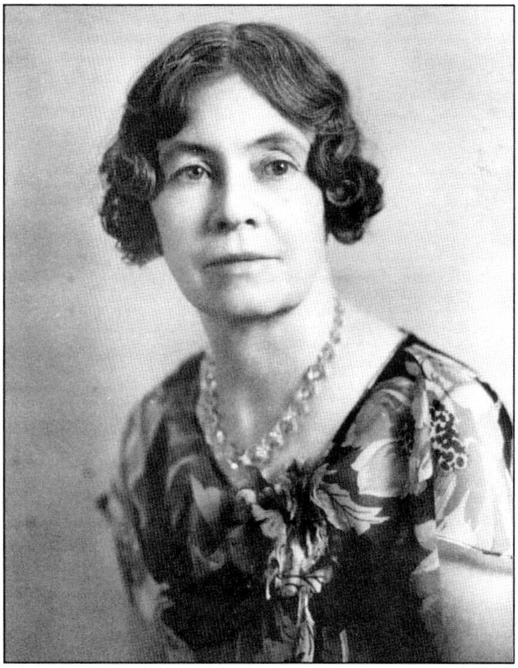

Casa Grande's first regular newspaper, the *Casa Grande Times*, was printed in 1912, and in 1913, the *Casa Grande Bulletin* was published. The most successful newspaper, however, was the *Casa Grande Valley Dispatch*, initially published in 1914. Prior to moving to Casa Grande, Angela Hutchinson Hammer (left), one of the few successful women entrepreneurs of the time, owned the *Wickenburg Miner* newspaper. Upon her arrival in Casa Grande, she became the first owner of the *Dispatch*. The *Dispatch*, which has evolved from a weekly publication to one published six days a week, has been owned by the Donovan Kramer family since 1962.

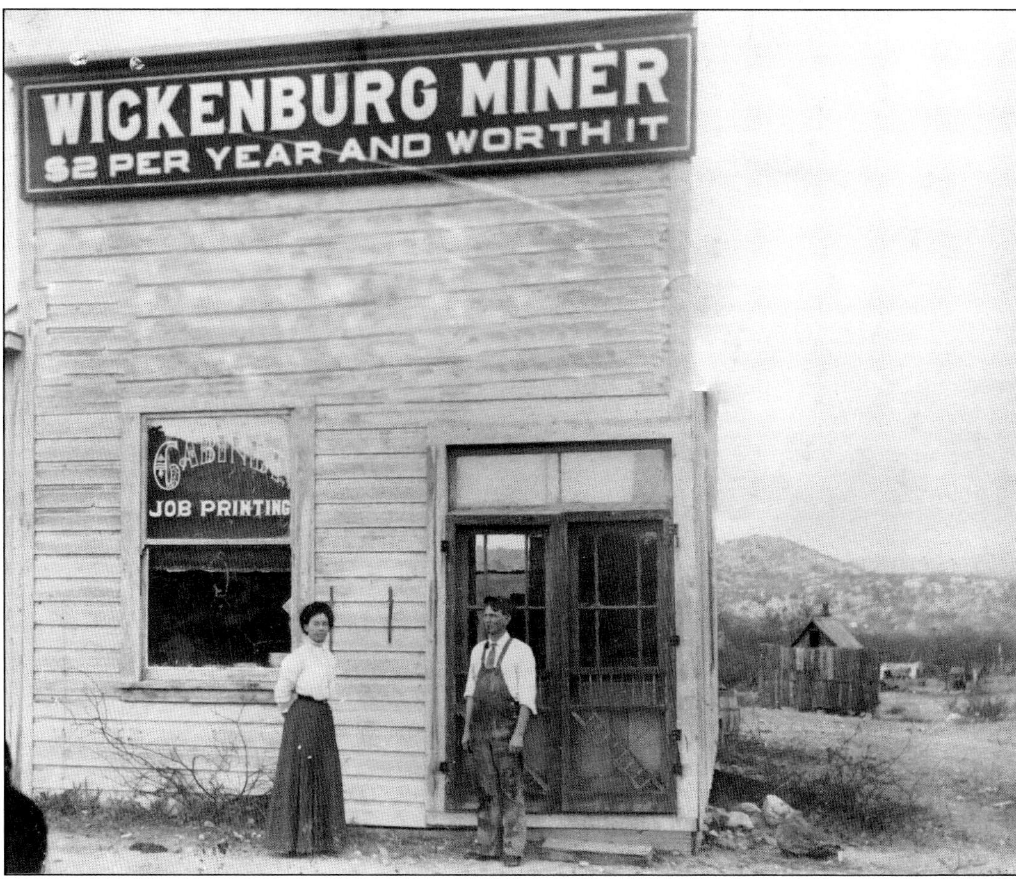

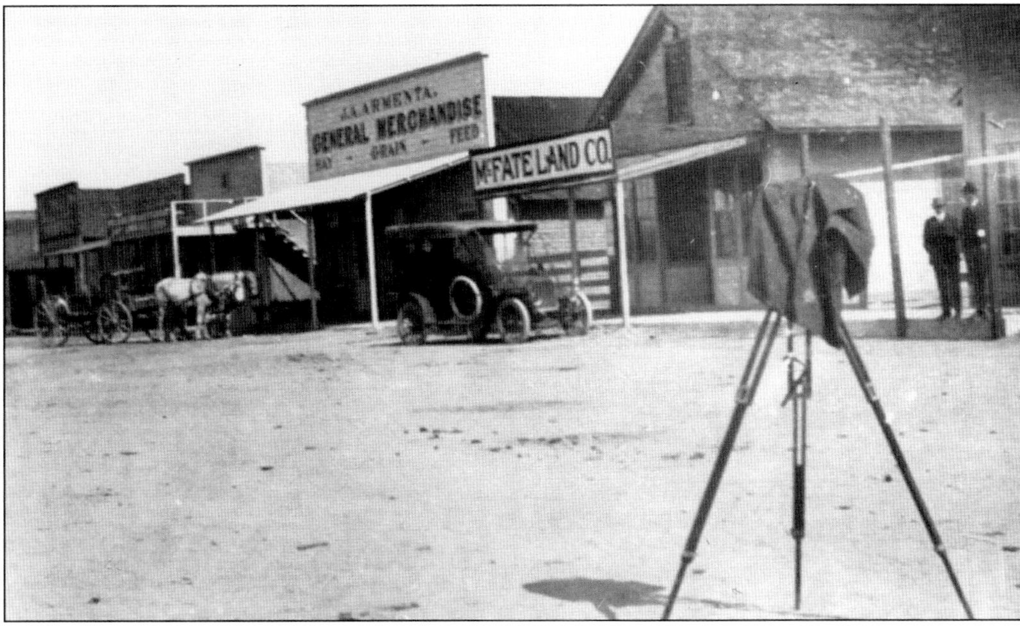

As early as 1914, land sales offices were offering brave, risk-taking speculators the opportunity to purchase open desert land. Those with foresight and a little bit of cash were soon to become the future leaders of the community. A back room of the McFarland Land Office was used as the first office of the *Dispatch* newspaper. A photographer, probably Cal Osbon, apparently felt that his camera was safe from traffic, as it appears to be abandoned in the middle of Main Street.

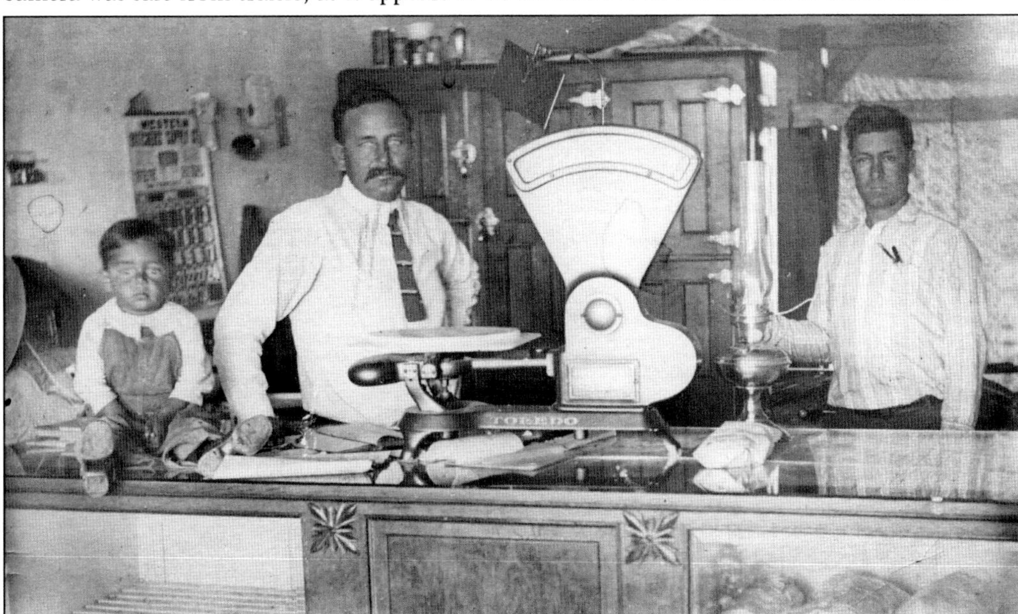

Main Street continued to be the hub of business activity in Casa Grande. The OK Meat Market, run by the Andrade family, was one of the busiest sites in town. Ramon Andrade ran cattle at Turning Point Mine, where he was the caretaker. He brought the cattle into town to be butchered by his brother Roberto as needed. Pictured from left to right are the Andrade brothers: Reynaldo "Blackie," Ramon, and Roberto.

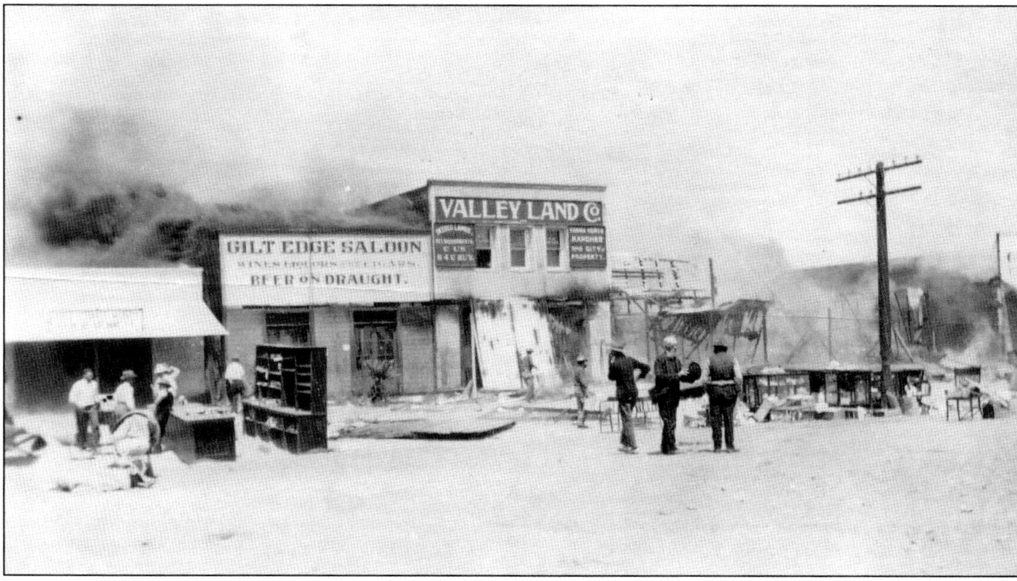

On April 28, 1914, a nearly catastrophic fire destroyed several of the buildings that comprised the downtown business community. In the photograph above, smoke can be seen still rising from the devastation as onlookers observe the damage. Some merchandise was salvaged and sits in the street. Seven buildings burned, including a bakery, a barbershop, a pool hall, Tom Meehan's Saloon, a meat market, and a secondhand store. Citizens fought valiantly with water bucket brigades, but without a fire truck and easily acquired water, there was little they could do to stop the fire from spreading.

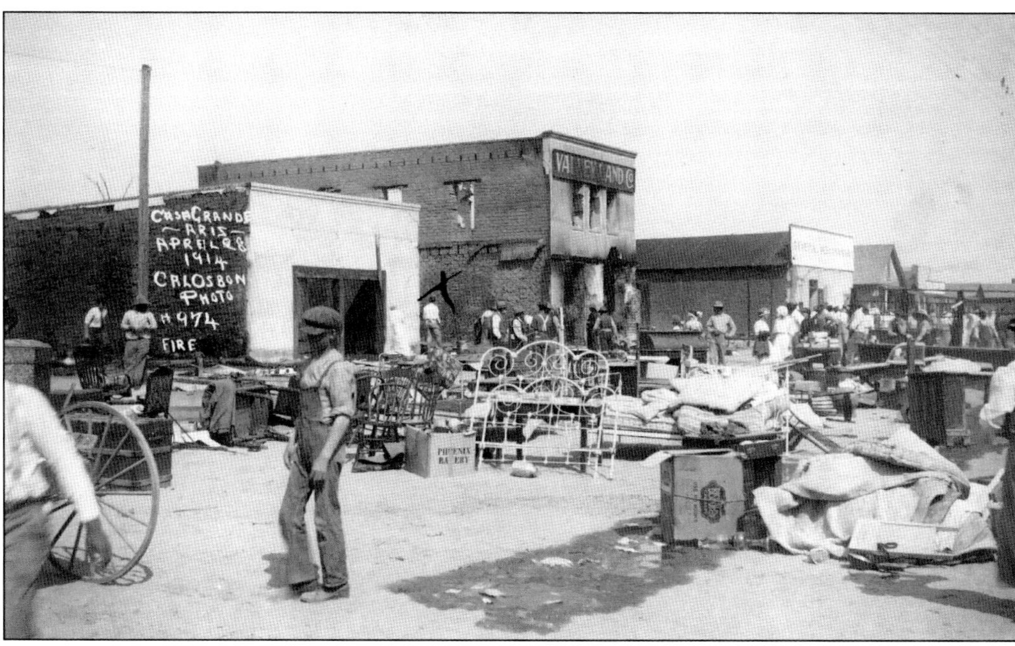

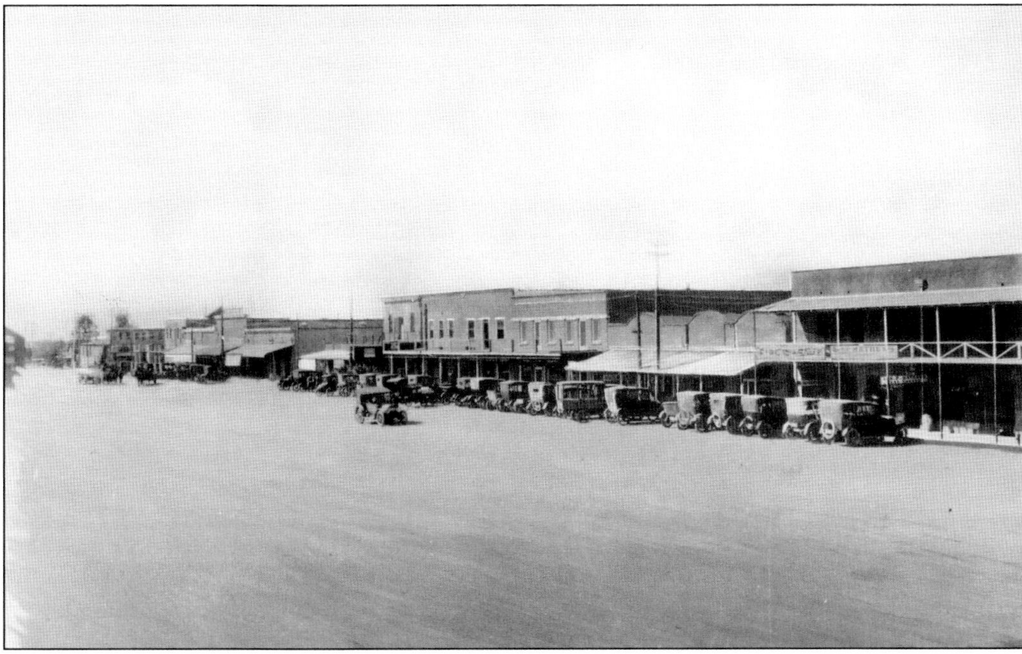

By 1916, the town had grown and, based on the number of automobiles lining Main Street, many of its citizens were apparently doing well financially. The town was not only growing out, but up, as seen in these two-story structures (several with balconies). Note the electricity poles along the street and especially those sticking through the roof of the second building from the right.

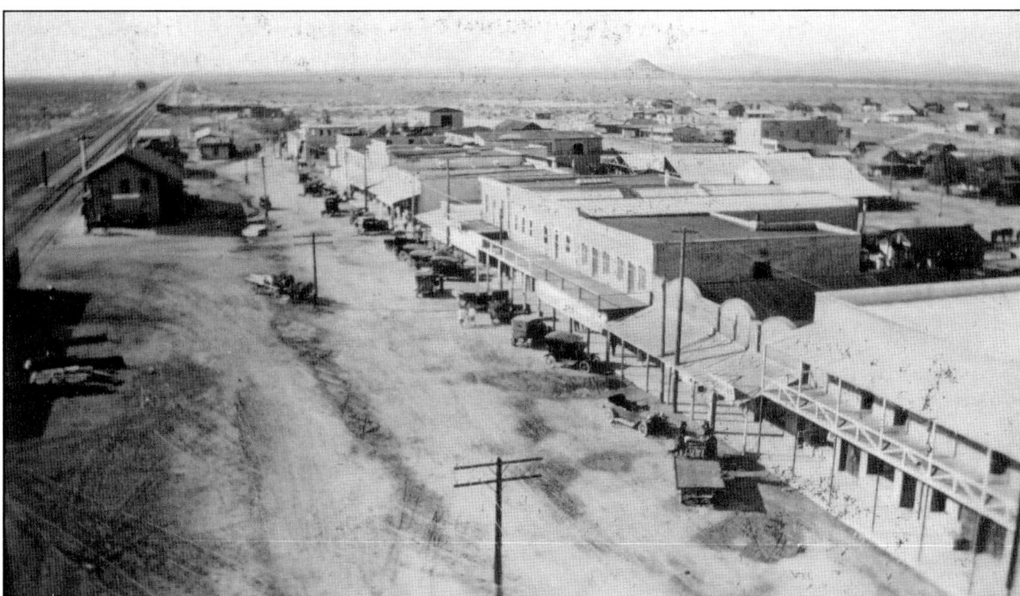

In what must be one of the earliest aerial photographs of the city, it is clear that Casa Grande is spreading into the surrounding desert. This 1917 photograph, probably taken from the top of the water tower, views the town looking west and north. The Southern Pacific Railroad depot is on the left, power poles line both sides of Main Street, and clearly the downtown is rapidly expanding. The emergence of purely residential areas is still poorly defined.

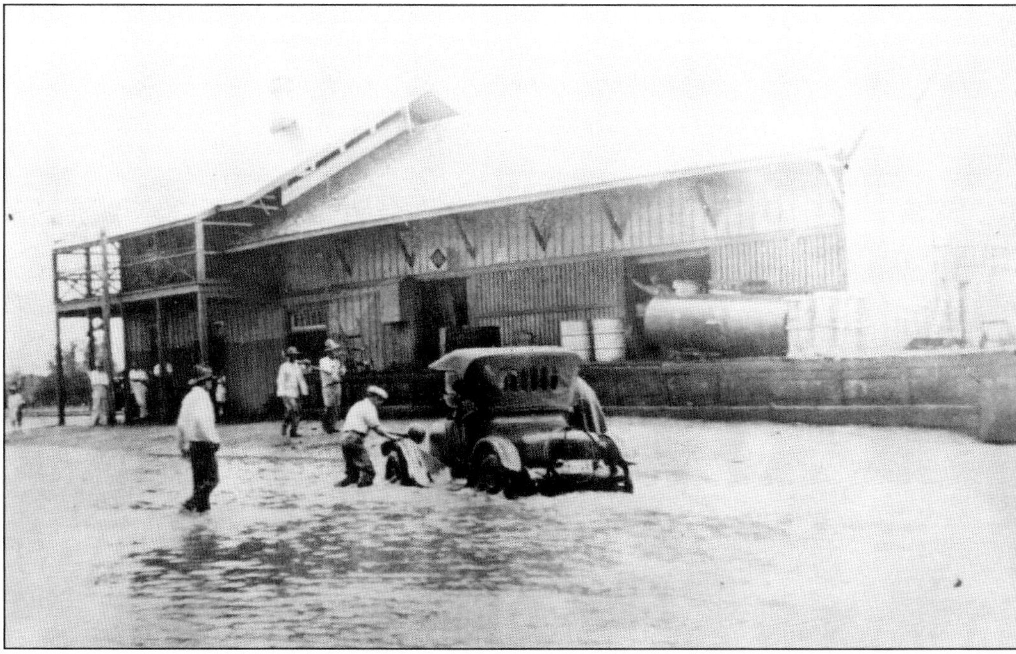

In 1917, a rare event occurred in Casa Grande. Excessive water is generally not an issue in desert towns; in fact, too much water is definitely an uncommon, unexpected, and unwelcome occurrence. A flooded Main Street no doubt claimed many automobiles on this day. Here, men are assisting one unlucky driver and his stranded Model-T Ford in front of the Southern Pacific Railroad depot.

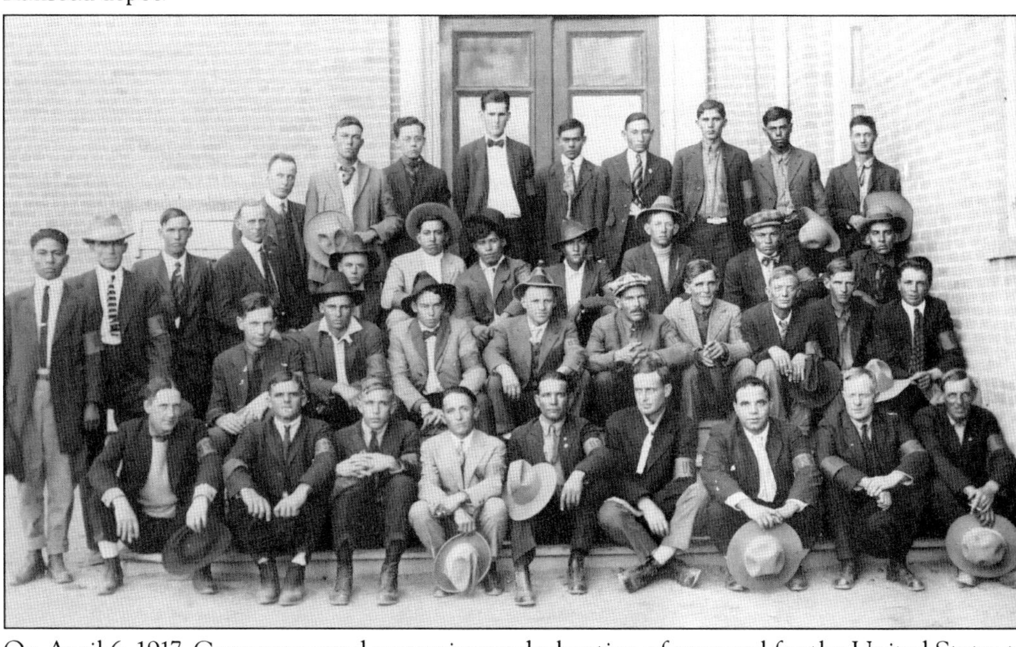

On April 6, 1917, Congress passed a unanimous declaration of approval for the United States to enter World War I, which had been inflaming Europe for the previous three years. By 1918, the war was winding down. The last group of draftees from Casa Grande and Pinal County posed for this photograph. Among the men are Guy Cates and Bill McNatt.

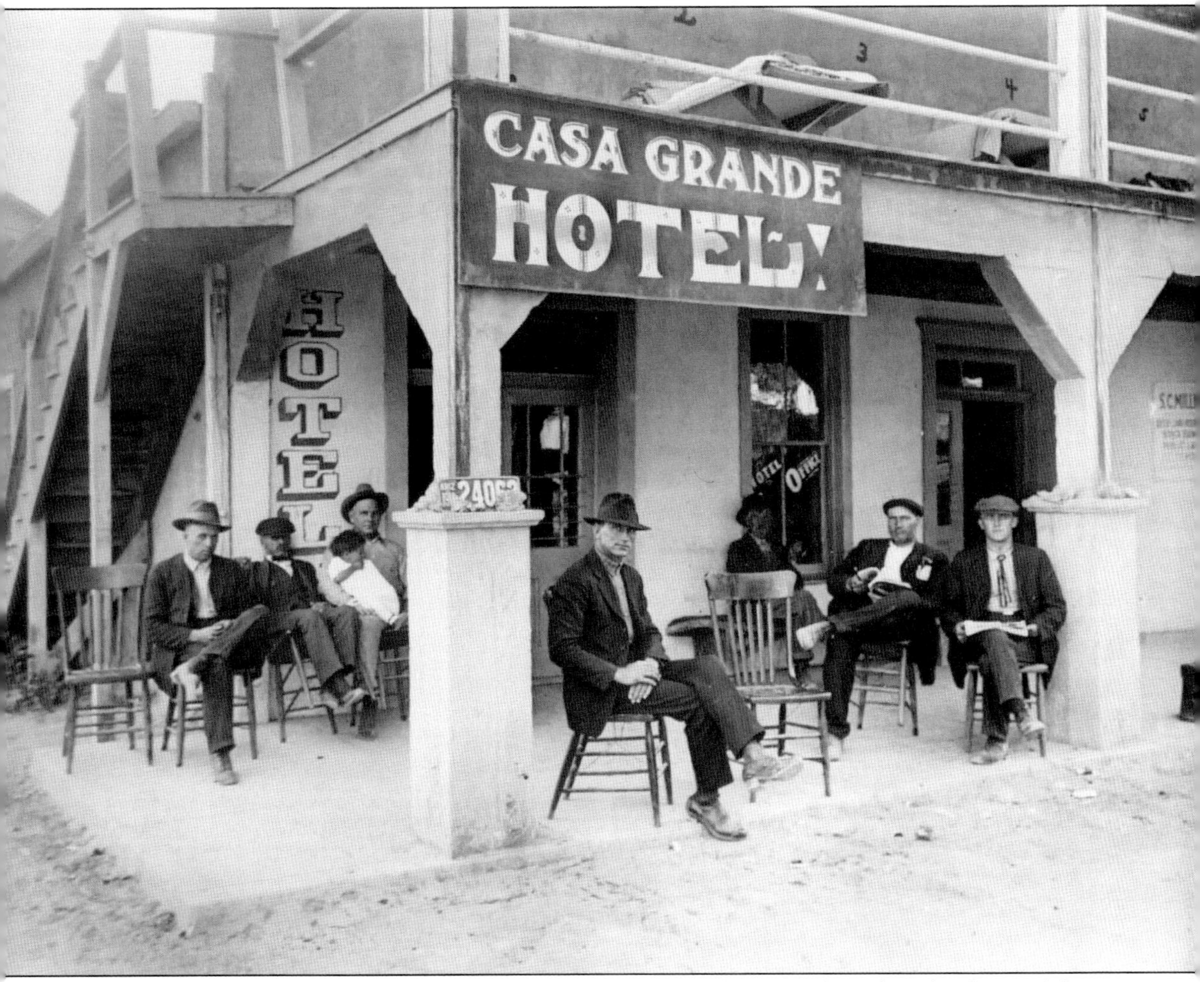

Looking like a scene from an old Wild West movie, town folk are gathered at the front of the Casa Grande Hotel. The adobe-style hotel was built in 1898, and one can imagine the men are waiting for the stage to arrive. However, it is 1920, and these men are just reading, relaxing, and gathering for conversation and people-watching. Note the beds on the balcony where guests could sleep in an attempt to escape the heat of an Arizona summer night without air-conditioning. In the background are Charlie Eastman Jr. and his daughter Ida. The man in the forefront in the black hat is L.H. Pottebaum. The Pottebaum family has a city street named for them. The long-vacant hotel, which was most recently used as a rescue mission, still exists at the corner of West Main Avenue and South Washington Street.

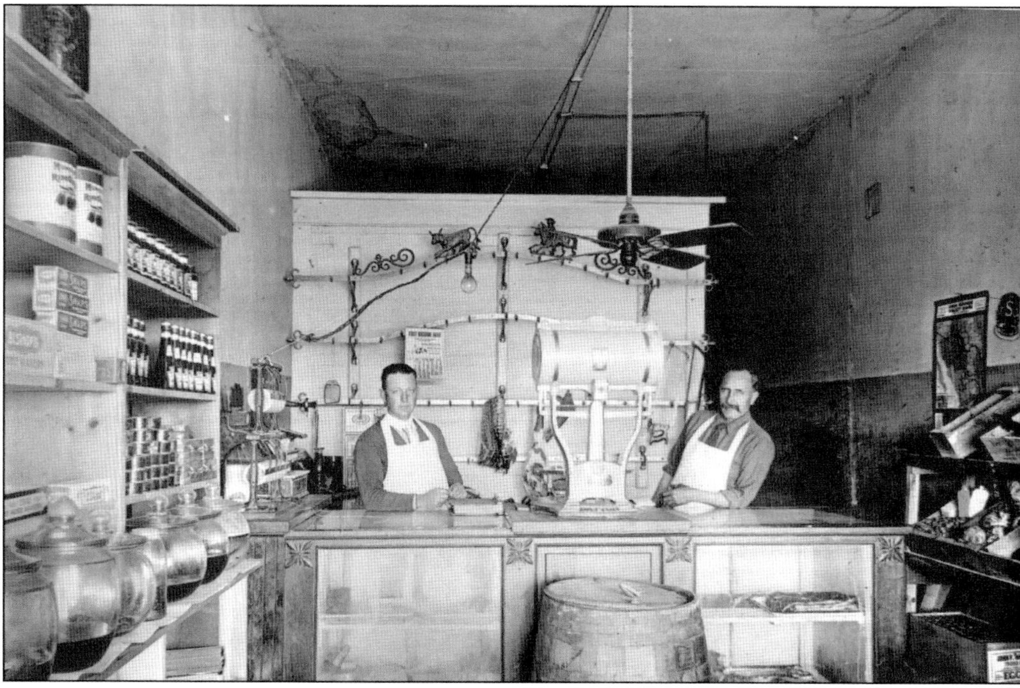

As the town grew, so too did the need for additional businesses to provide for the influx of new residents. In 1920, the Prettyman Market (above) was one of the new businesses that was thriving. Owner Don Prettyman Sr. and Ramon Andrade Sr. are manning the counter. The store stood at Main Street just west of Florence Street. Business was so good that eventually there were two Prettyman Markets. The Hancock Pharmacy (below) was another active business in 1920. From left to right, the gentlemen are a Mr. Young, O.L. Hancock, and Bruce Franz.

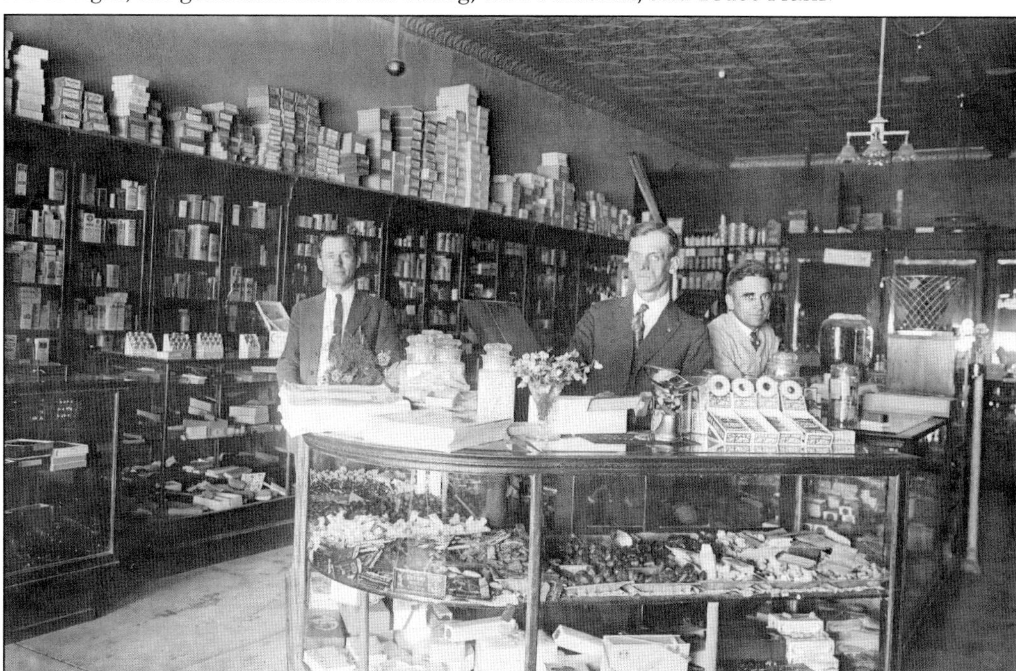

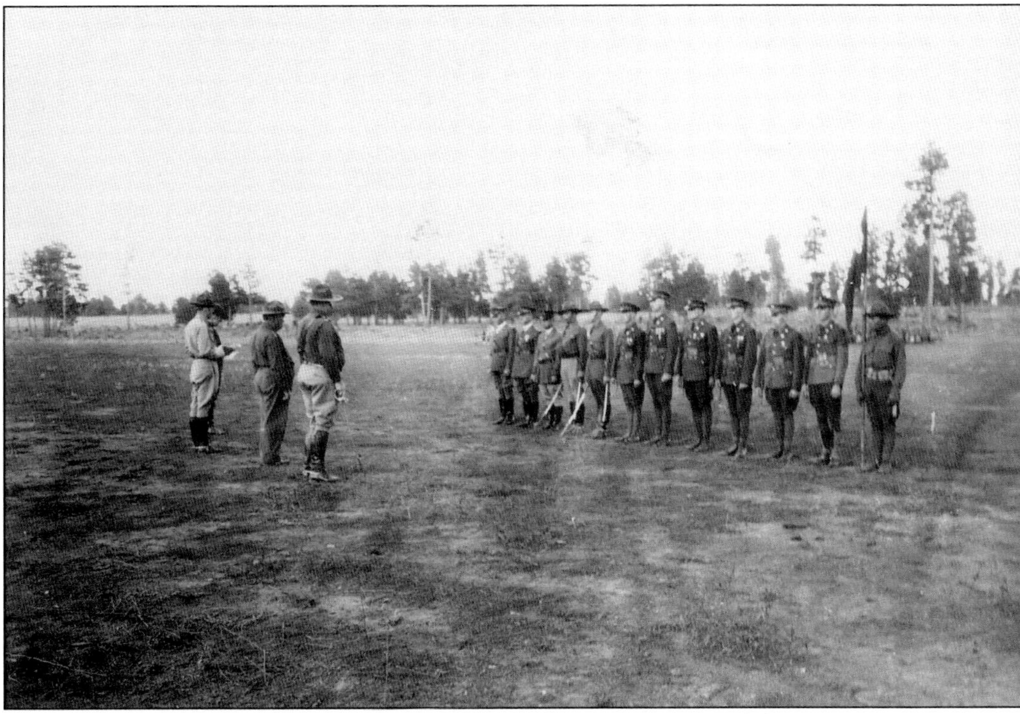

Although World War I had ended three years earlier, patriotic men of the community continued to serve as members of the National Guard. Here, in 1921, under the guidance of Capt. Jesse Hill, several of them are participating in a field exercise.

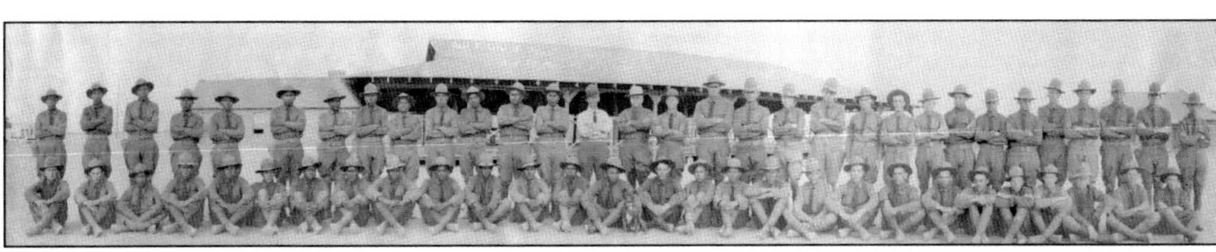

Company H, 158th Infantry Battalion of the Casa Grande National Guard, later designated Company D, 158th Infantry Battalion, attended its first summer camp at Camp Harry J. Jones in Douglas, Arizona, from May 29 to June 12, 1921. Pictured in no particular order are Capt. Richard H. Peart, 1st Lt. Dan T. Peart, and 2nd Lt. Merrill C. Windsor.

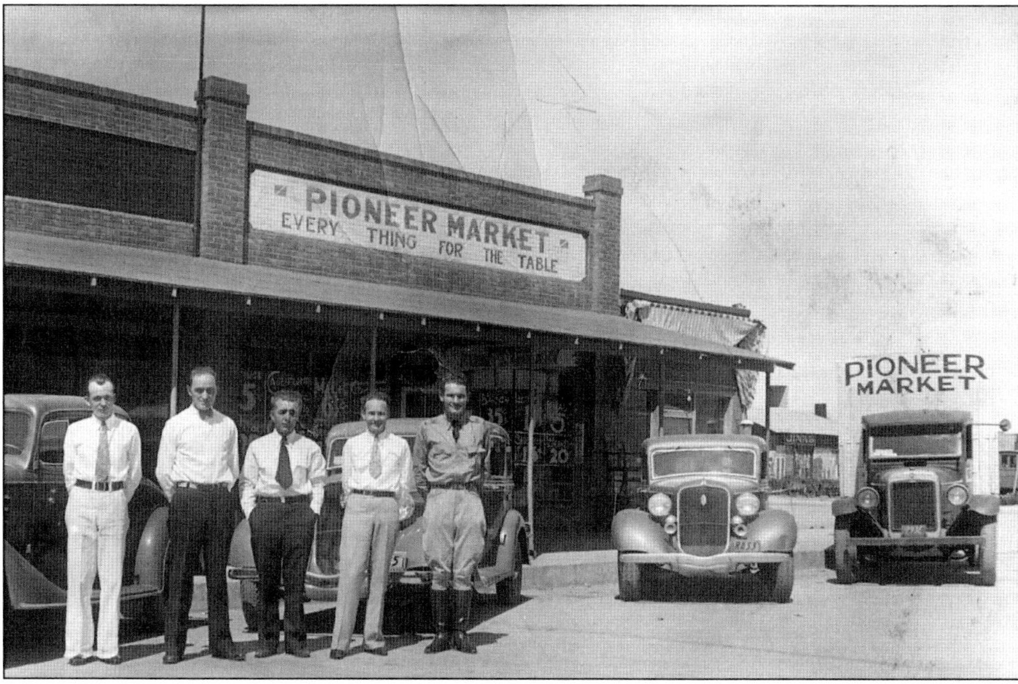

In 1922, a new brick building was built downtown. It consisted of two bays, one of which held the Pioneer Market and the other was a bank. The Pioneer Market, which was one of the most popular grocery stores in town, was located at 117–119 North Florence Street. It had pressed tin ceilings and wood floors. The store closed after 30 years because competition with chain stores made the enterprise unprofitable.

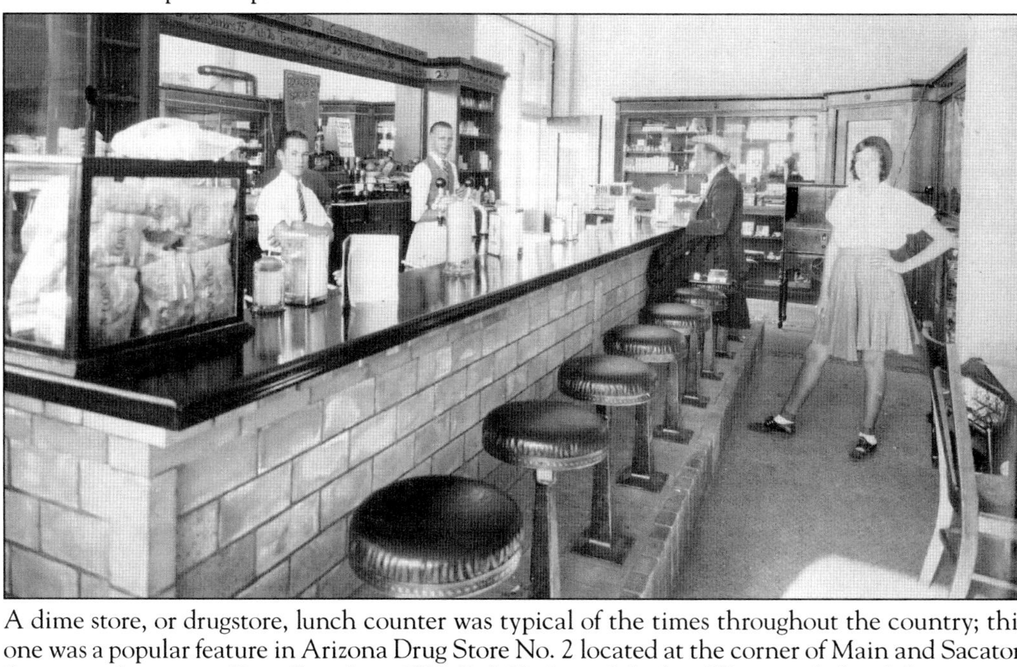

A dime store, or drugstore, lunch counter was typical of the times throughout the country; this one was a popular feature in Arizona Drug Store No. 2 located at the corner of Main and Sacaton Streets in downtown Casa Grande in 1929. Bob Hicks and Arthur Elliott are behind the counter. The two patrons are unidentified.

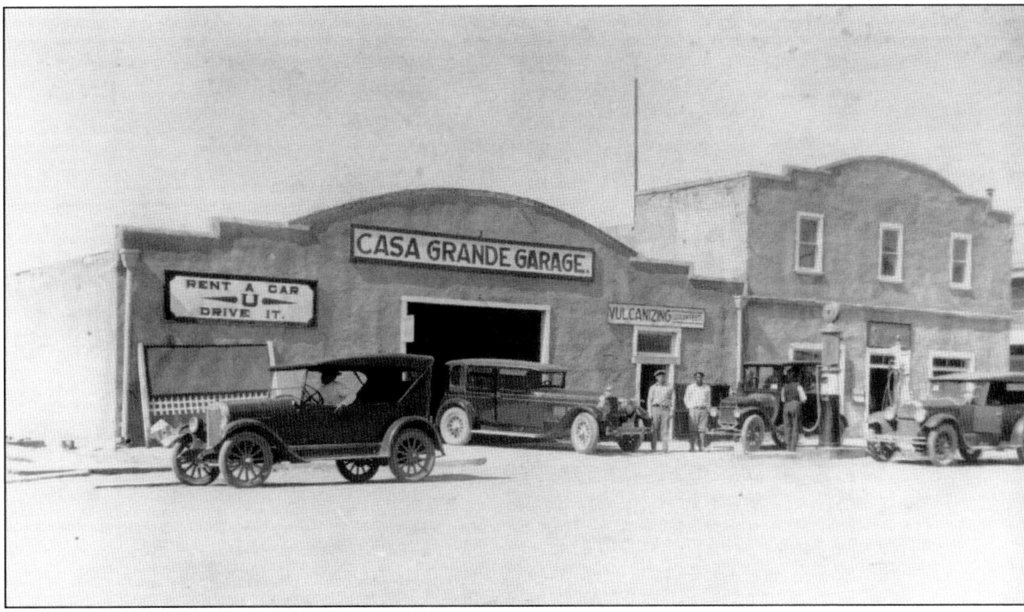

As automobiles became an affordable necessity and more Casa Grande residents owned them, the need for gasoline, service, and repairs grew. Among those providing that service was the Casa Grande Garage (above), located at the corner of First and Sacaton Streets. This all-purpose garage provided gasoline, tire vulcanizing, and even a rental car service. It was conveniently situated a block away from the San Carlos Hotel, from which one can assume guests might want a rental car. Not to be outdone, Dick Vasquez's service station, located on Florence Street between Second and Third Streets, seems to have been a precursor of today's ubiquitous gas station and convenience store. As seen in the photograph below of the interior of his station, he sold more than automotive services and supplies. J.C. Penney's later occupied this location.

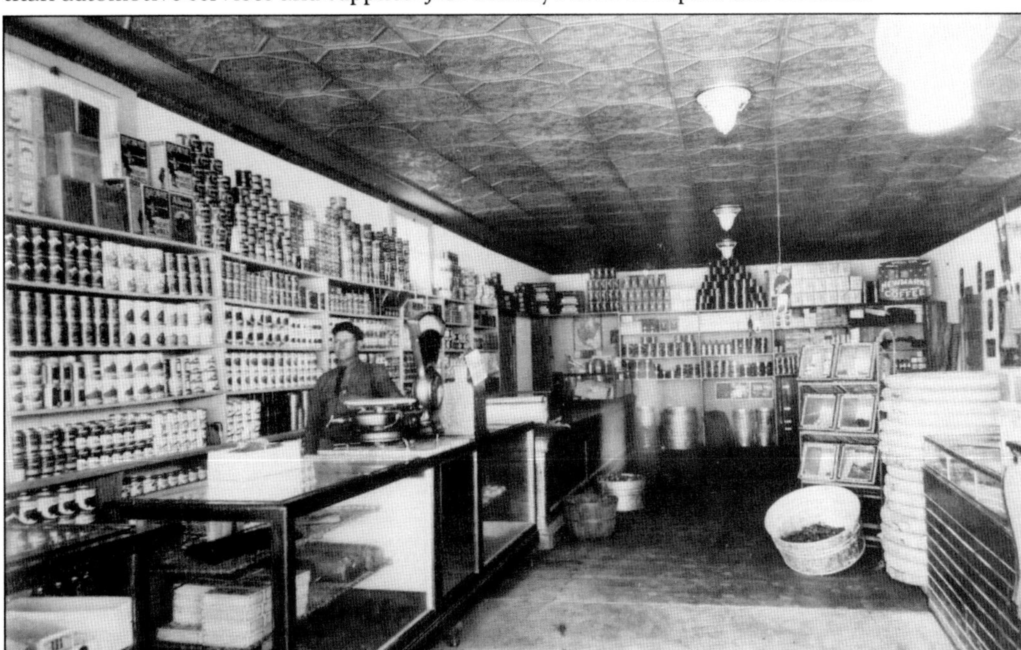

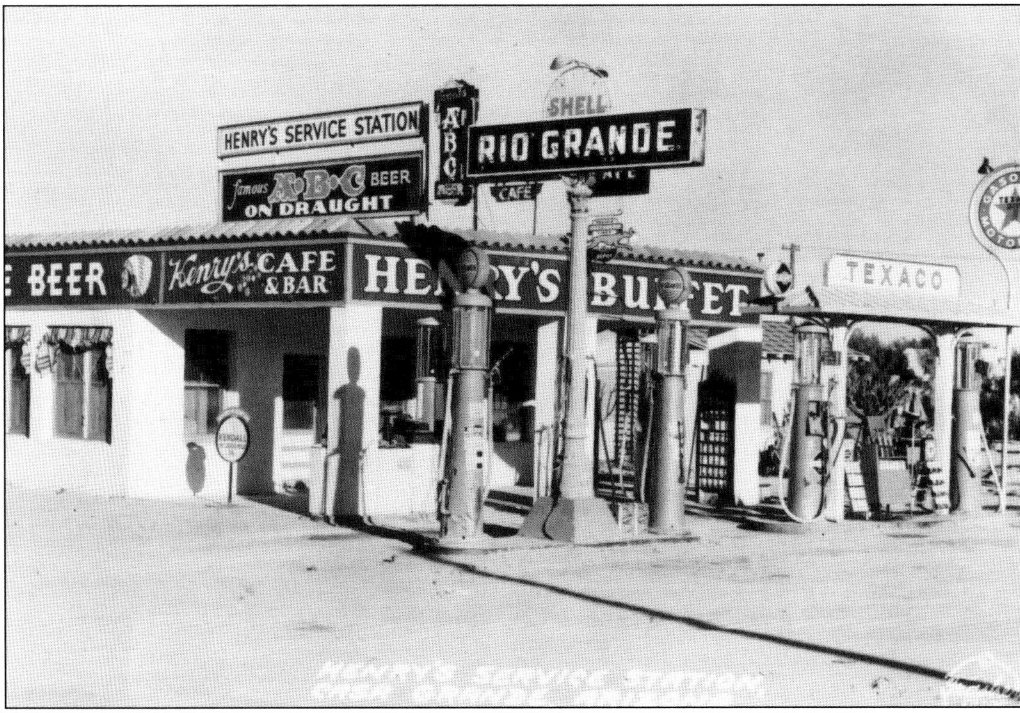

At the beginning of the 1930s, many more cars were on the road. Fortunately, Casa Grande did not lack for gas stations. Henry's Service Station (above), owned by Henry Armenta Sr., was located on East Main Street. It served as a service station, a bar and liquor store, a café with a buffet, and—almost incidentally—sold Texaco and Shell gasoline. Taking advantage of the increasing popularity of automotive travel and the arrival of tourists, Henry Armenta Sr.'s entrepreneurial tendencies kicked in, and he built several motel cabins next to his service station (below). Although they were lacking in the amenities that one expects when traveling today, they no doubt provided a weary traveler a fairly comfortable place to rest after hours of driving through the desert.

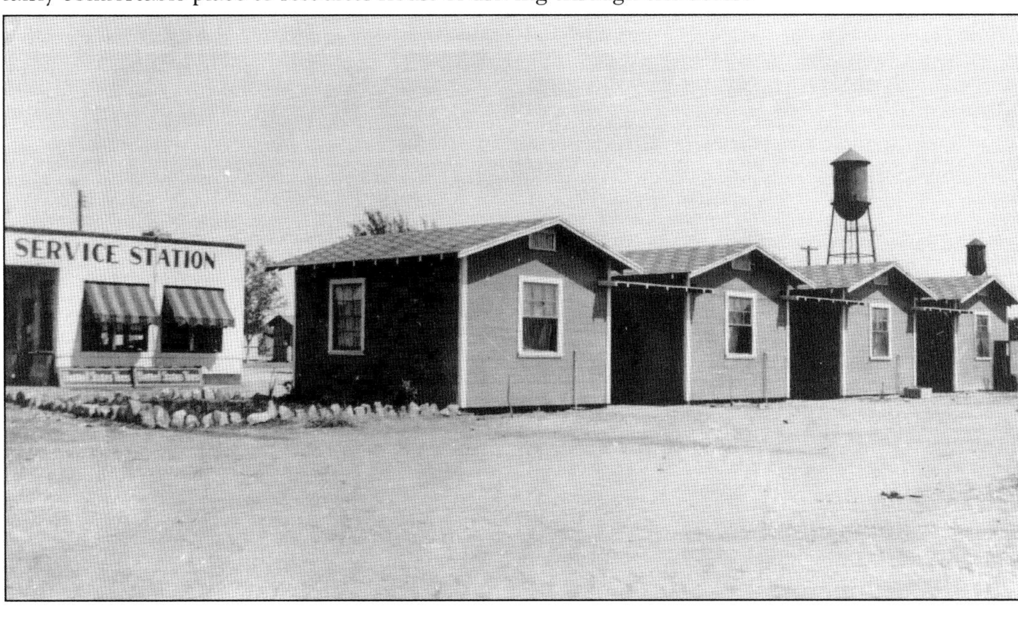

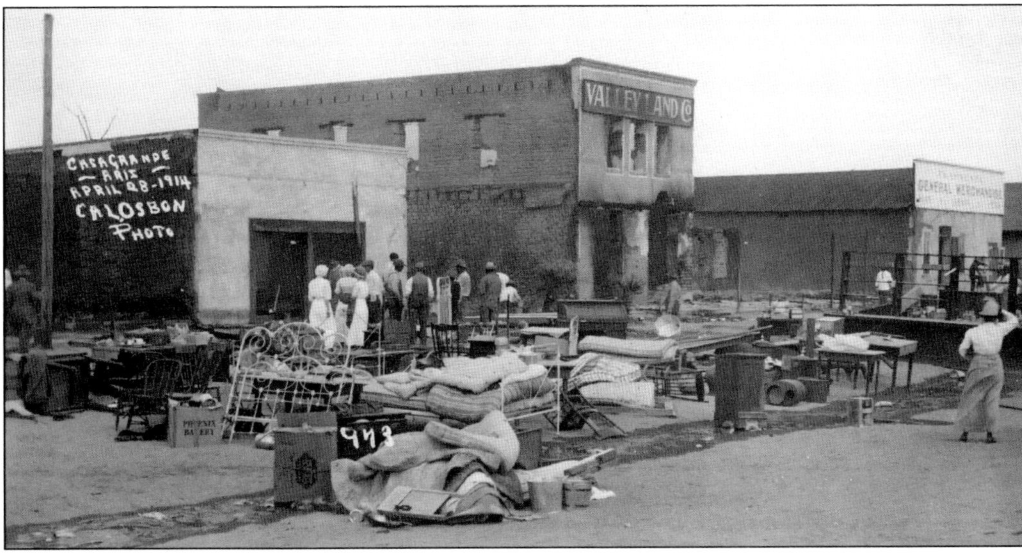

Among the first and most necessary public services that a new community needs is a fire department. In 1914, Casa Grande did not have a fire department, and townspeople with nothing more than bucket brigades were unable to stop a fire that destroyed much of the downtown (above). In 1932, the City of Casa Grande purchased its first fire truck. In the photograph below, from left to right, are the following proud members of the volunteer fire department: Barney Tindall, T.H. Burton, Jess Hill, Al Arnston, Hokey Overland, Howard Hess, and Bob Tindall with the 1929 LaFrance that served the community for many years. The fire truck is now housed at the historical society and is a highlight of almost every parade held in the town.

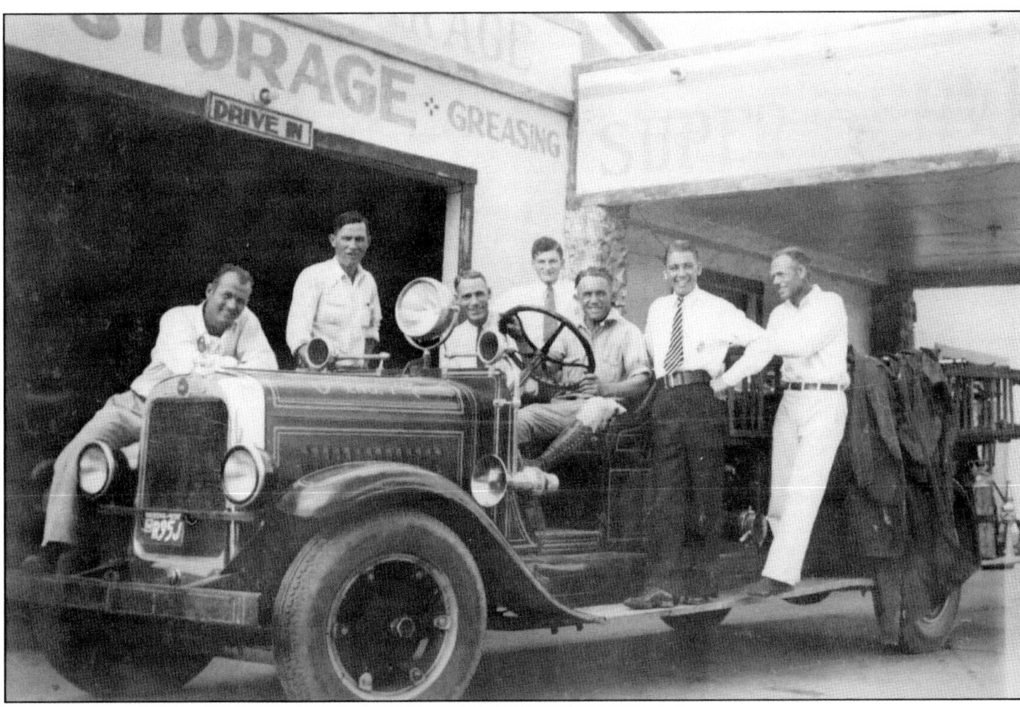

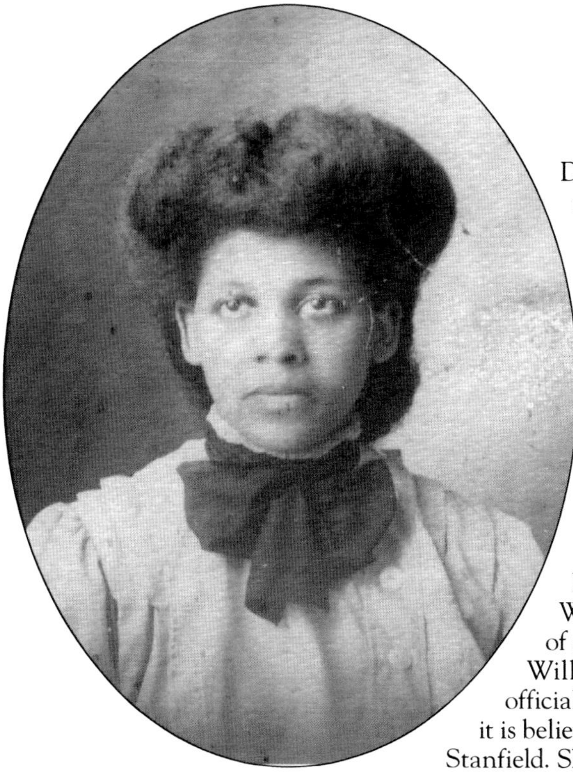

During the years that segregation was the national norm, Casa Grande schools were no different. Nevertheless, a young black woman from Alabama made her mark in Casa Grande even before those troubled times. In 1935, Rebecca Dallis was one of the first African American women to earn a master's degree from the University of Arizona. In 1939, she began teaching in a one-room wood building on the grounds of South School (now Ocotillo School). The building, which was called the Southside Colored Grammar School, is now preserved on the grounds of the historical society. Rebecca and her husband, W. Curtis Dallis, ultimately became principals of schools—she of East School and he of the William Huey School in Stanfield. Rebecca officially retired in 1962 at the age of 65, although it is believed she continued to occasionally teach in Stanfield. She died in 1971.

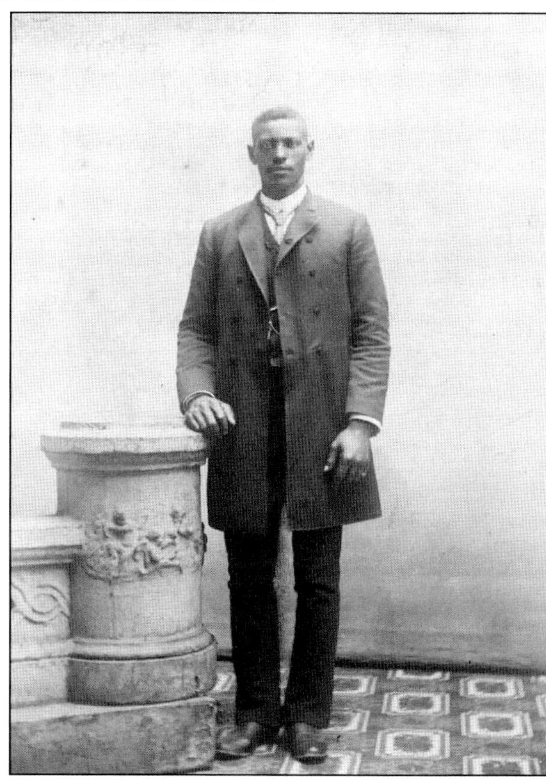

The year 1936 saw the unexpected arrival of one of the most famous people in the world. Famed aviatrix Amelia Earhart made an emergency landing in the pasture of Judge J.T. Overfield. This photograph was taken at the Rodeo Grounds outside of Casa Grande. Joe Curry is on the horse in the background. Overfield Road is named for the judge.

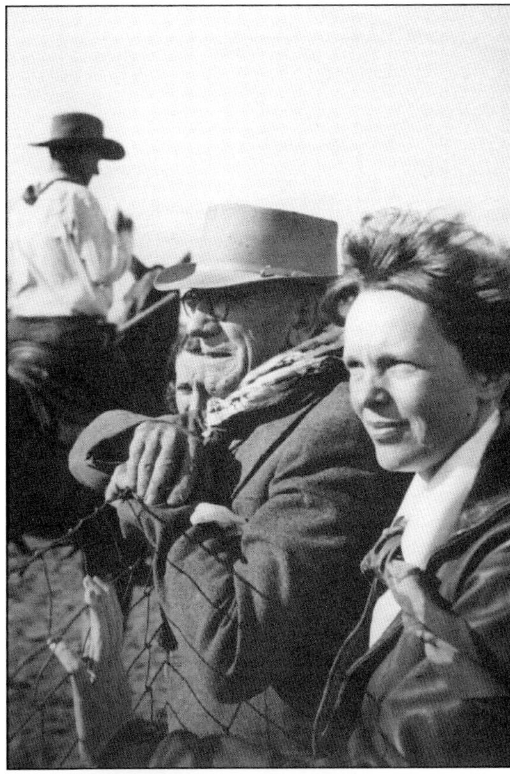

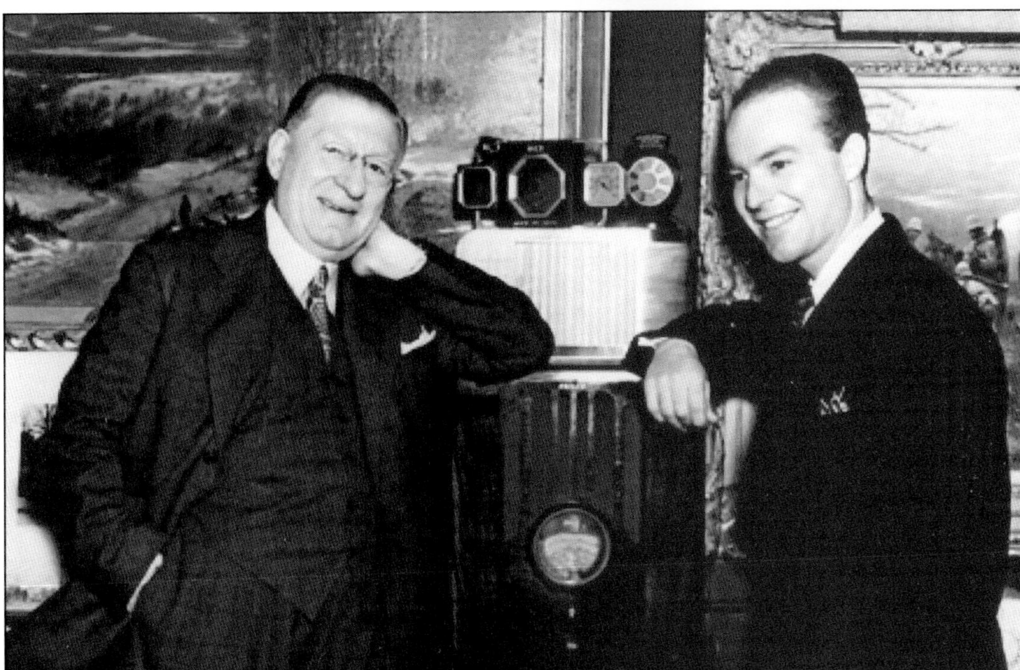

That same year, the popular radio program *Major Bowes Amateur Hour* arrived in Casa Grande to present one of its broadcasts. Ralph Edwards, the show's effervescent master of ceremonies is on the right, and Major Bowes is on the left.

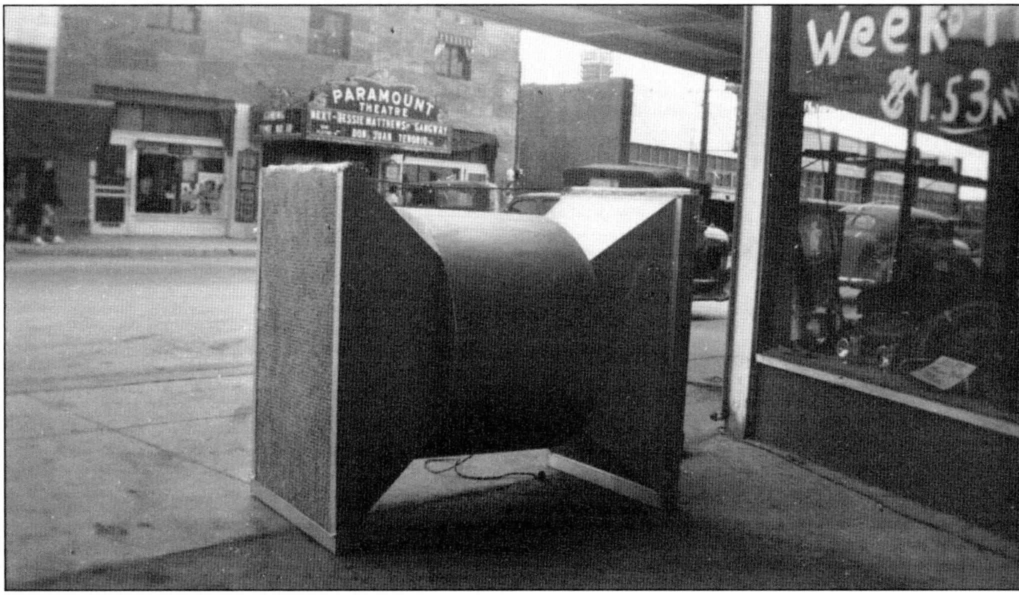

Businesses in the bigger cities located in the Arizona desert were about to undergo a big change as air-conditioning—or "refrigerated air," as it was called at the time—became an option. In 1937, a new cooler awaits installation at a service station on the corner of Fourth and Florence Streets across from the Paramount Theater. By about 1940, air-conditioning was becoming ever more common and many businesses were having units installed. Air-conditioning was still too costly for most family homes, but it provided a welcome respite when folks went shopping, dining, or to the movies. Below, this unit is ready for transport, although it is questionable whether the small pickup can handle the job.

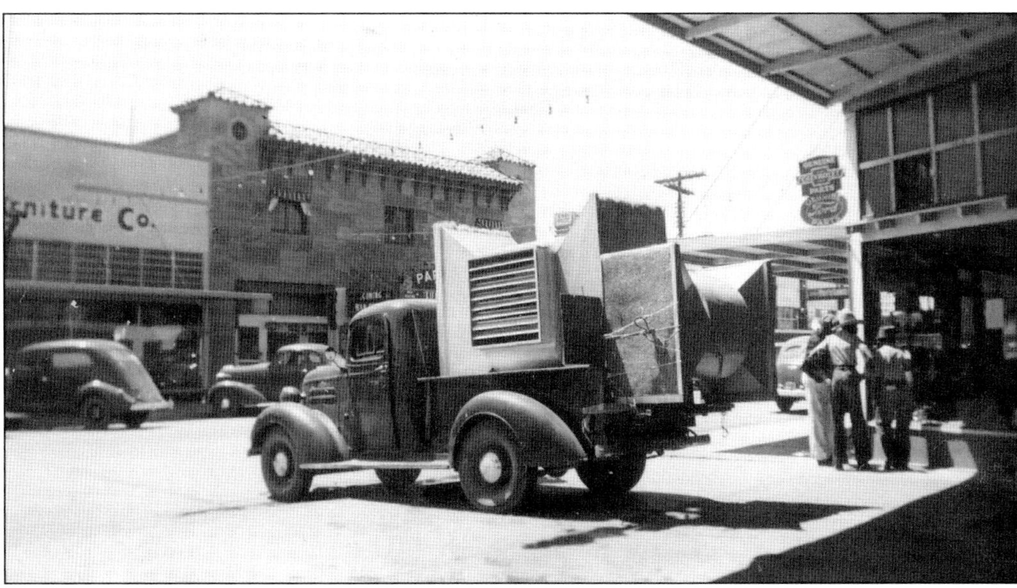

Six

Growing Pains of a Desert Community

World War II had a huge impact on the country at large, and Casa Grande was not exempt from the upheaval of that event. Many young men had joined the military, leaving their family farms and other local farmers without the workers they needed to maintain their fields. After the war, these same men found land too expensive to buy and many were forced to work for large landowners. Some were able to purchase property together until one or the other could afford to buy his own land. Because of the shortage of men, the war created the opportunity for women to find work outside the home for perhaps the first time.

As men returned from the war to begin their lives anew, agriculture, commerce, construction, and general economic improvements were still pending. Nevertheless, by the 1950s, new housing subdivisions were springing up throughout the community, creating the need for more schools and businesses to provide goods and services. The addition of new churches, hospitals, entertainment venues, restaurants, and public services—and the people needed to run them—ensured an economic recovery was on its way. Modern appliances were about to become affordable, and Casa Grande merchants were happy to provide them to the housewives who now worked in and out of the home.

Although agriculture still defined Casa Grande and Pinal County, a major contributor to the growth of the region was the new interstate highway system inaugurated by Pres. Dwight Eisenhower in 1956. Once again, Casa Grande was on a trail to somewhere when Interstate 10, stretching from the Pacific Ocean to Jacksonville, Florida, passed through the city. Soon, Casa Grande would have to decide if it was going to remain strictly an agricultural community, become a bedroom community of Phoenix and Tucson (as it was often viewed), or perhaps diversify into a vital combination of rural and urban development. Fortunately, the last option was chosen by city officials, and now Casa Grande is a testament to the foresighted citizens and dedicated public officials who envisioned the dynamic city of today.

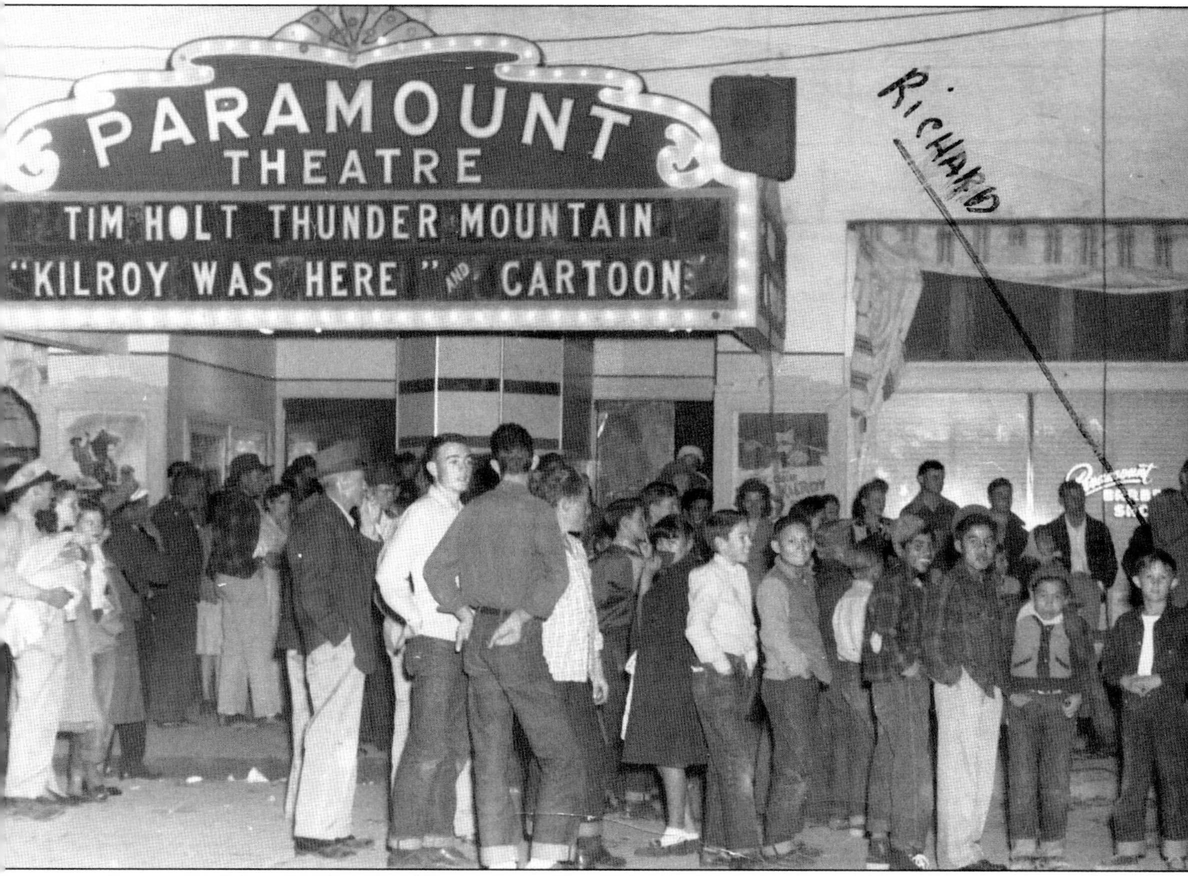

During and shortly after World War II, Hollywood once again began making Western movies as a respite from the war. *Thunder Mountain* was one of those films. It is considered a classic B-western and starred the B-movie cowboy hero Tim Holt. Around 1940, the Paramount Theater's marquee tells passersby that if they buy a ticket they will see the main feature, a secondary feature, and a cartoon. Most likely a newsreel would also have been shown. *Thunder Mountain* was based on a compilation of two stories by Zane Grey, who wrote many of his popular novels while living in Arizona. The movie tells the story of a man attempting to save his Arizona ranch from evil-doers who wanted the land so they could build a dam. The story was not far-fetched, as the construction of dams has been a divisive issue throughout Arizona's history.

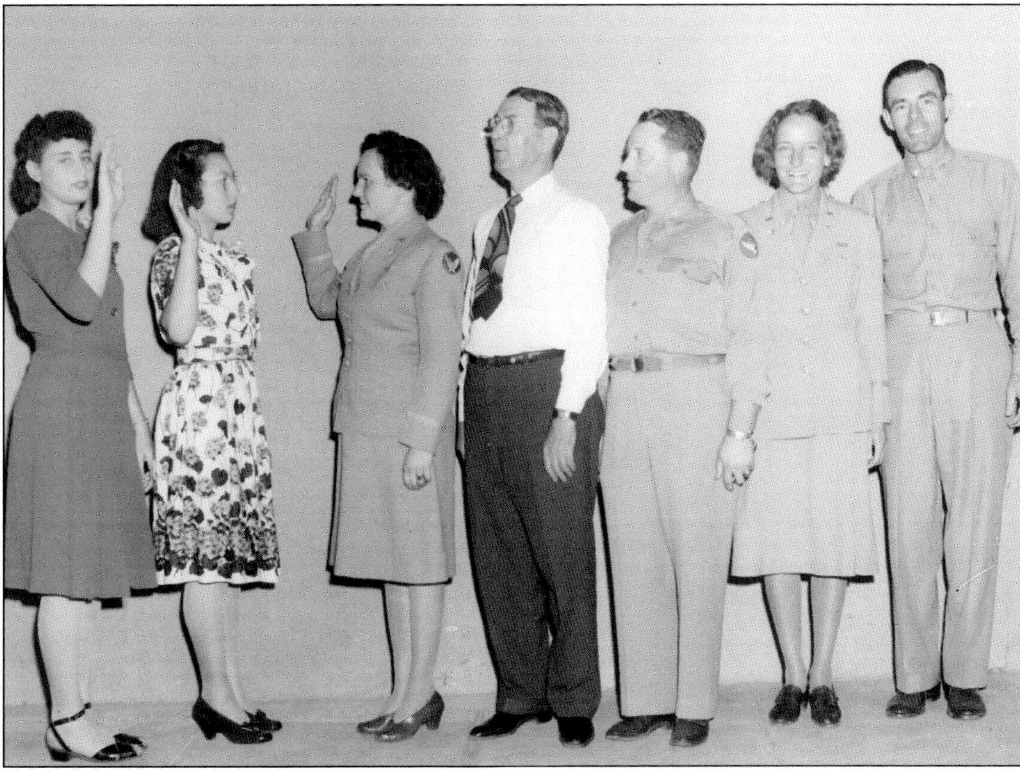

In 1944, the war was still active in Europe and Asia, and patriotic men and women of Casa Grande were either already serving their country or preparing to do so. The photograph above shows the swearing in of the first Woman's Army Corps in Casa Grande. Franklin Don (right), a member of one of the earliest families in Casa Grande, proudly poses in his dress uniform. Franklin attained the rank of sergeant in the US Air Force. After the war, he returned to Casa Grande to work in the family business, Don Market. Franklin, now in his 90s, often attends the annual Old Timers' picnic sponsored by the historical society.

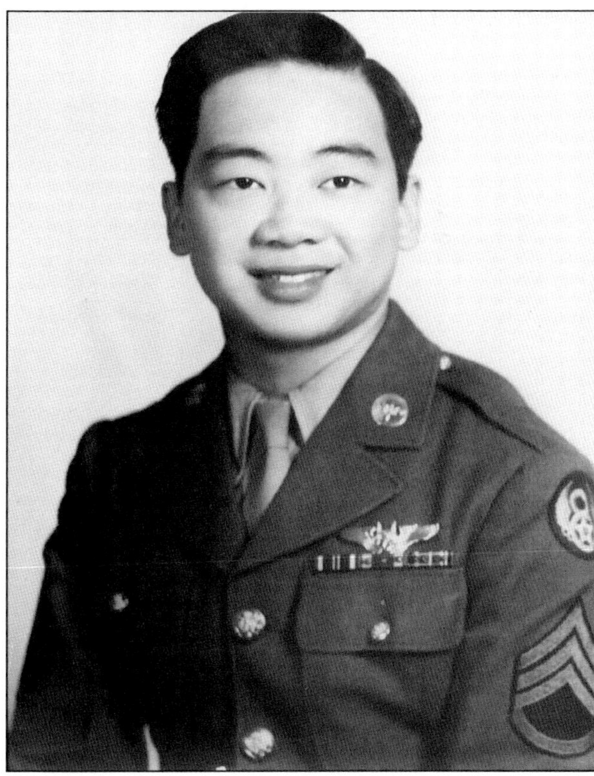

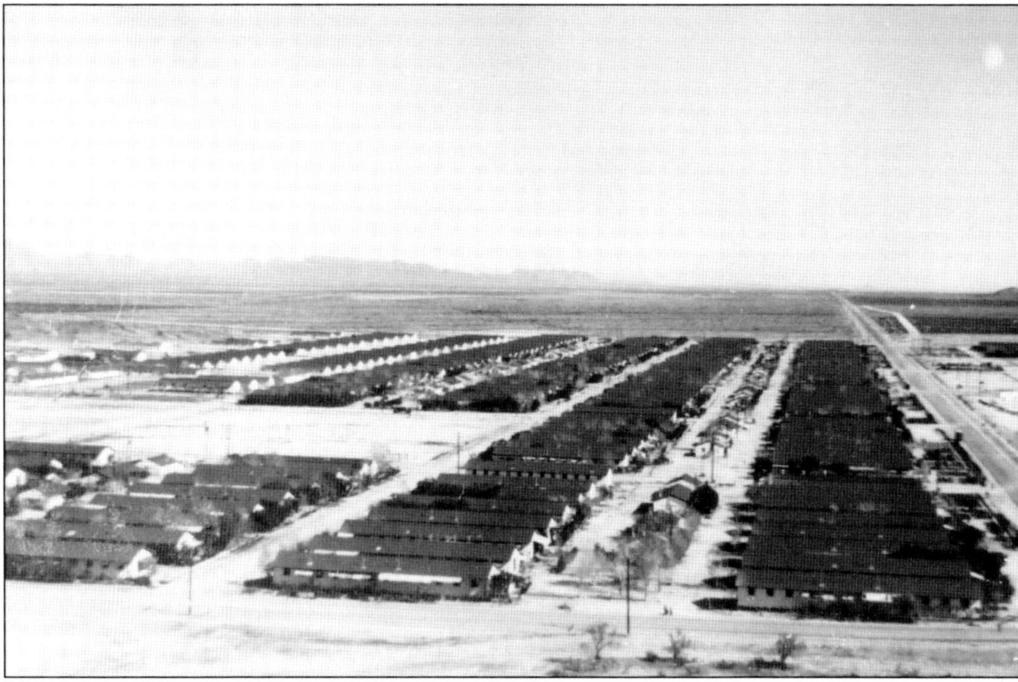

The war created an air of suspicion regarding some of the nation's citizens. Casa Grande had the unfortunate distinction of being a part of what is now viewed as shameful treatment of Japanese Americans. Across the country, people of Japanese descent were rounded up and sent to internment camps. Although Casa Grande was not the site of an internment camp, one was located on 15,000 acres of Gila River Indian Community land (above), and the city and its citizens benefited from its establishment just 15 miles away. Laborers were hired to build more than 990 buildings, including schools (below), a hospital, and living quarters. Farmers provided food, and city merchants sold material for construction. Several townspeople worked at the camp in various capacities, including administrative positions. Begun in 1942, the camps were emptied by November 1945.

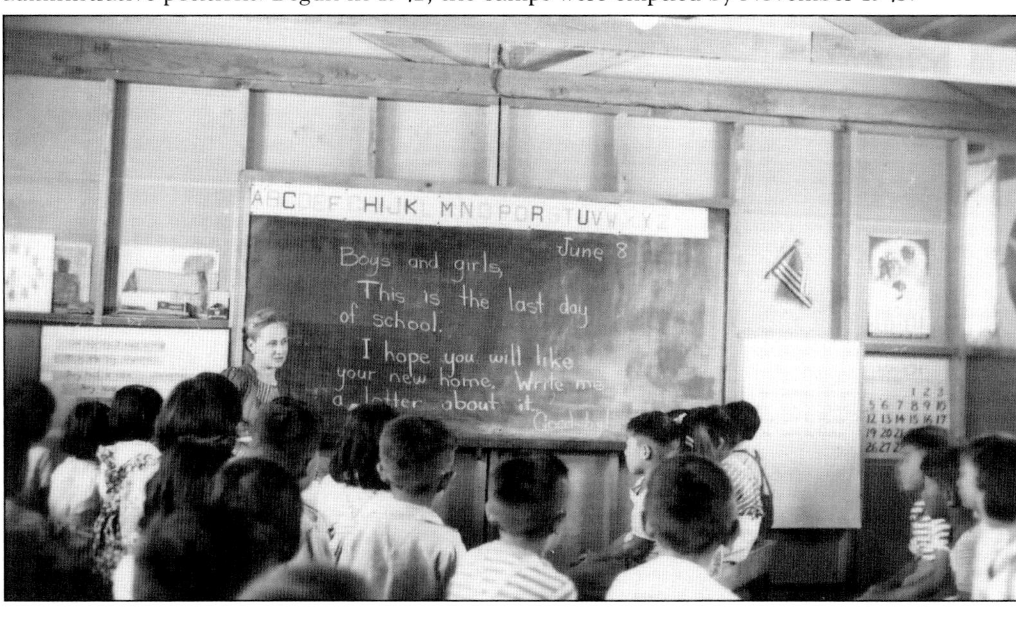

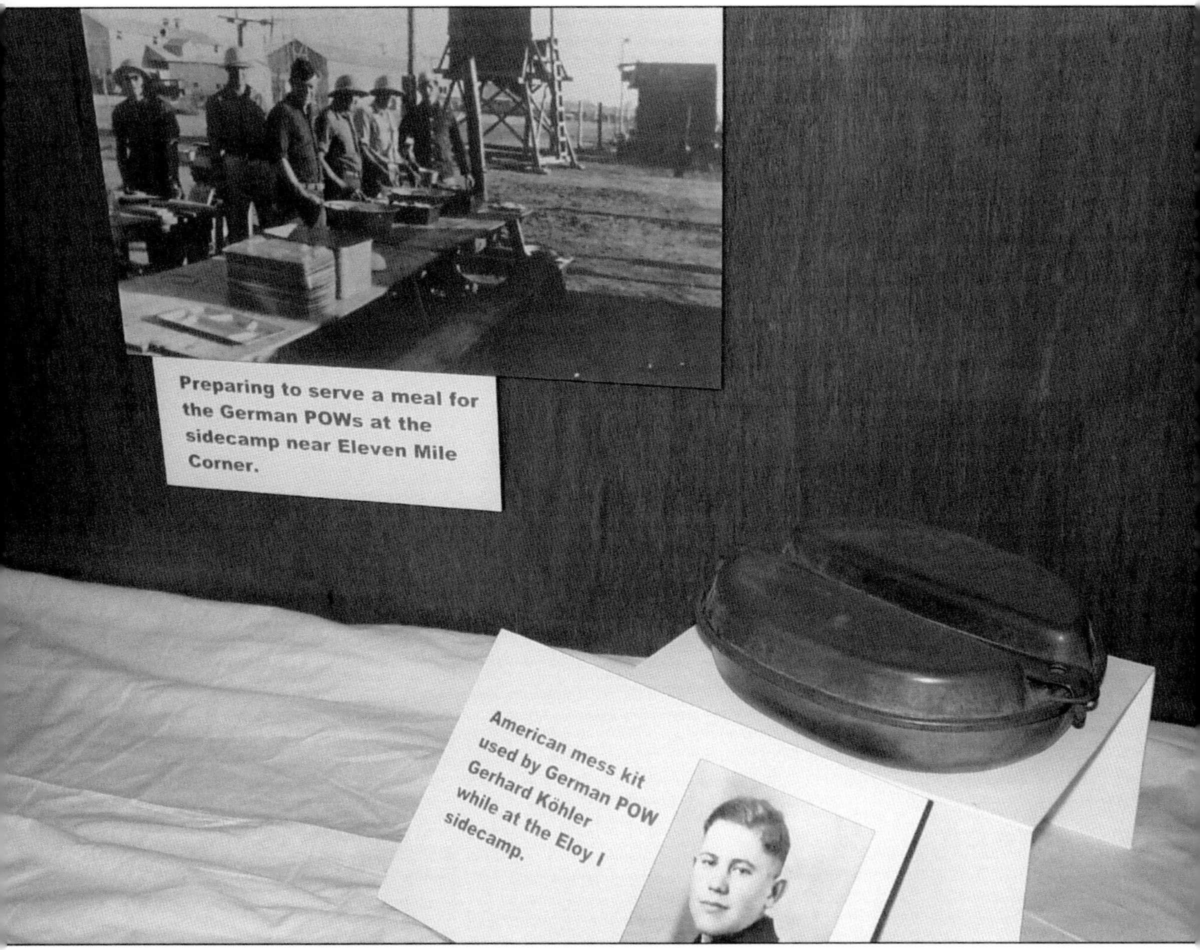

During World War II, nearly 400,000 prisoners of war (POWs) were housed in camps scattered throughout the United States. Arizona was home to 24 camps initially built for Italian POWs and then later for German prisoners. Most of the camps were known as main camps, such as the ones at Florence and Papago Park in Phoenix. Others, like those at Eleven Mile Corner, Eloy, and Casa Grande, were considered side camps largely dedicated to agricultural pursuits. By the end of the war, German POWs had picked almost 90 percent of the Arizona cotton crop. Here, a prisoner waits in the chow line at Eleven Mile Corner side camp. A book compiled by Steve Hoza contains a brief history about the camps as well as interviews with many of the prisoners who speak well, and even fondly, about their time in Arizona. The book, a ship model, and several artifacts can be seen at the museum.

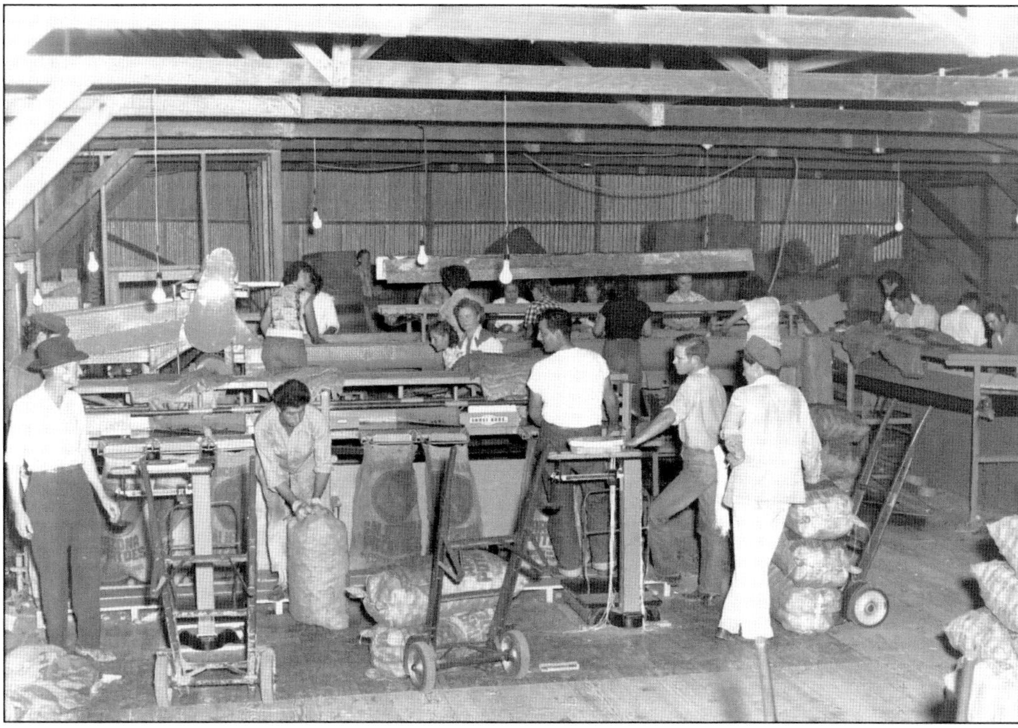

Agriculture continued to be a major source of employment for local residents as the nation was recovering from the hardships of the war. Here, men are working in a potato shed sorting and bagging potatoes for shipment throughout the country. Although a variety of food was harvested, cotton proved to still be king of the crops grown in the area.

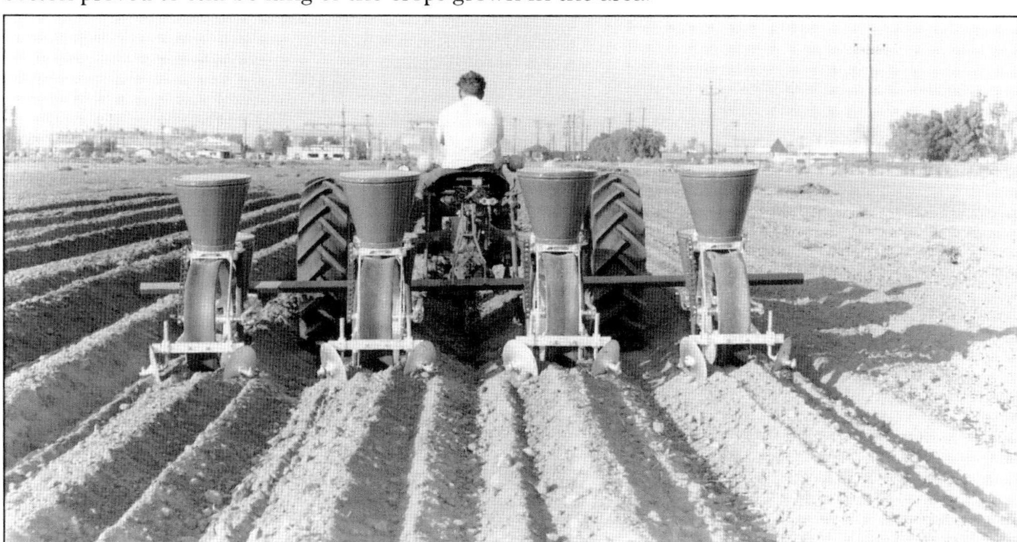

Farming had become easier and more efficient with the variety of new mechanized equipment that was available. One man driving a Burch Plow Works tractor is single-handedly planting a crop that used to take several passes to accomplish. Now, four rows of seeds could be planted and covered at one time. This enabled larger crops to be planted, thereby increasing productivity as well as profit.

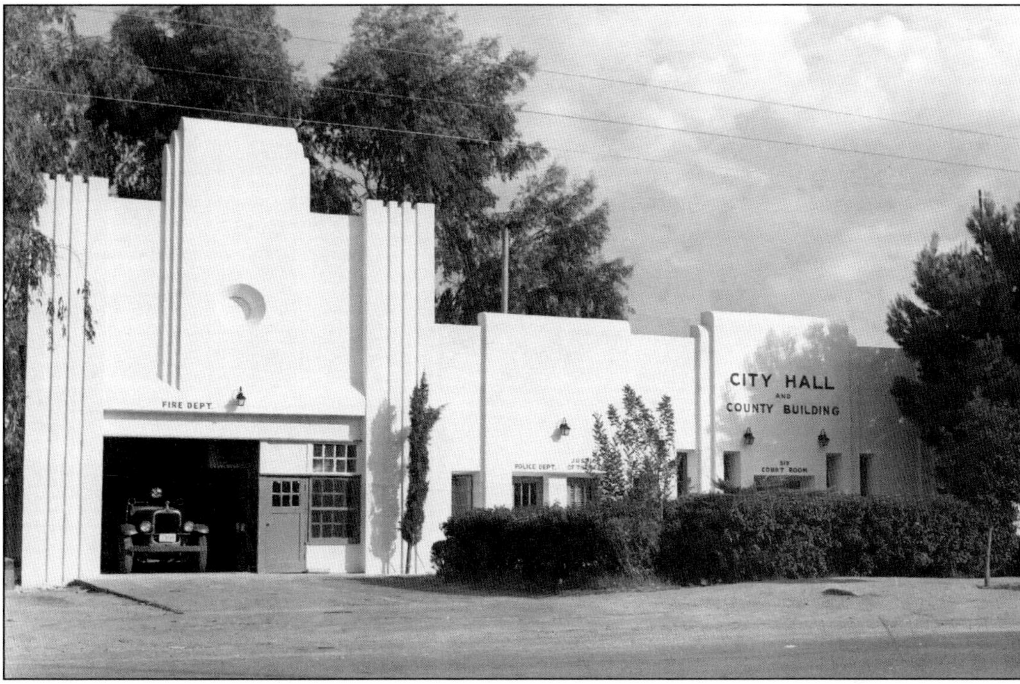

A city is defined by the effectiveness of a dedicated city government and its concern for the education of its youngsters. This Art Deco–style building housed city hall, the county government offices, the fire department, the police department, and courtrooms. Today, each of these entities has at least one building dedicated to its specific purpose. Among other prominent buildings in the city during the early 1950s was the Casa Grande Union High School located on Florence Boulevard. Today, that building is city hall, and the city has four high schools, with a fifth under construction.

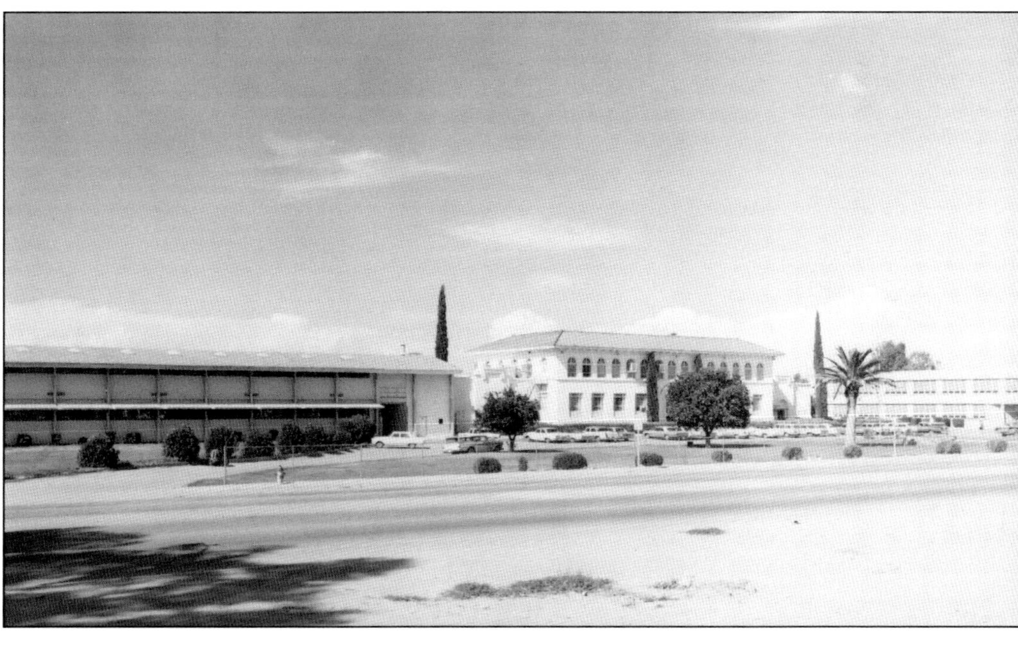

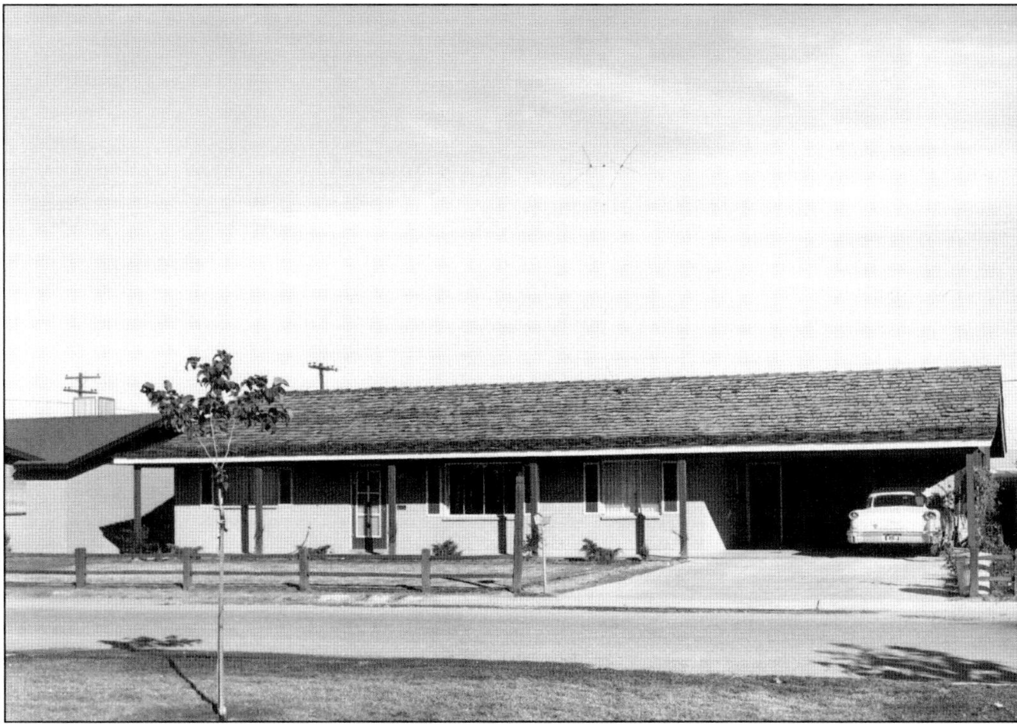

New subdivisions were springing up throughout the city or rather, what was at the time, the outskirts of the city. Buying a ranch-style house with a carport and making it into a home was now a possibility for the men who had returned from the war anxious to start a family. This new neighborhood (above) off of Manor Drive west of Trekell Road is typical of the types of houses being built. Many of the houses had a kitchen like the one below, which in a model is an enticing selling point; however, any family with children was unlikely to have a kitchen that looked like this for very long.

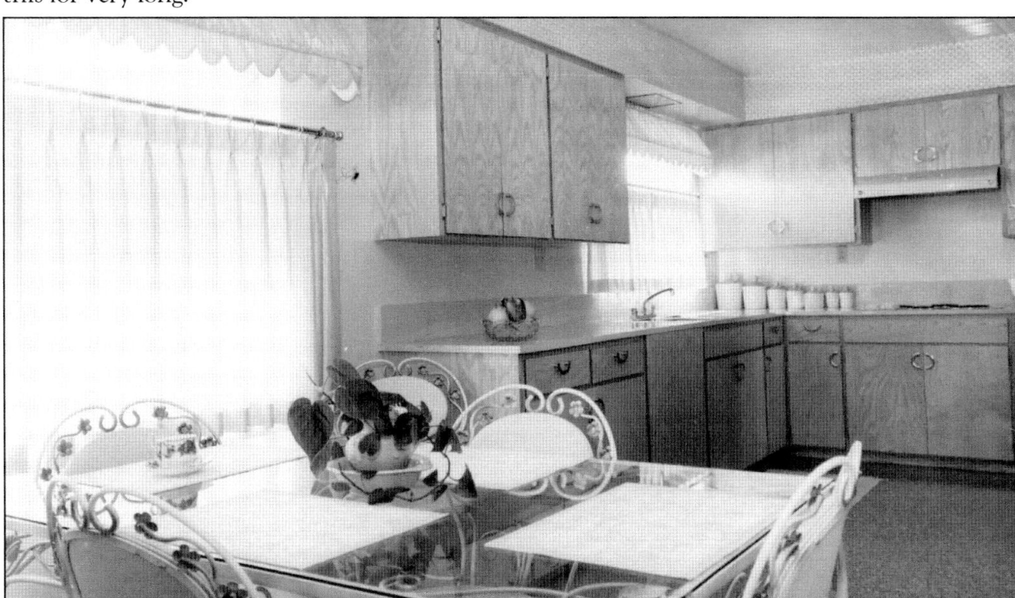

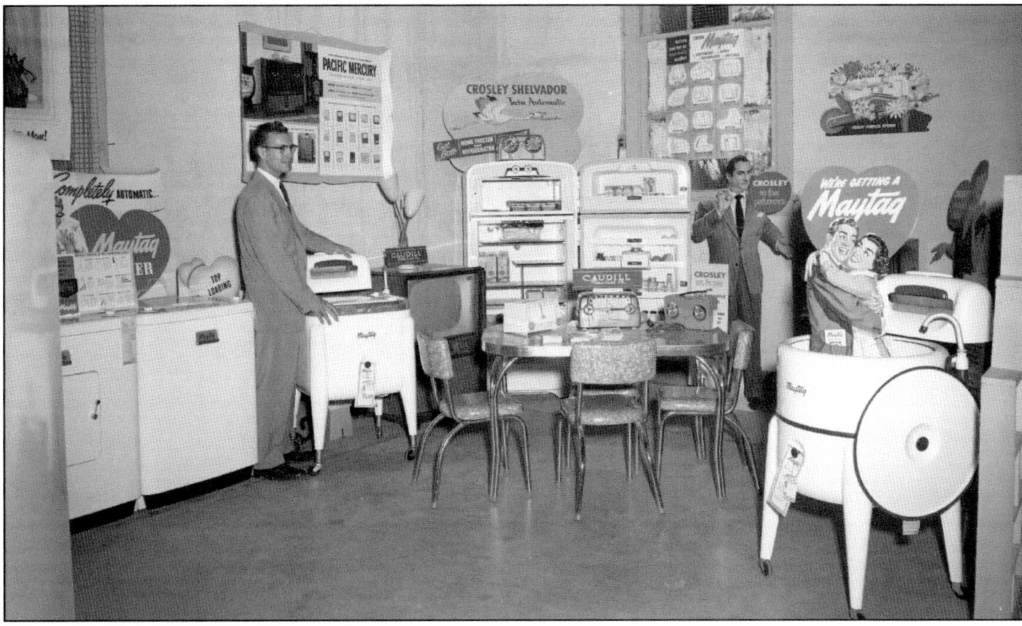

Although a woman's work was never done, by 1957 many new appliances were available to make her work easier. Wringer washing machines in a choice of square or round were available, as were even more modern washers and dryers and new electric refrigerators. Utilitarian Formica and metal kitchen tables with padded, plastic-covered chairs could be purchased as well and were often the highlight of any new home.

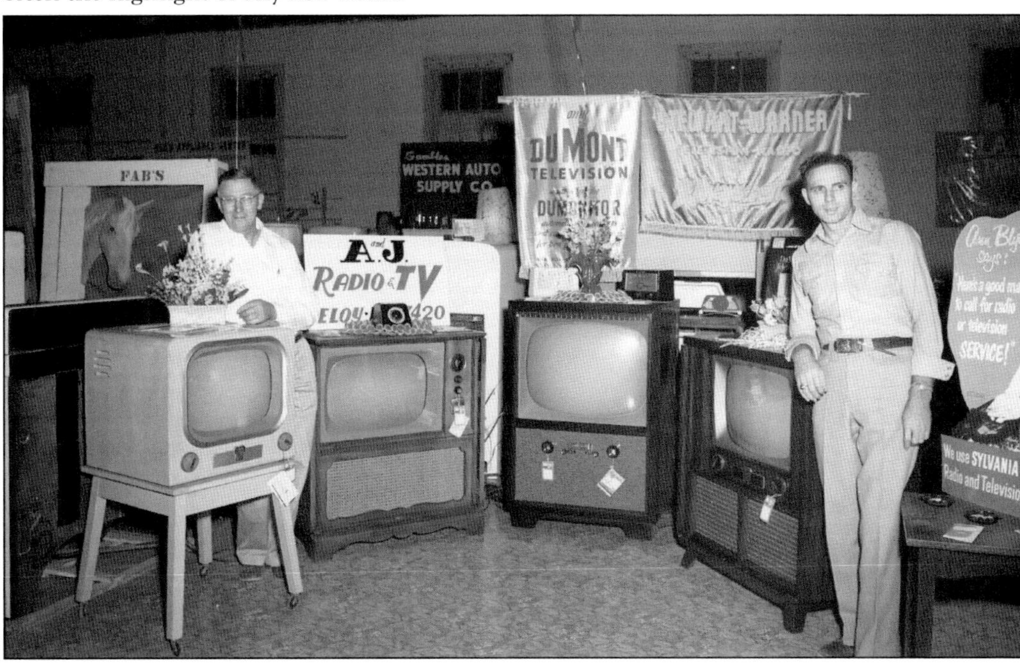

With the advent of affordable television sets, home entertainment was becoming an integral part of family life as well as big business for area retailers. Console and tabletop models of black-and-white television sets were featured at many of the local stores. The Western Auto Supply Store has a couple of salesmen anxious to sell a choice of Sylvania or Dumont products.

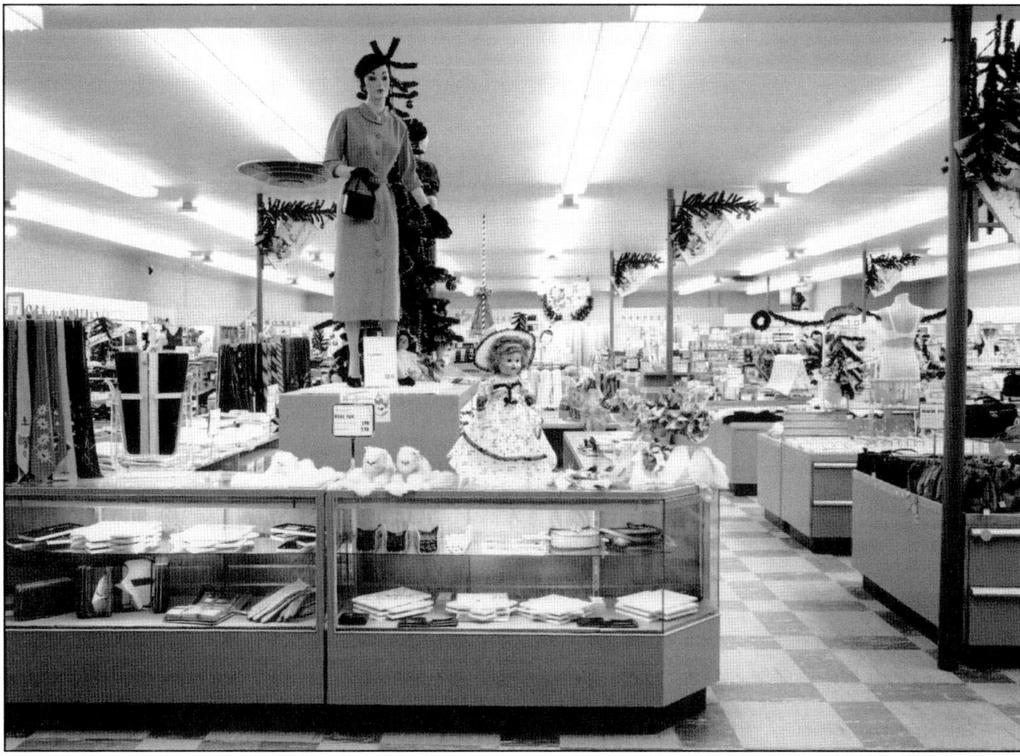

One of the many advantages of living in Casa Grande was the variety of stores and products available locally. Decked out for Christmas shoppers, J.C. Penney's department store on Florence Street was one of the few large chain stores to do business in Casa Grande in the early 1950s. Although this depicts the women's department, men and children were not forgotten; each had a section of its own. In addition to clothes and shoes, accessories such as cuff links and costume jewelry were sold, as were linens and fabric. Other businesses catered to a specific clientele, such as this sporting goods store seen below. This small corner of the store seems to contain something for everyone, from a bear hunter to a fisherman to a tennis or baseball player. Specialized equipment was also available for target shooters, horseback riders, golfers, and boaters.

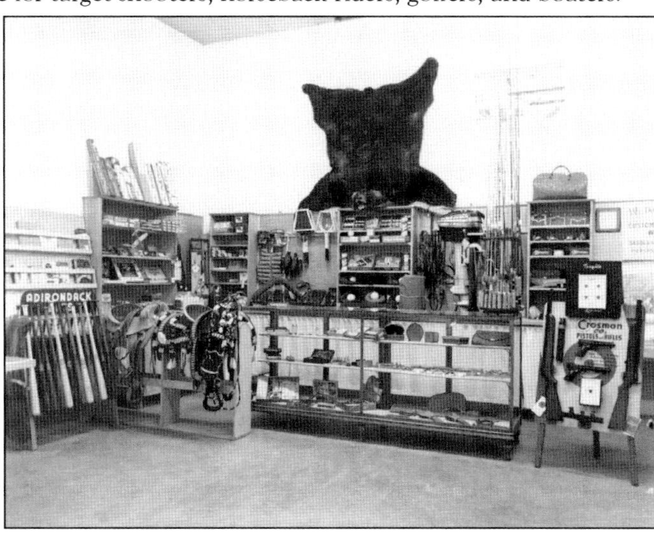

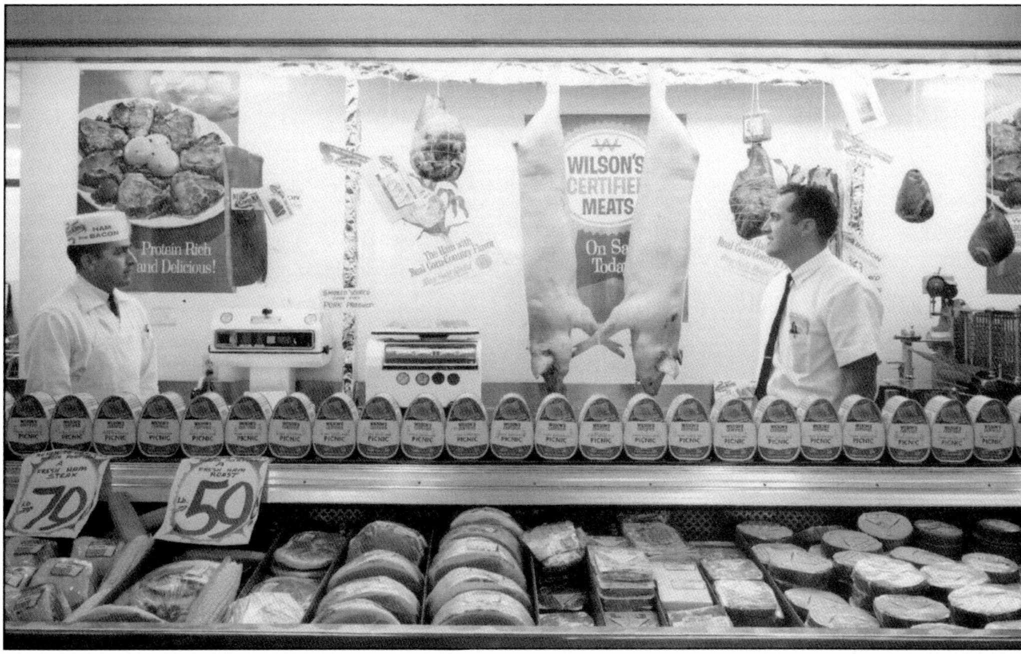

For years, Prettyman's had been the go-to grocery store in Casa Grande, but Bashas' was another popular Arizona-owned, full-service supermarket. It was located at the corner of Florence and Second Streets, a space now occupied by Food City. A display of fresh meat at the butcher counter is a sight one is unlikely to see today. Henry Carrera (left) and Paul Quintana were typical of the friendly neighborhood butchers often found at local groceries.

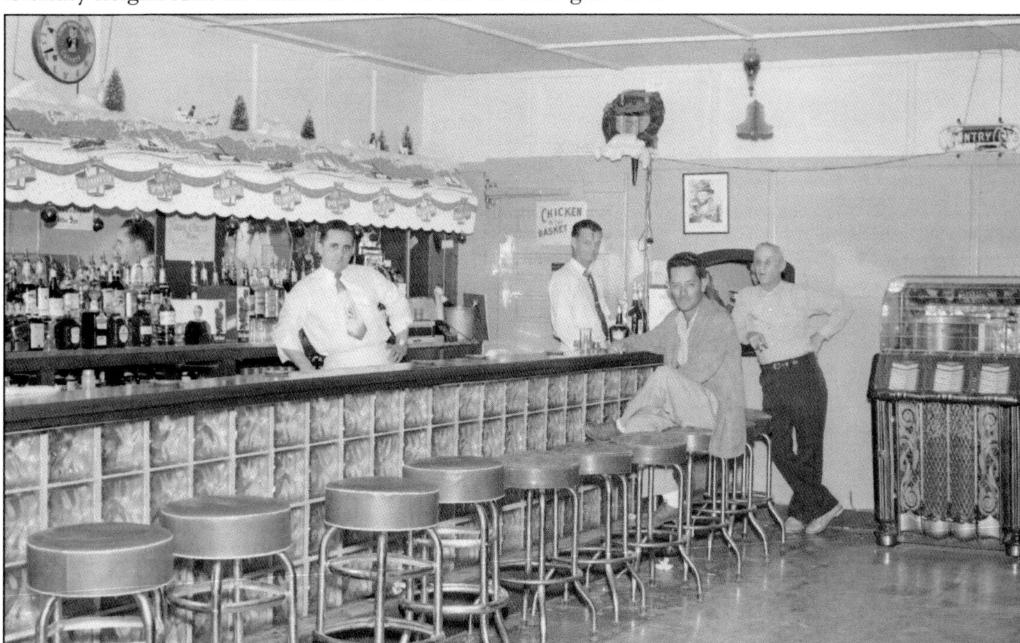

Although it is sparsely attended in this photograph, Club 84 was a popular bar and restaurant that provided a place for the hard-working men and women of the community to unwind after a busy work week. It was located on old Highway 84 near Arizola Road.

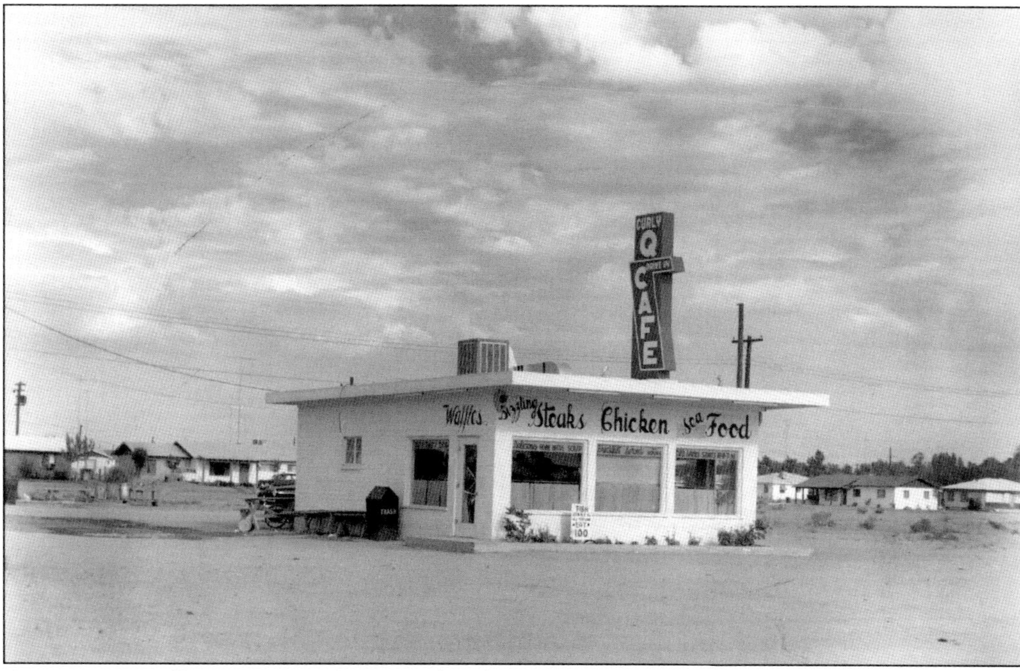

As in many small towns across America, family-run restaurants were common. The Curly Q Café was one of several of these types of eateries in Casa Grande. This one was located at the corner of Pinal Avenue and McMurray Boulevard across from the junior high school. Some local folks remember walking there for a hamburger during lunch time. The Casa Grande Jewelry and Pawn Shop now occupies that spot. Another popular eating spot in town in the 1950s was the 5-Points Café, located at the junction of Highway 84, Florence Boulevard, and Second Street. It, too, was typical of small, popular local restaurants.

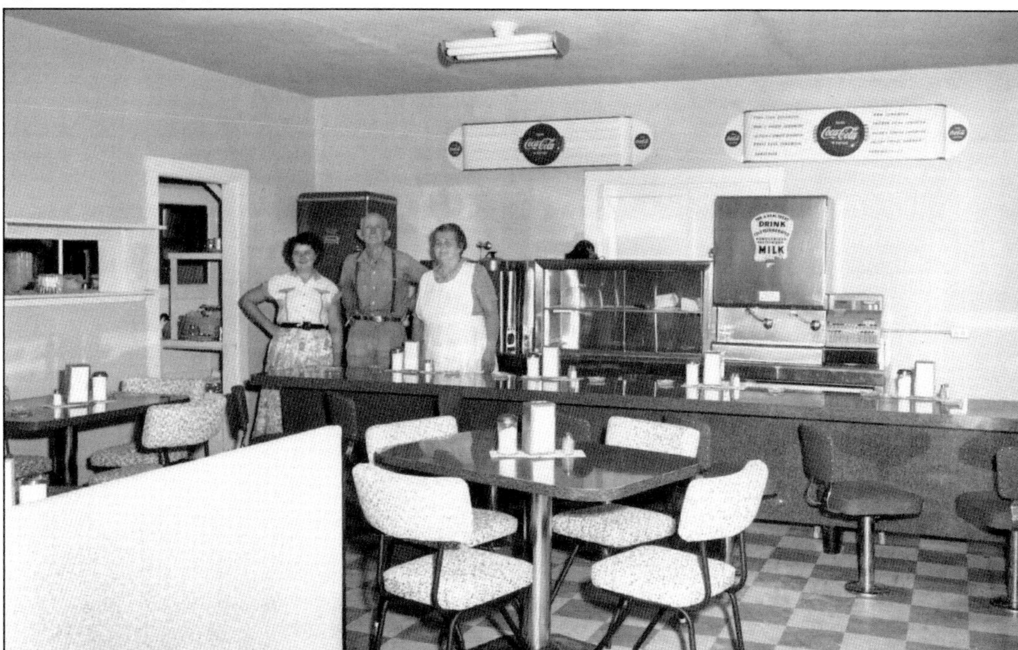

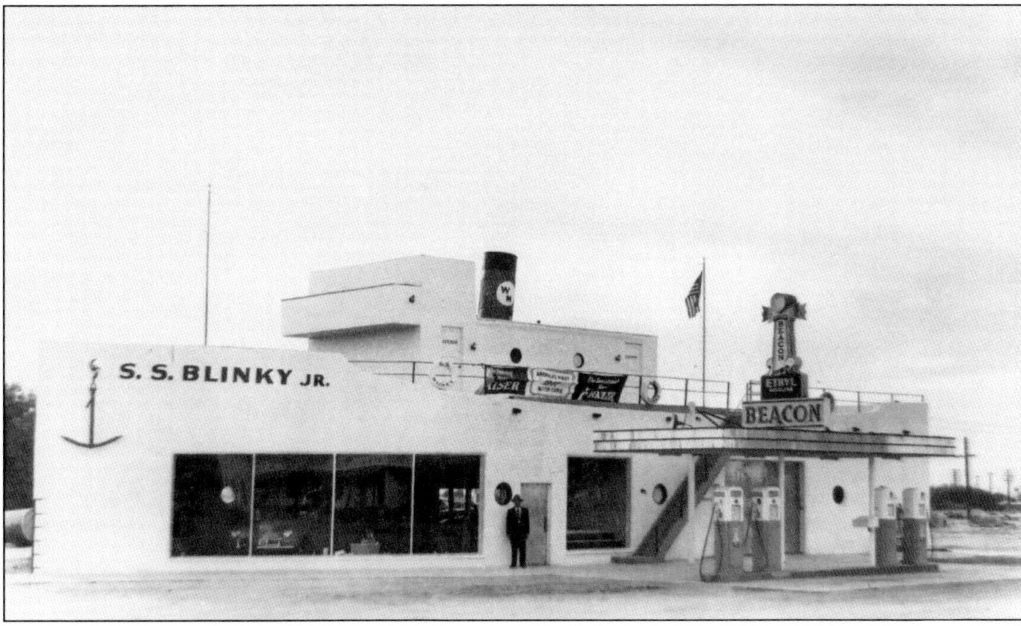

Many communities have what can be considered unusual or interesting buildings. Casa Grande has several prominent buildings made of stone, including the historical society. The city has had its share of Art Deco and Pueblo Deco buildings as well. Two of the older, iconic structures still in existence are the S.S. Blinky Jr. building on the corner of Highway 84 and Wilson Street. Blinky Wilson is in front of what was a gas station and automobile salesroom built in the form of a ship. It was constructed to honor the owner's son, who was serving in the Navy during World War II. The other is the always-popular Dairy Queen, which is still located at the corner of Marshall Street and Florence Boulevard with little modification to its iconic look, although its surroundings have changed.

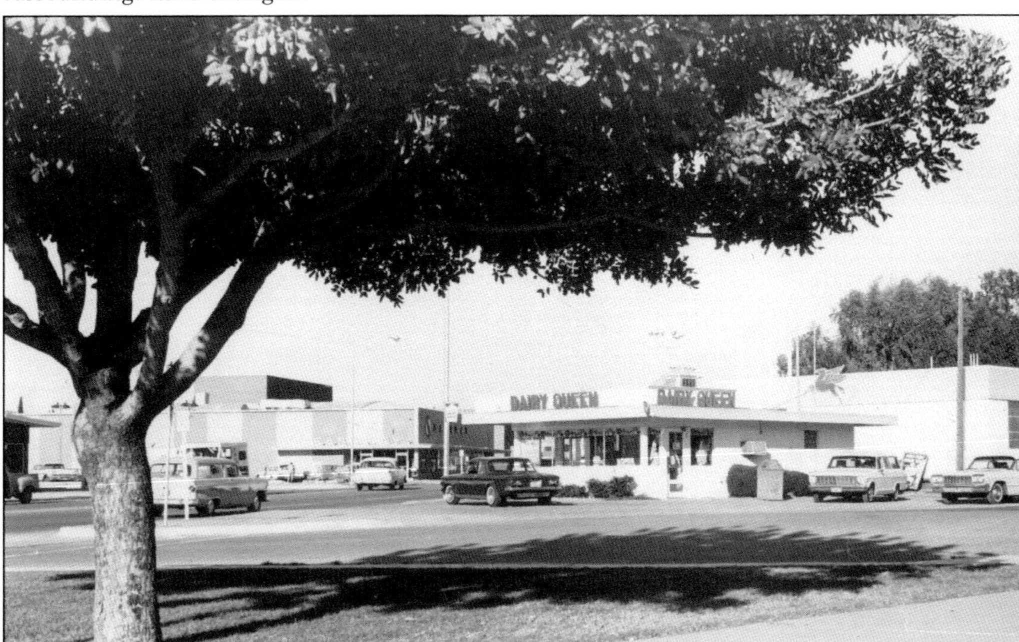

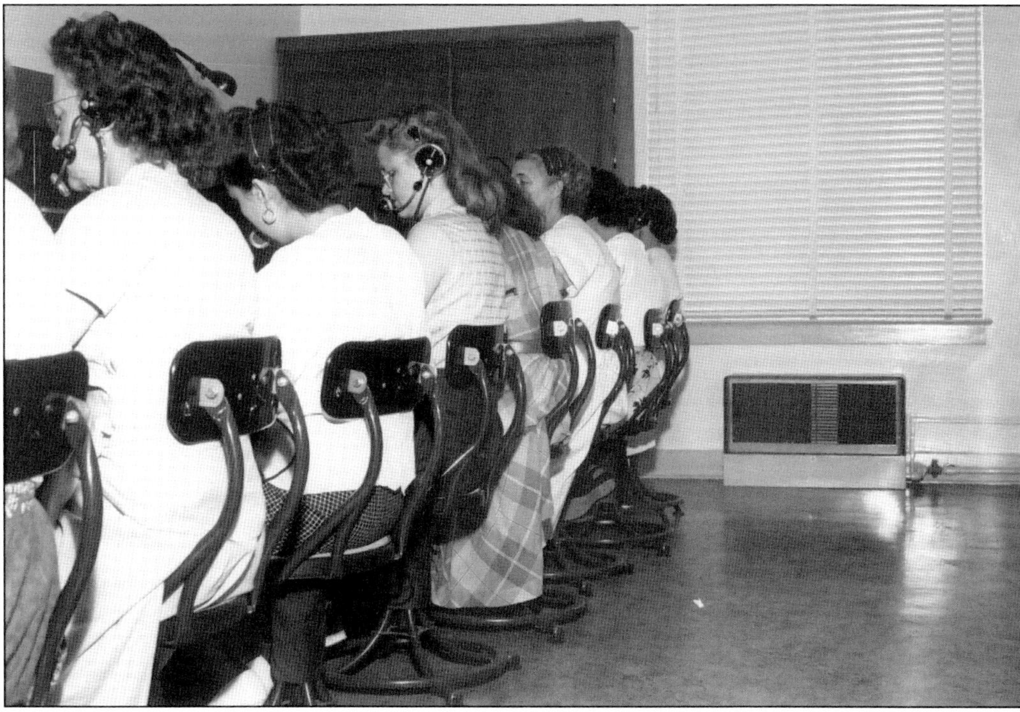

Beginning in the mid-1940s and into the 1950s and beyond, World War II and its aftermath had created work for women in the absence of men at war or lost in the war. Prior to that, Casa Grande had few jobs for women if they were not schoolteachers or nurses. The local telephone company (above) was an exception, and it provided women, many of whom had never worked for pay before, with a source of income to help support their households. Another position deemed "woman's work" was microfilm reading (below).

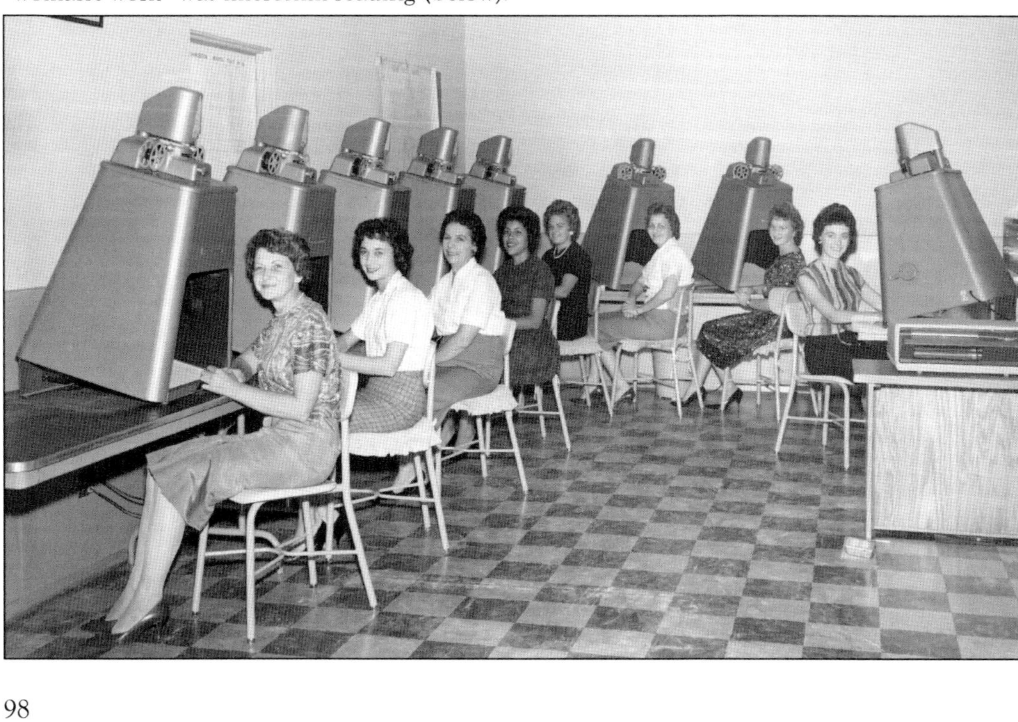

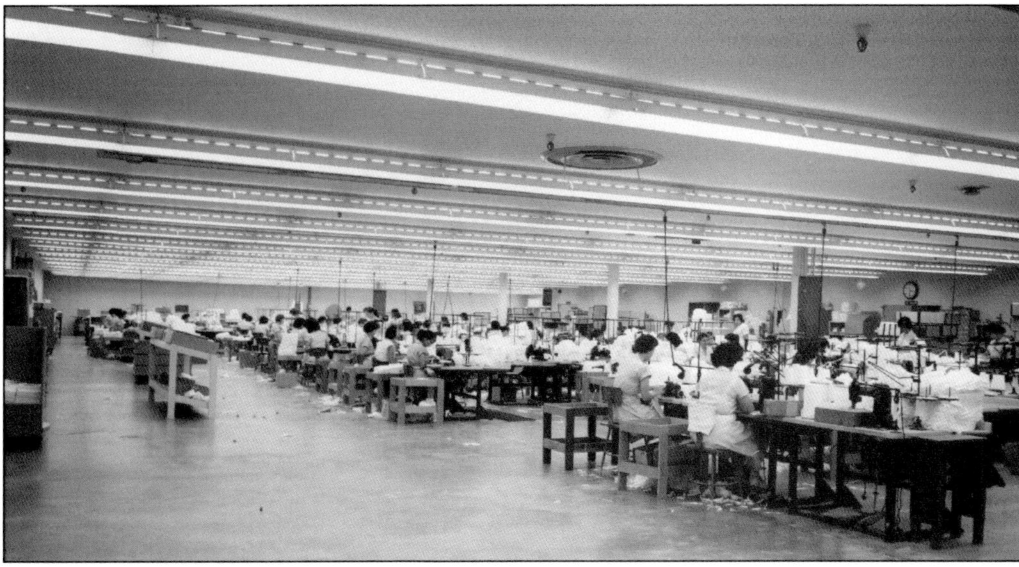

Shortly after the war, several new manufacturing companies opened in town, which employed men and women but rarely at the same factory. Women were generally relegated to what was considered woman's work, while the men worked at jobs that were considered more appropriate for them. Casa Grande Mills was one of the first large-scale manufacturing plants in town, although it employed mainly women as seamstresses making T-shirts and underwear. The enterprise, which was in existence for about 20 years, was located where the post office is now. Men were employed at places like Arizona Iron Works (below).

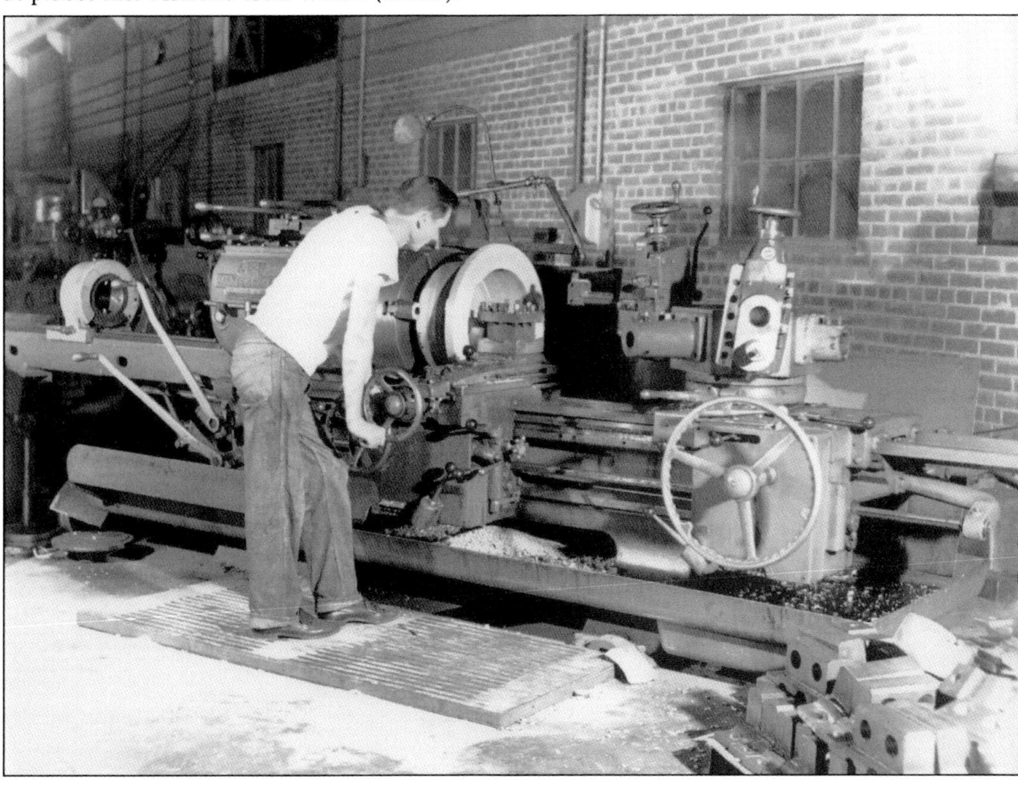

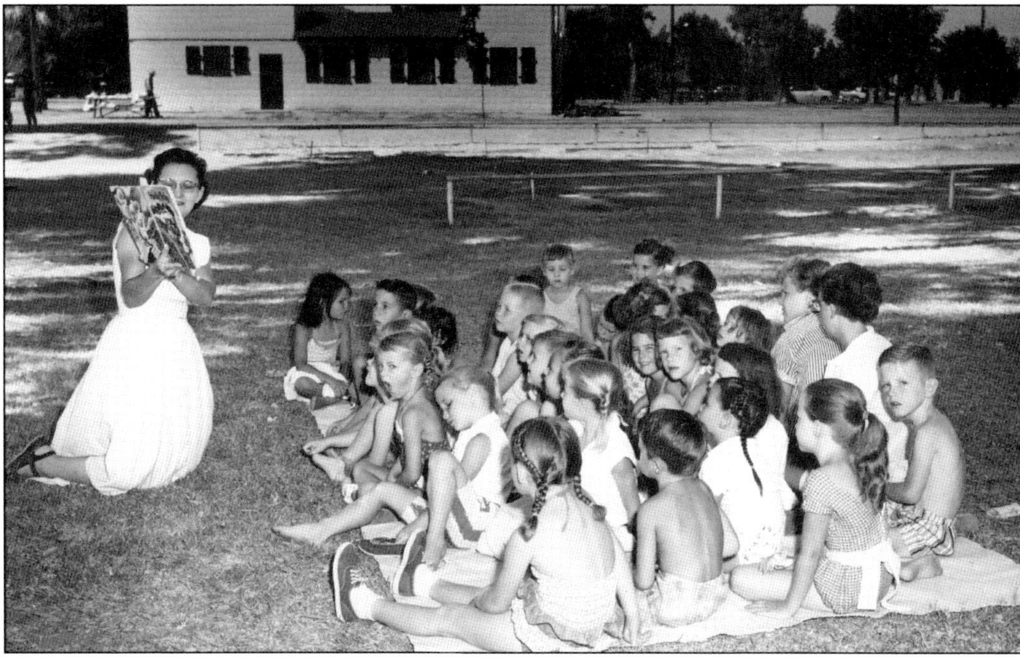

Then, as now, kids are known to lament that there is nothing to do in their spare time, but Casa Grande has always provided various sources of entertainment for its youth. The parks and recreation department hosted many events for children, teens, and adults, ranging from swimming classes to volleyball and tennis to sewing and photography. Even the smallest children had events. Here, they are listening to someone read to them. Teen dances were often held and were generally well attended. The old National Guard Armory Building (below) was one venue for the dances. This is a far cry from today's style of dancing, but these young couples seem to be enjoying the opportunity to slow dance, which required them to snuggle up to their partners.

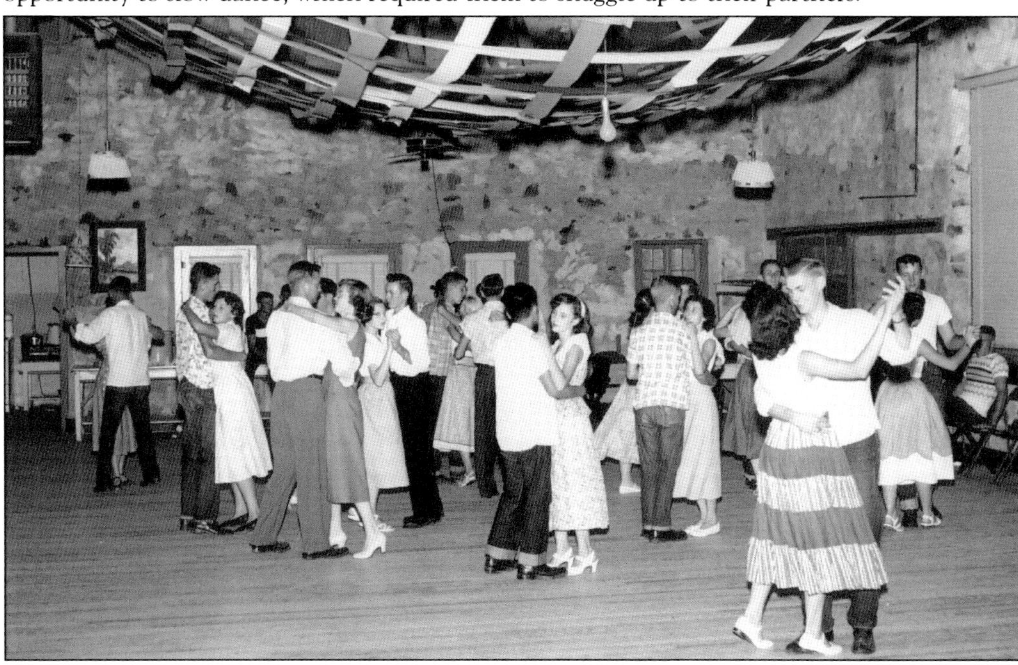

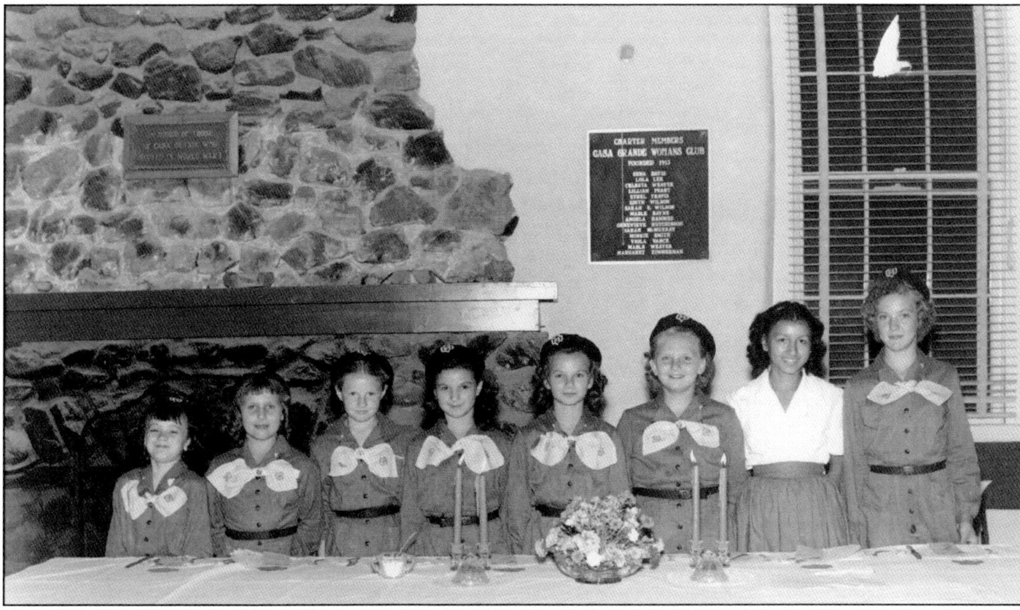

Among the many recreational and educational activities provided for the youth of the community was scouting. A Girl Scout troop (above) poses for a photograph prior to an awards ceremony at the Casa Grande Woman's Club. In 1952, twenty lucky Casa Grande Boy Scouts and their leaders attended the third annual Boy Scout Jamboree in California. The Casa Grande scouts who could not attend the Jamboree pitched tents and set up field kitchens in Peart Park as a poor but enjoyable substitute for the trip.

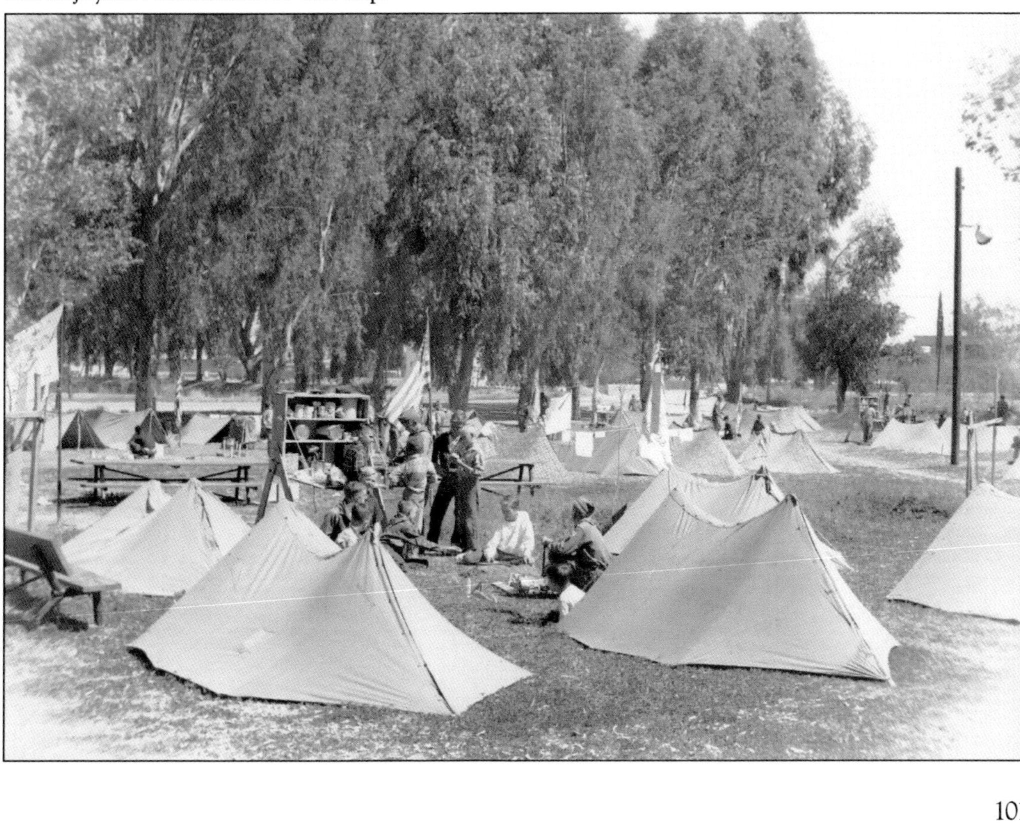

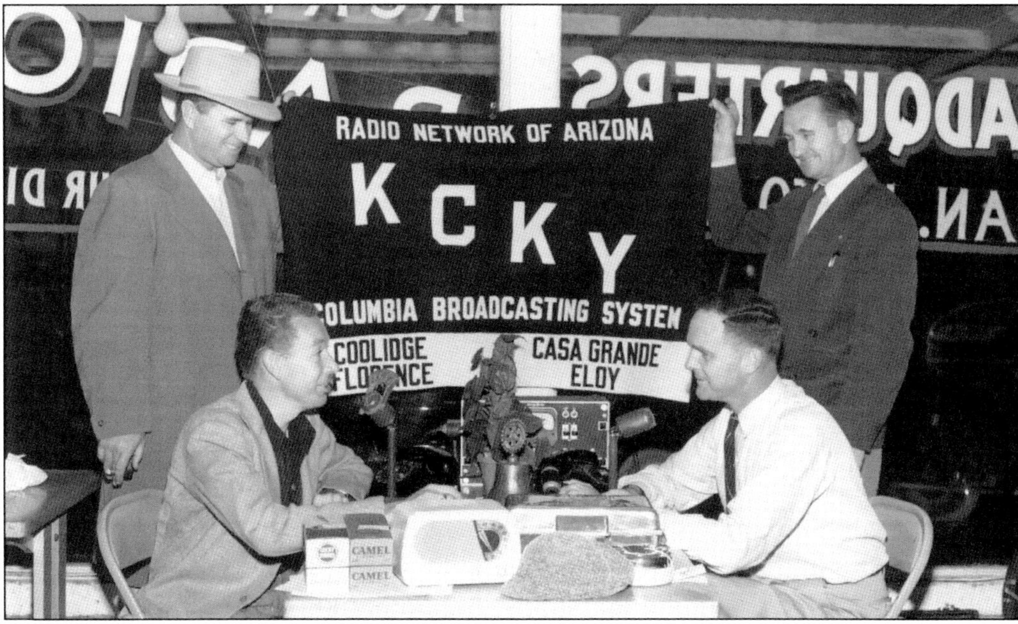

KCKY, a local radio station affiliated with the Columbia Broadcasting System, conducted a radio auction in conjunction with the Kiwanis Club to help pay for the municipal ball field. Proceeds from the auction not only paid off the debt, but enabled the club to support the Cotton Kings and Little League baseball teams. Those identified are Guy Acuff (standing on the right) and Bill Paraday (seated). Below, the Cubs, one group of Little Leaguers who benefited from the fund drive sponsored by KCKY, pose for their team picture.

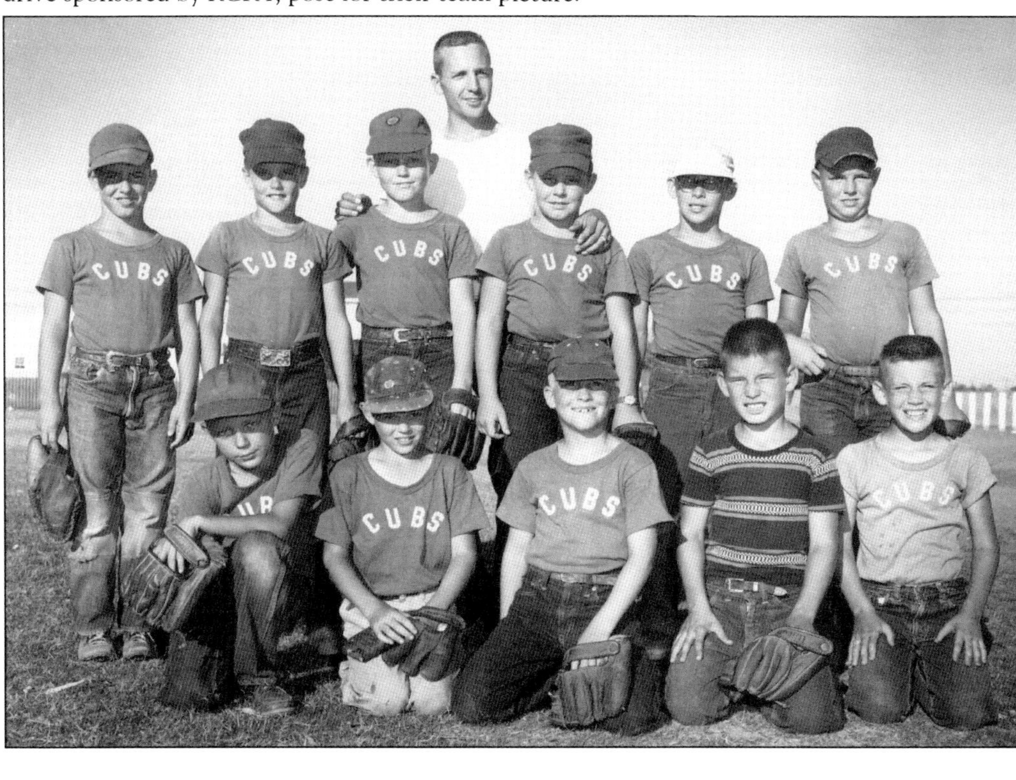

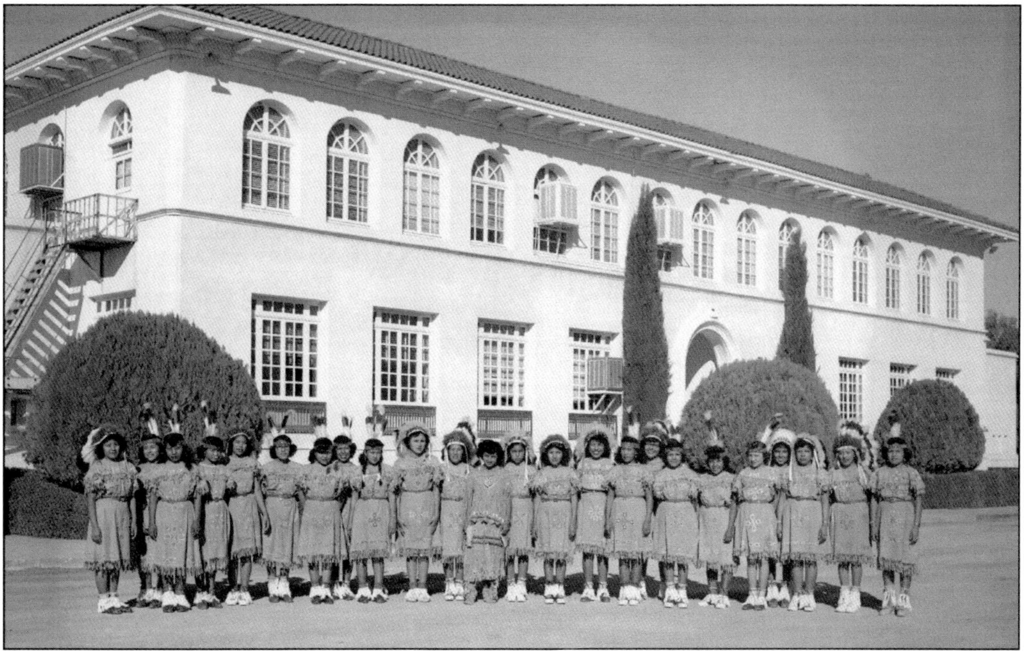

Beginning in 1947, the Junior Chamber of Commerce sponsored a Cotton Carnival with a variety of activities and a parade. Casa Grande still celebrates special events and entertains its citizens with parades during the year. Young women dressed in Native American costumes pose in front of the high school in the early 1950s as they await the start of the fifth annual Cotton Parade.

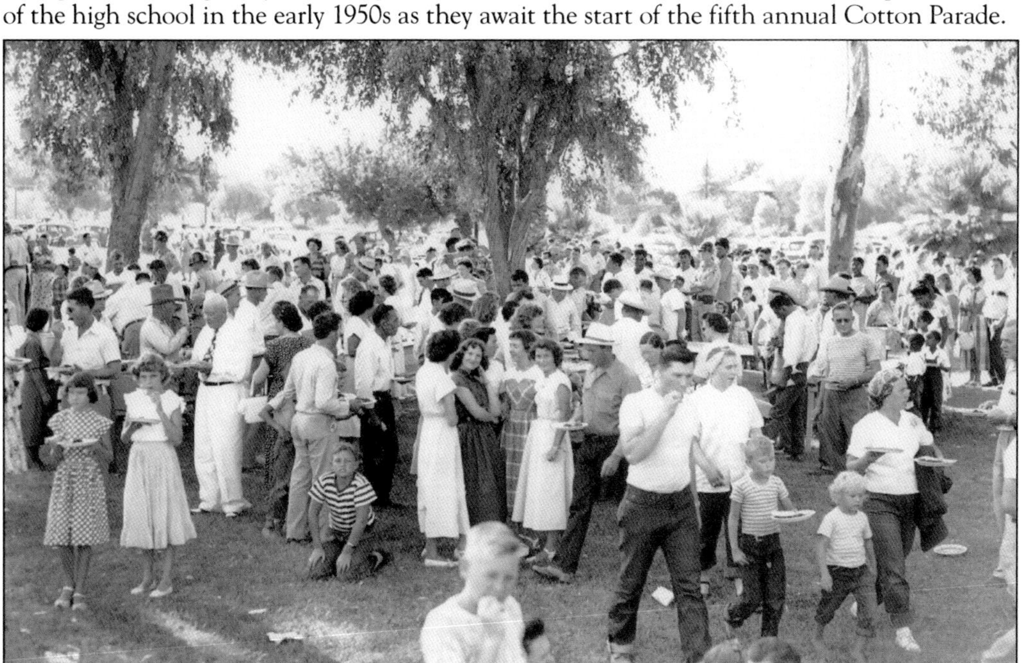

The Fourth of July picnic sponsored by the Junior Chamber of Commerce was always something to look forward to as a special family event. The picnic was usually held in Peart Park with free barbecue for all. A watermelon-eating contest drew eager contestants and enthusiastic spectators. Attendees of all ages attest to the popularity of the event.

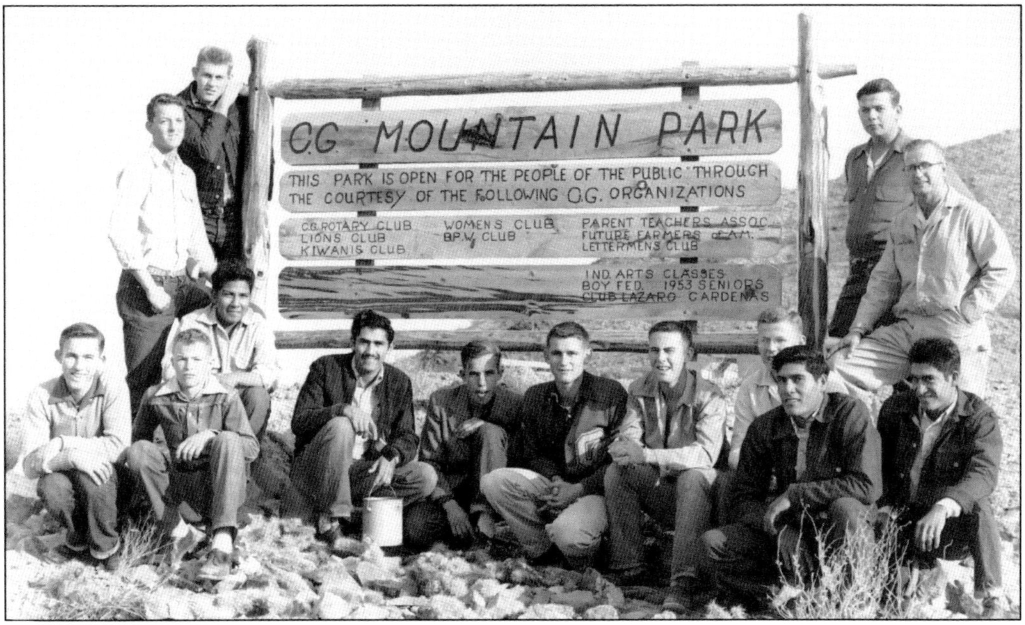

Casa Grande Mountain Park, located northwest of town, has long been a refuge for birdwatchers, hikers, and picnickers. These men and boys pose for their picture after policing the park in 1953. Only some of the people are identified: in the first row are J.W. Ritchey (second from left), Toco Rendon (third from left), Ralph Barker (fifth from left), and Charlie and George Singh (seventh and eighth from left, respectively).

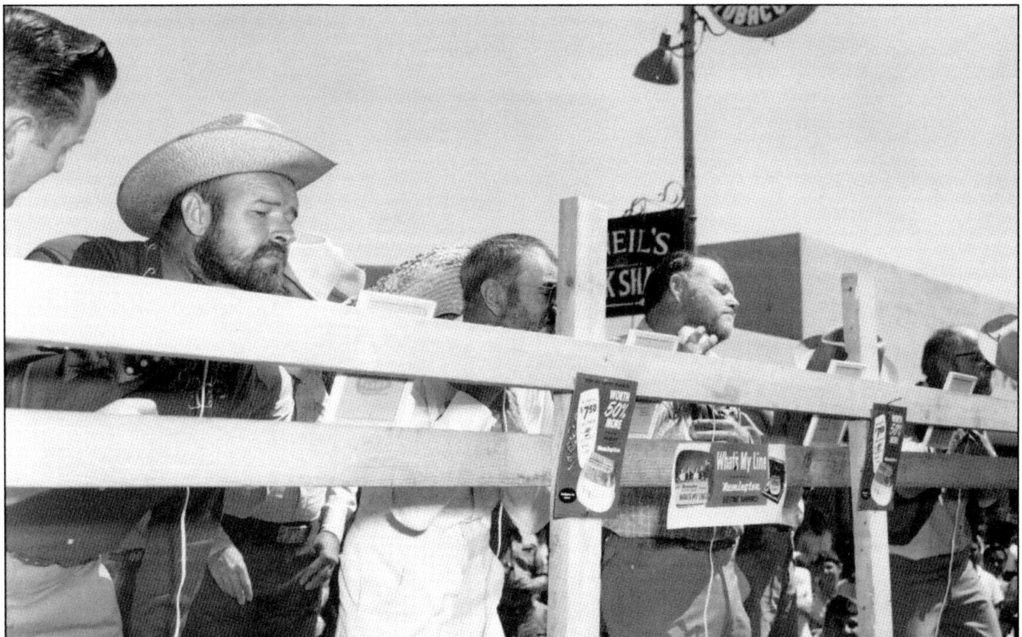

As a publicity stunt to attract attention to the newest electric Remington Razor, Lawrence Jewelers, located on West Florence Street, conducted a beard-shaving contest. A small crowd gathered to observe the contest, which drew several men who were willing to trim or shave their beards.

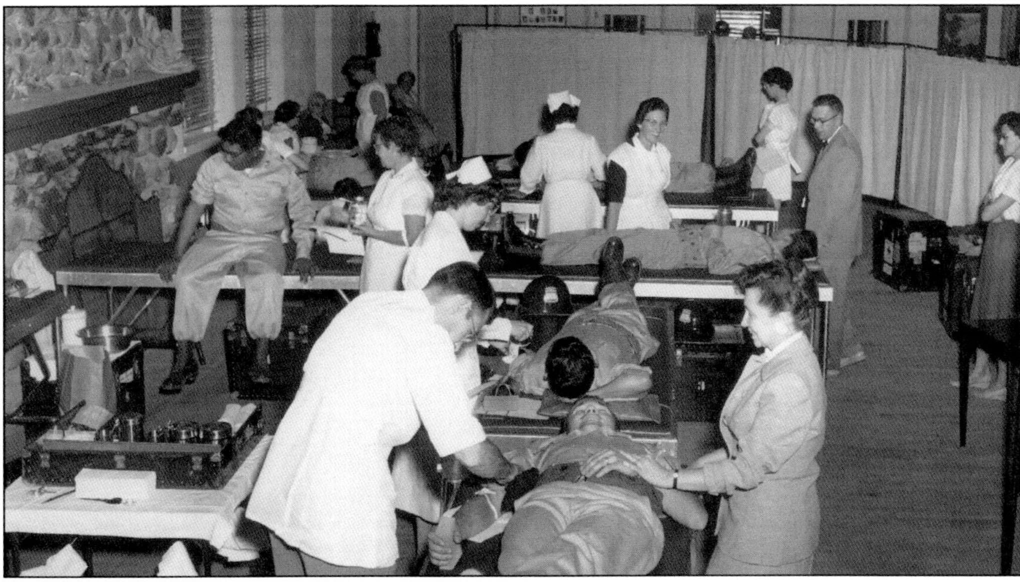

Health issues are always of major concern to a community. In addition to serving their country, members of the Casa Grande National Guard are giving blood at the Woman's Club during a blood bank drive (above). Dr. R.F. Schoen is in the suit on the right. If a patient could not make it to the doctor's office, the office would come to the patient. The Arizona chest X-Ray bus made periodic visits to various locales throughout Pinal County to more easily enable those who needed an X-ray to acquire one. Below, several men and boys are lined up to take advantage of the opportunity.

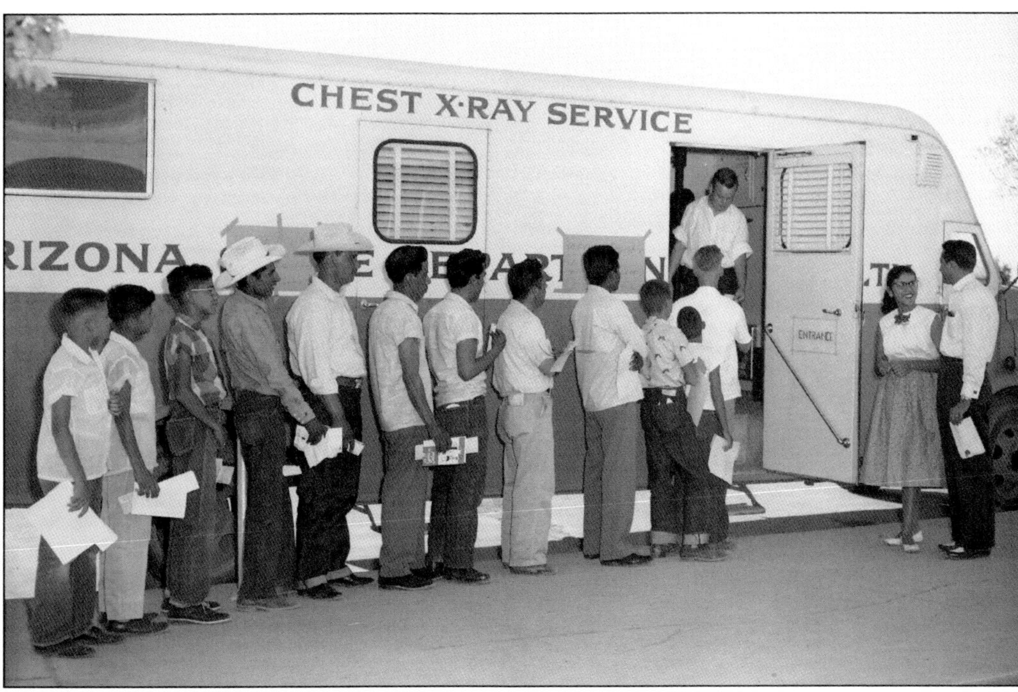

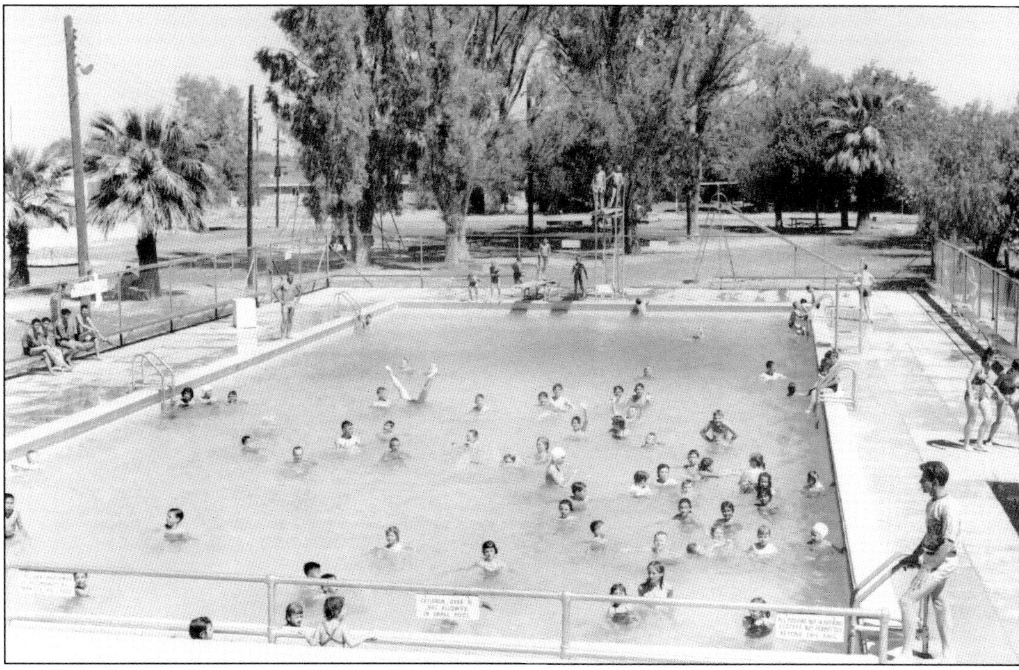

Many people would say that a Casa Grande summer would not be endurable without a community swimming pool. Casa Grande residents, and especially the children, always enjoy going to the pool, and the folks above are making the most out of the experience. In the photograph below, kids are fishing in the same pool. It is unclear if they are fishing for real fish or perhaps items that could be caught and kept as prizes. Today's tradition does not include fishing in the pool, but residents are encouraged to bring their dogs for a swim before the pool is closed for the winter.

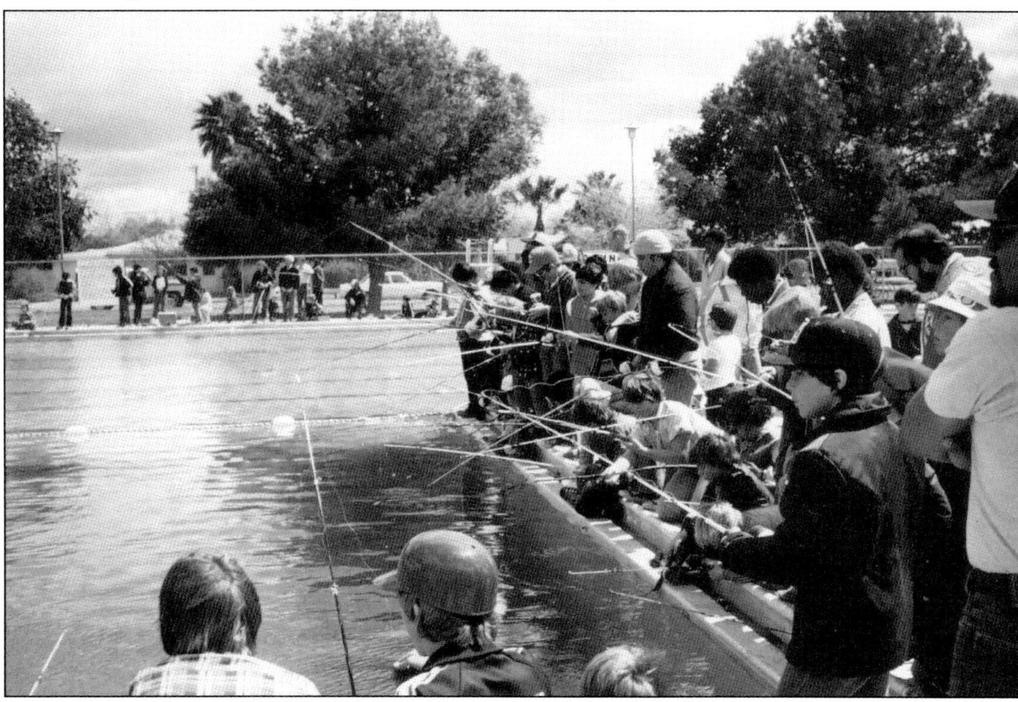

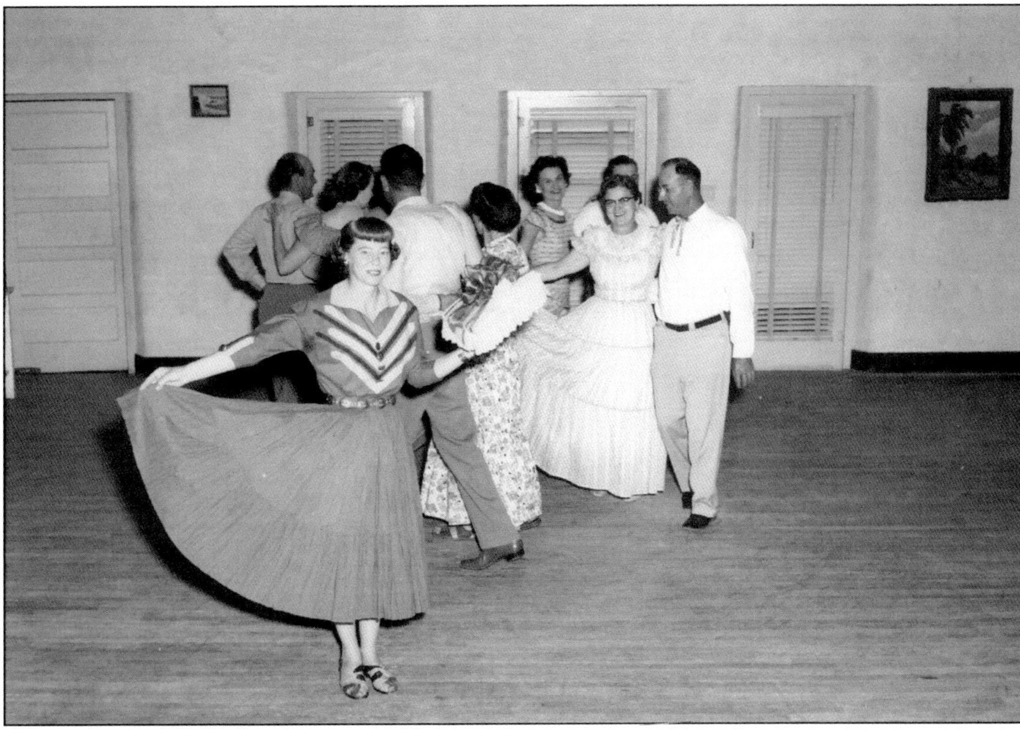

Through the years, the adults of the community have not been forgotten when it comes to entertainment. The Box Social Group, a gathering of square dancers, takes advantage of the Woman's Club as they do-si-do their way around the floor. The ladies show off their fancy skirts, and the gentlemen have on their dress cowboy boots.

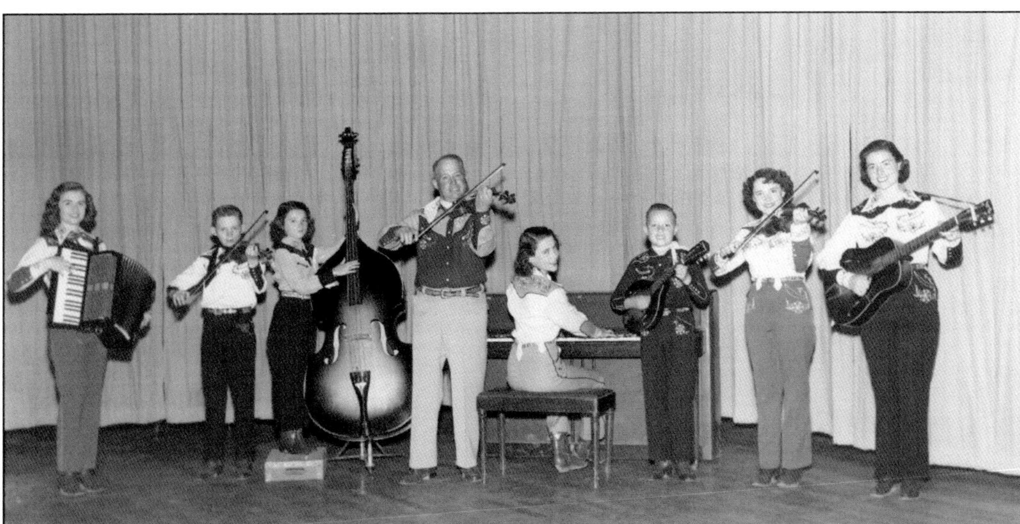

Family entertainment events were common, and many a toe-tapping evening was enjoyed by the city's residents as they listened to the Montgomery Family Western Band. Dressed in their Western-style clothes and led by dad on the violin, the group was well known in Pinal County. Everyone played at least one instrument, and all family members played and sang to the delight of their audiences.

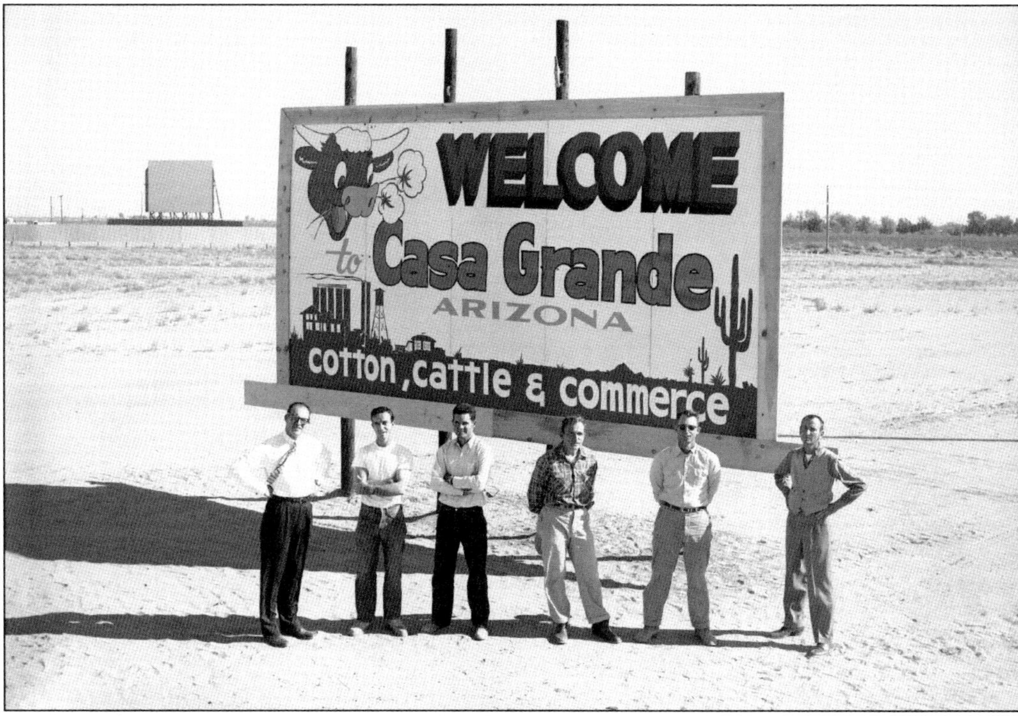

By the mid-1950s, Casa Grande was in the throes of a growth spurt; however, the local Junior Chamber of Commerce was anxious to continue the trend and posted the sign above. The Desert Drive-in Theater can be seen in the background. Around 1954, this corner of Pinal Avenue and Cottonwood Lane was in the country. Now the site is home to a convenience store and gas station along two of the busiest thoroughfares in town. The Casa Grande West Sales Office staff (below) was poised to welcome those who accepted the invitation to move here. Based on the size of the staff, they were prepared for an onslaught of newcomers.

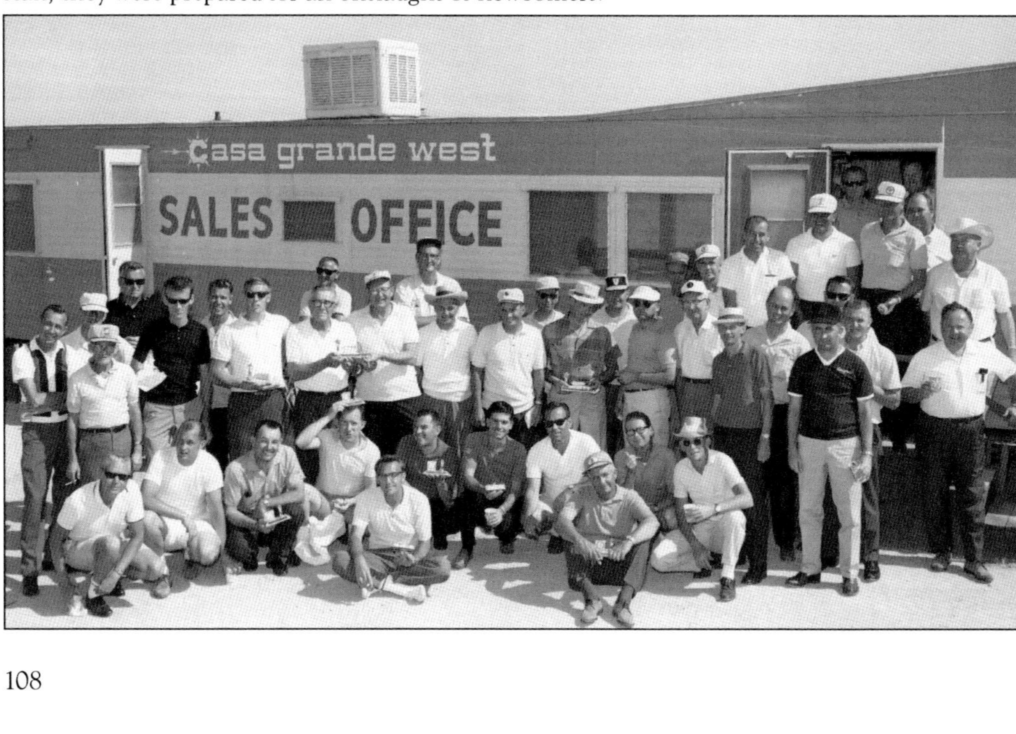

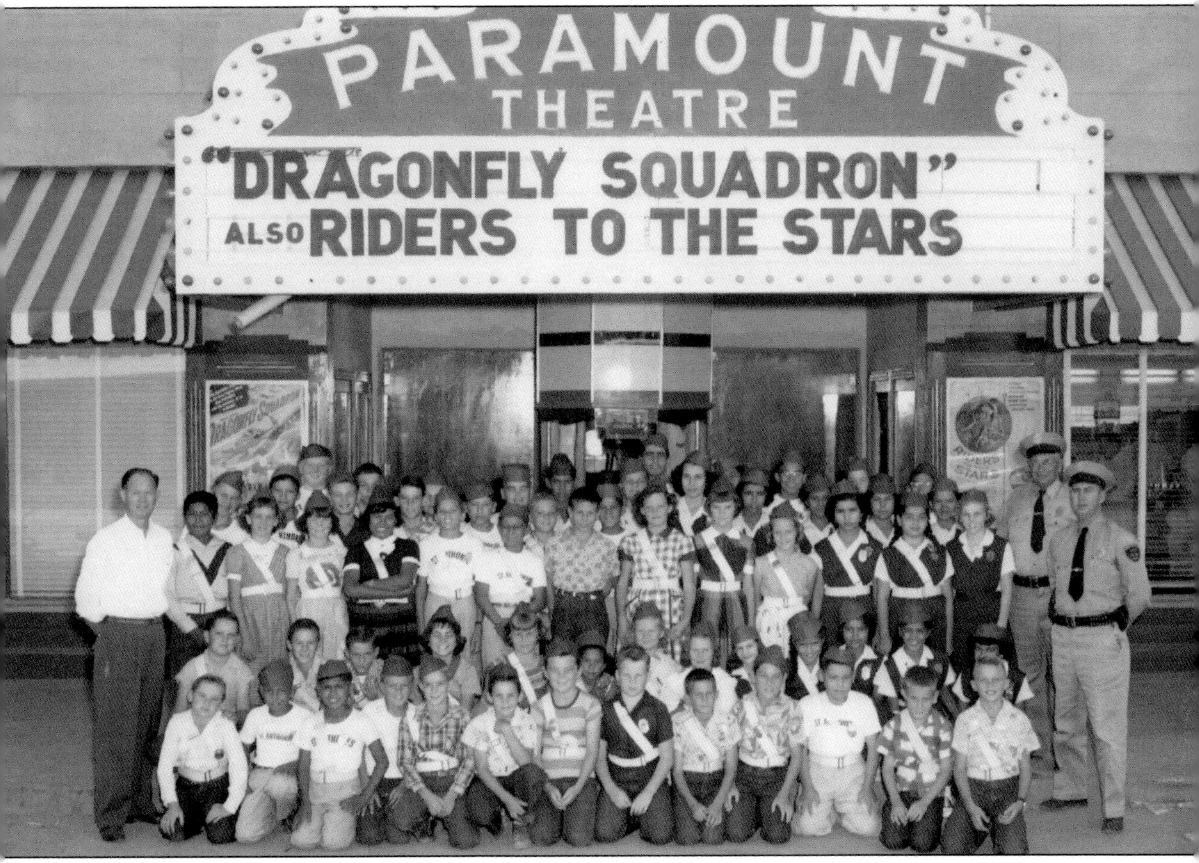

By 1954, World War II and the Korean War were events of the past, but the Cold War was in full swing. Here, a group of school safety patrol students are photographed in front of the Paramount Theater as they prepare to see a double feature. *Dragonfly Squadron* tells the story of pilots during the Korean War. *Riders to the Stars* is a science-fiction movie about an experimental rocket that falls to earth in the southwestern desert. On the left is Harry Bowers, the theater manager, and on the right are police officers Louis Davis and Glen Rogers. Elementary school patrol members could see movies for free on Friday night and at Saturday matinees. There are no African American students in the picture. That is because the theater was segregated, and minority children could only see movies at the Chief Theater, which was operated by the same people who operated the Paramount and Desert Drive-in.

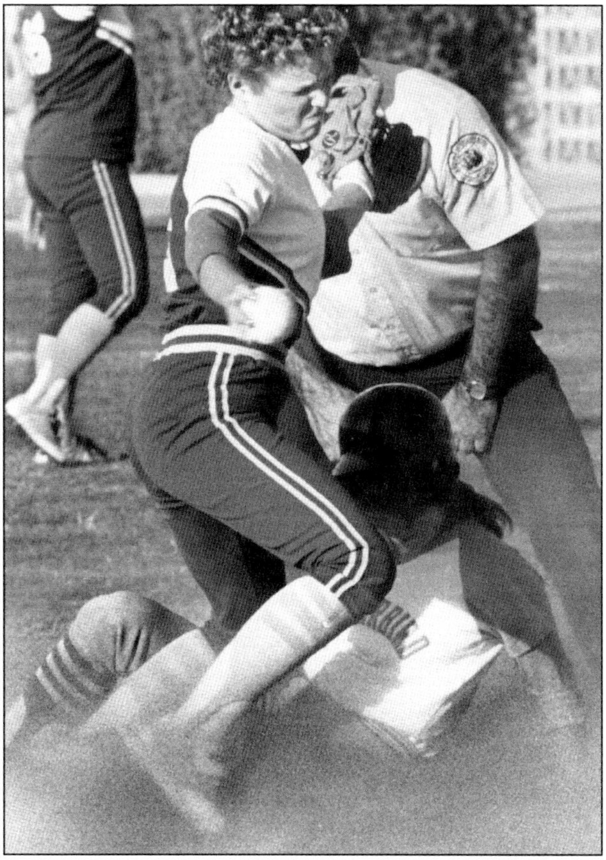

Girls and women were becoming more involved in sports. Several leagues for volleyball and softball were for girls only. It is clear in this photograph that girls were willing to get just as down and dirty as the boys. A hard slide and attempted tag is closely watched by the volunteer umpire. While sports were now girls' games as well as boys', some sexist behaviors lingered. Today, it would be politically incorrect, but then it was a common practice to present cedar chests to female high school graduates (below), not too subtly implying they would be getting married soon.

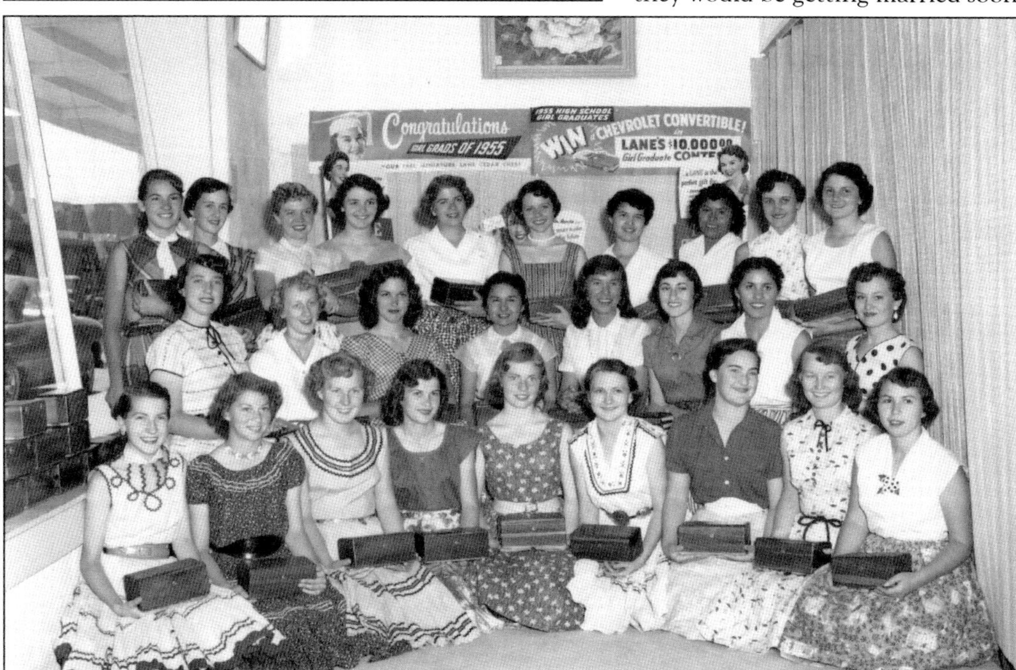

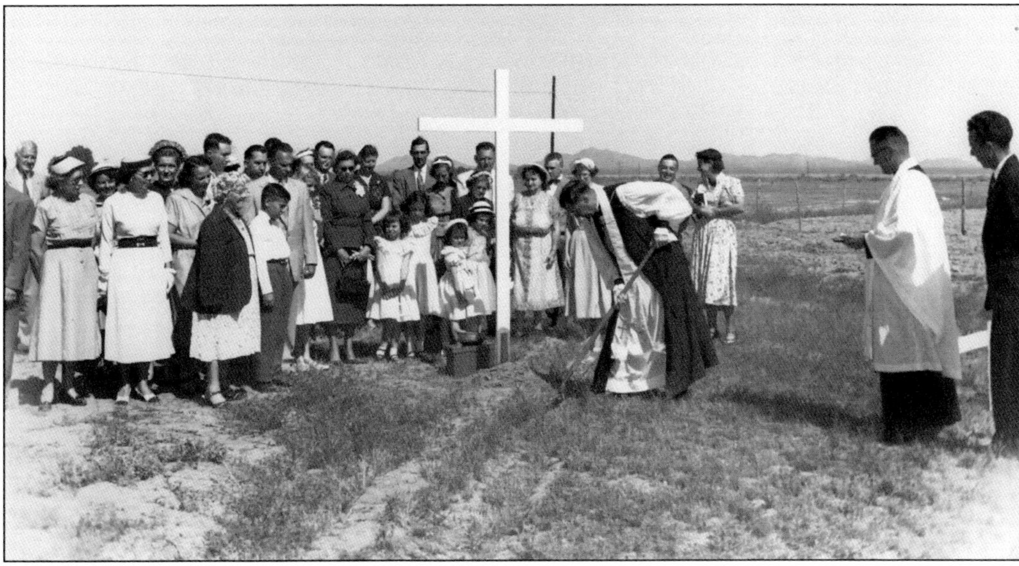

Religion and faith have played a major role in the history of Casa Grande. These two pictures represent just two of the many churches that have provided comfort to the residents of the community through the years. In the photograph above, the dedicated flock observes the groundbreaking ceremony for the new Episcopal church. In the photograph below, friends and family attend a wedding at St. Anthony's, the Catholic church that had already served the community for many years. In 2010, the historical society took photographs of more than 35 places of worship in Casa Grande.

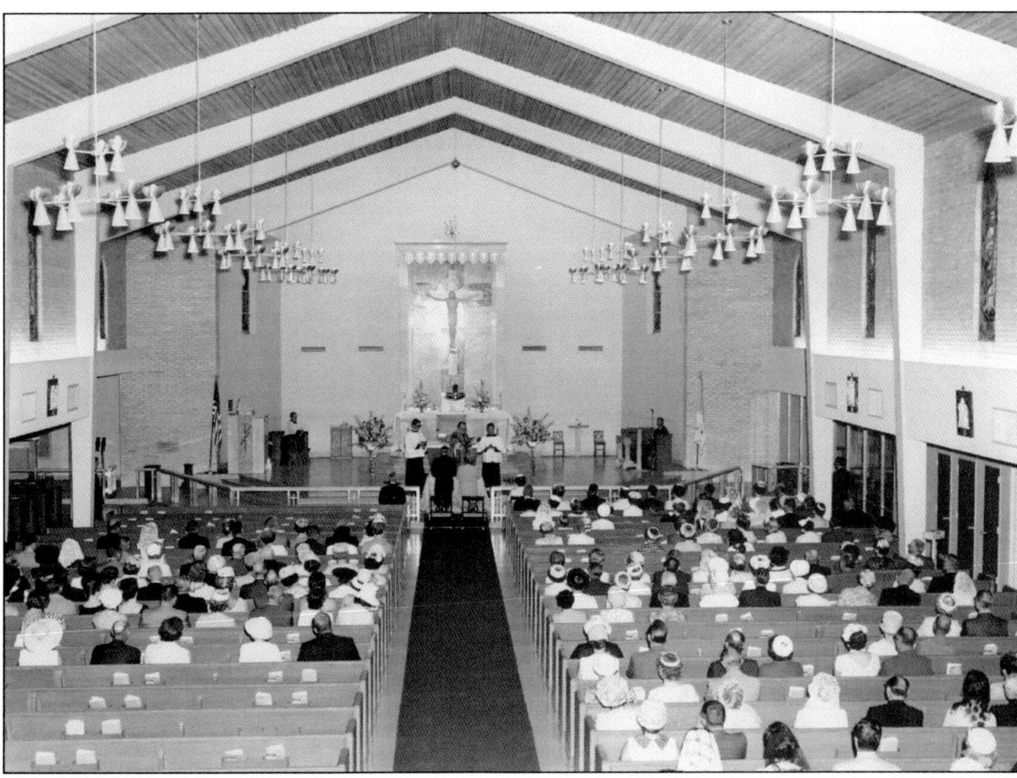

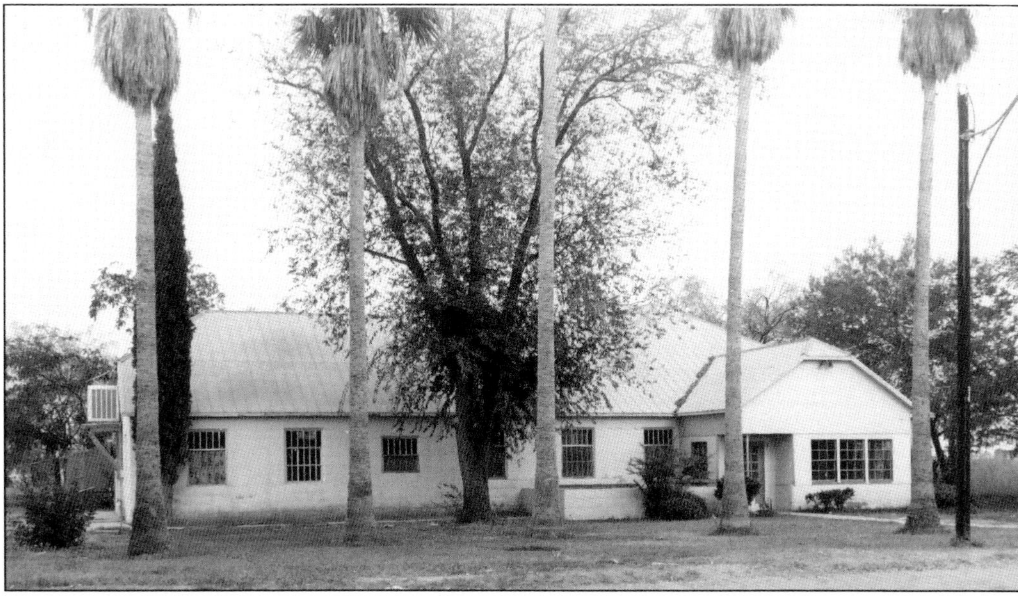

Almost every enterprise starts small and hospitals are no different. This house above on Brown Avenue served as the Lincoln Hospital, but before the city had a hospital, family practitioners provided all of the medical care for the citizens of Casa Grande and Pinal County. Dr. James O'Neil (below) was one of those early doctors. Here, he takes time from his practice to play what appears to be a lonely game of chess. Doctor O'Neil practiced medicine in Casa Grande for 18 years in his office located at 113 West Second Street and later at the clinic at 1023 East Florence Boulevard.

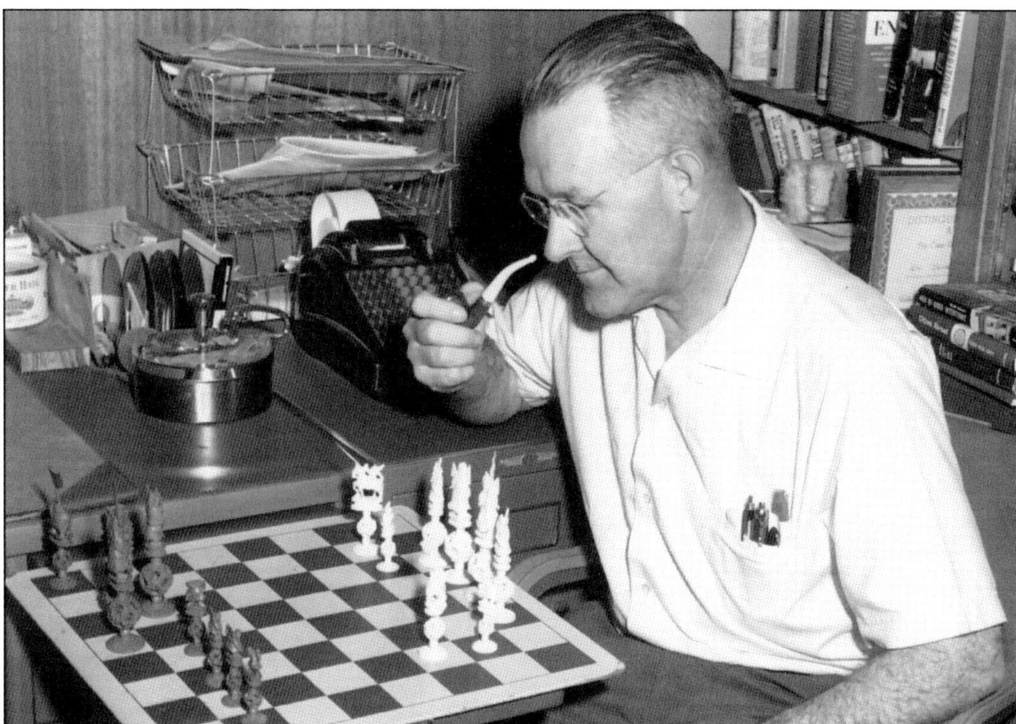

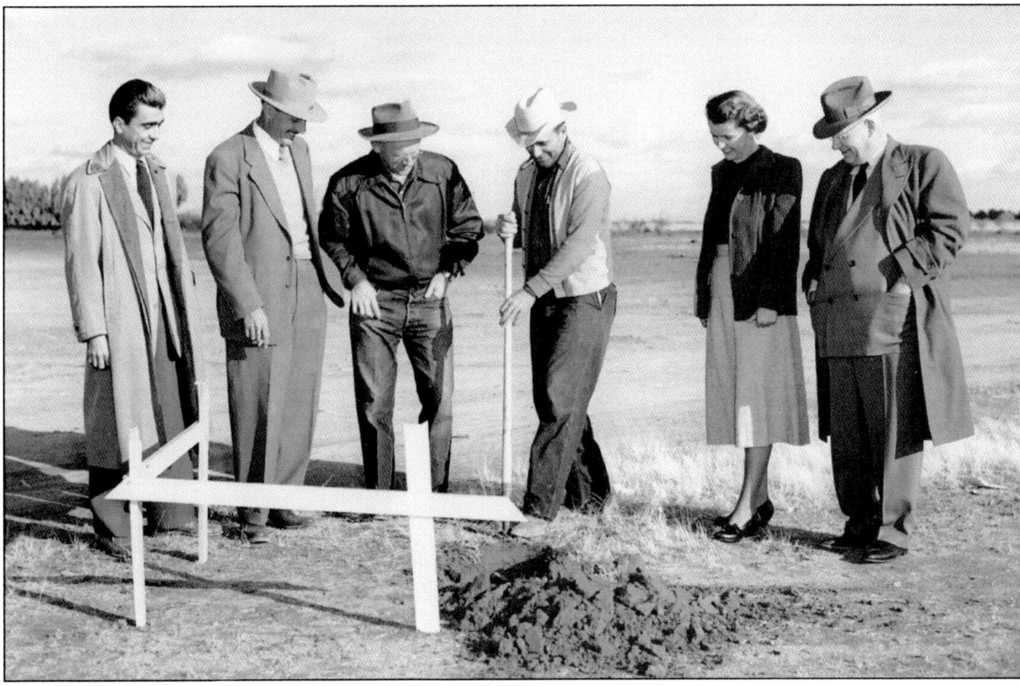

In 1948, a drive to build a bigger hospital was underway and in 1951 ground was broken for that endeavor. Pictured at the ground-breaking ceremony (above) are, from the right, Pappy Guin, Blodwen Thode, Guy Gilbert, and Pete Peters; the rest are unidentified. Edna Blodwen "Blodie" Thode, who was the driving force in getting the new hospital built, named it Hoemako Hospital. Hoemako, which is similar to "one" or "first" in the Papago language, is said to be the first word in the Papago Bible. Hoemako Hospital, located at the corner of Trekell Avenue and Florence Boulevard (below), quickly became a thriving success. Eventually, the need for a more comprehensive facility resulted in the creation of the Casa Grande Regional Medical Center, which is a well-respected, non-profit, full-service facility serving all of Pinal County.

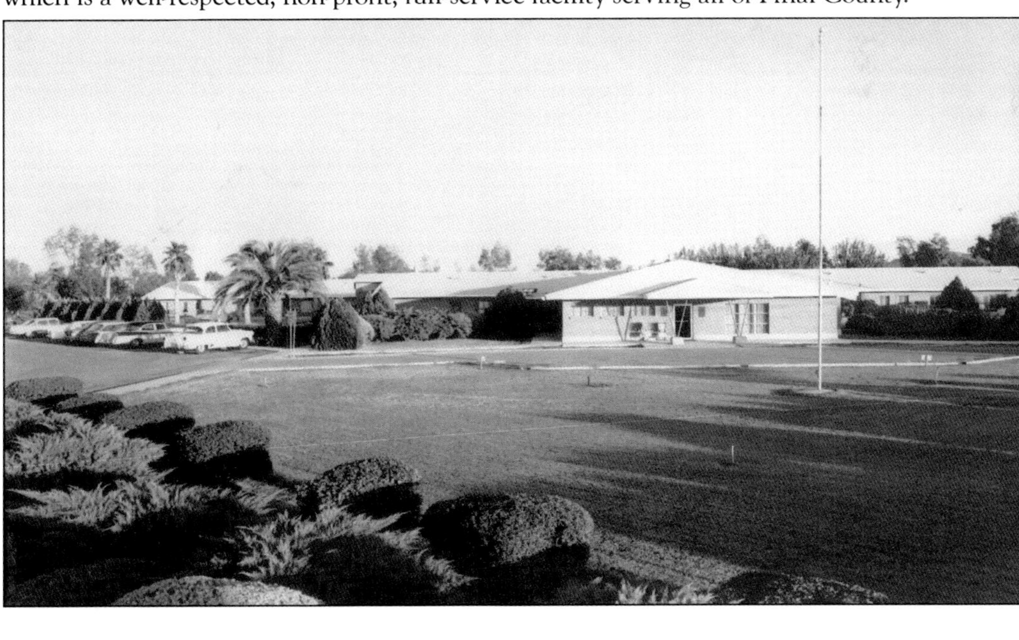

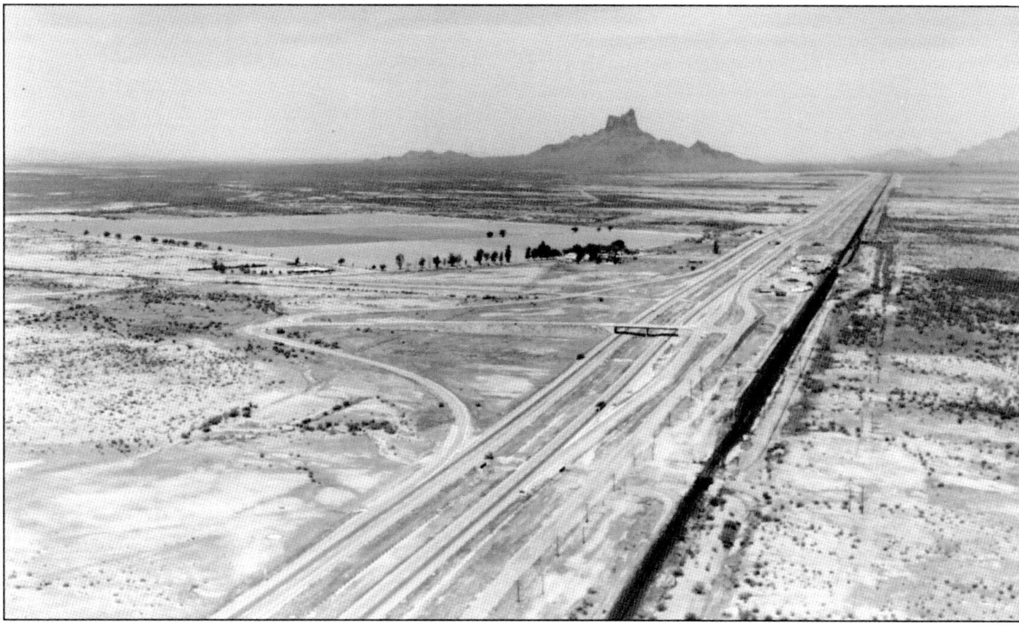

In 1956, Pres. Dwight Eisenhower inaugurated the interstate highway system. In Casa Grande, the road was a continuation of the trail system that led to and through the area throughout the centuries. In Pinal County and Casa Grande, the road, which runs from the Pacific Ocean to Jacksonville, Florida, was initially known as state highways 84 and 93. When the upgrade of the state highways was completed in 1961–1962, the road was cosigned as Interstate Highway 10, the fourth-longest highway in the interstate system. The highway parallels several historic trails across the area, including the Butterfield Stage and the Pony Express routes. From Interstate 8 east to New Mexico, the road closely follows old stage routes where travelers could rely on known water holes for their horses. Sections of the highway are currently being widened, and new interchanges are being constructed.

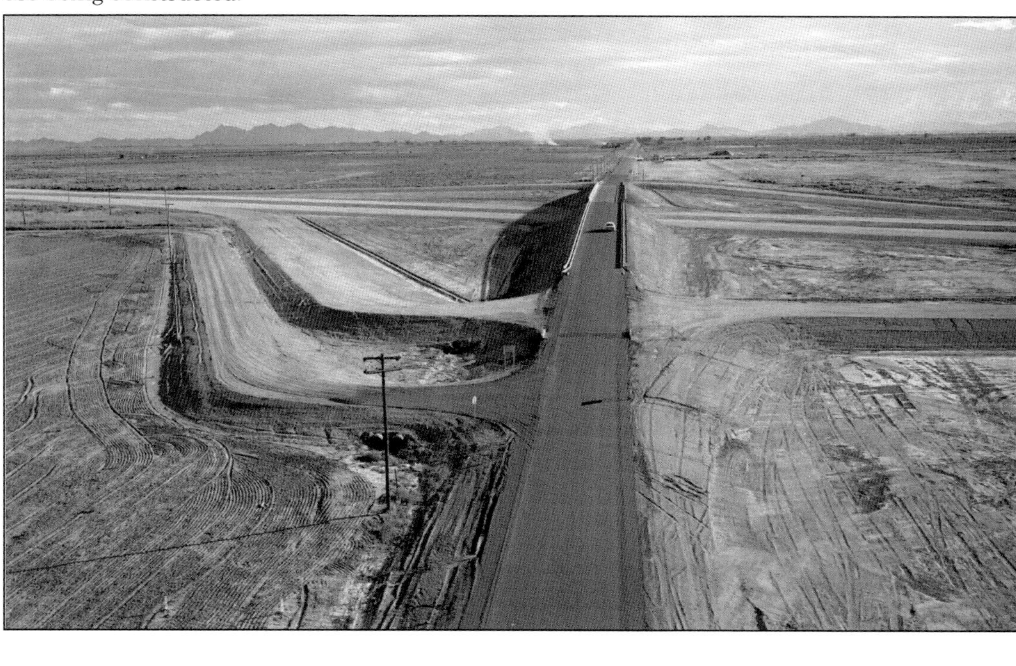

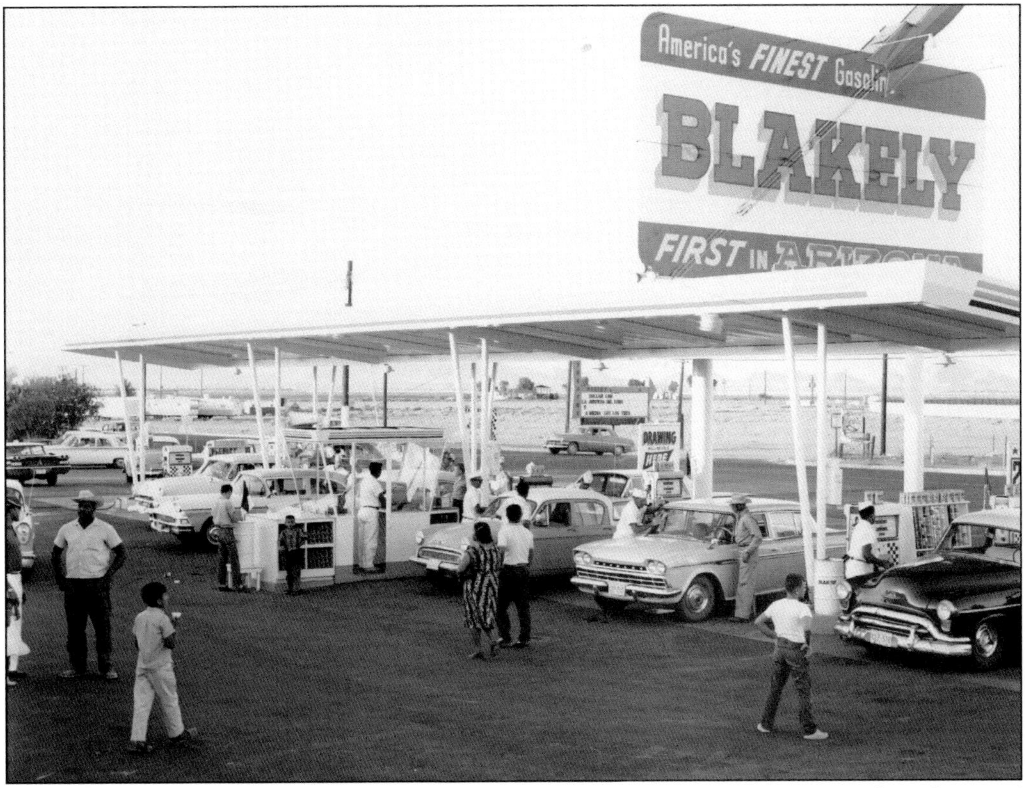

With the establishment of Interstate 10, more travelers passed through Casa Grande and created the need for more gas stations. The grand opening of Blakely's full service gas station drew a large crowd when it opened on the southwest corner of Pinal Avenue and Cottonwood Lane in 1963. Attendants in white uniforms are washing windows and checking oil as well as pumping gas. The Desert Drive-in Theater is across the street where the sign indicates the entrance fee is $1 per car. In 1957 (below), this Gilbarco Calco-metered gas pump is apparently inaccurate since the $3.30 charge does not calculate if gas is 22¢ or 23¢ per gallon, regardless of whether the meter reads 5.8 gallons or 58 gallons, as is unclearly indicated on the pump.

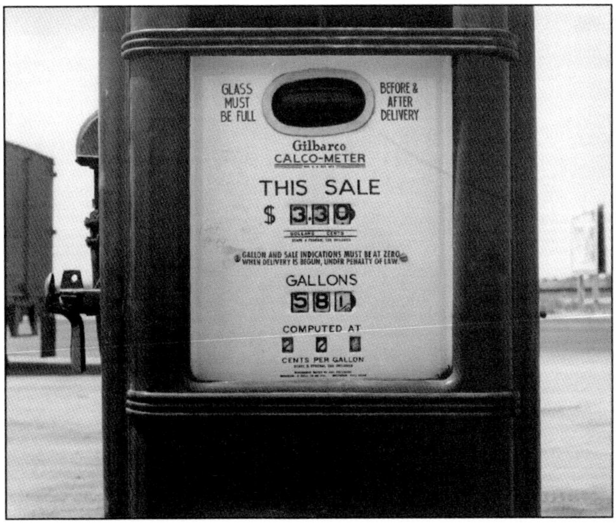

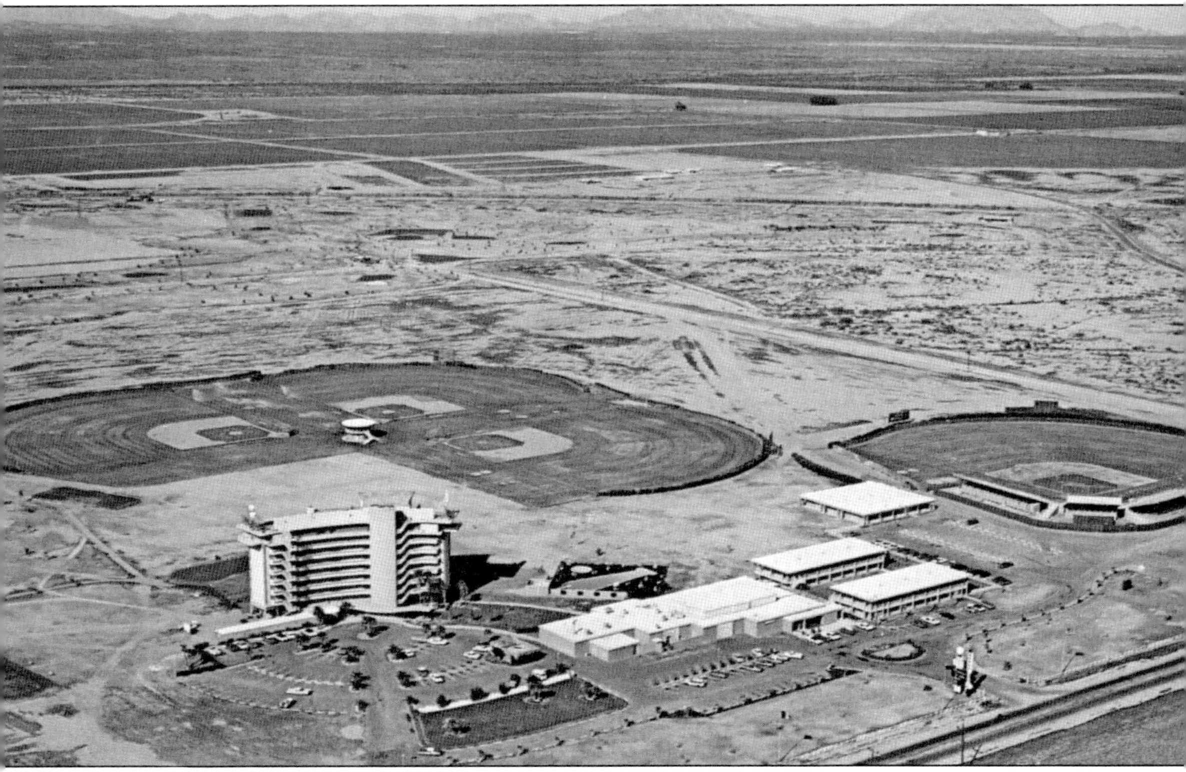

In 1959, Horace Stoneham, the owner of the San Francisco Giants baseball team, agreed to build a training facility in Casa Grande instead of Wickenberg. Horace was initially enticed by the prospect of an interstate highway passing through the western part of the city. He was further encouraged when city officials and businessmen offered him $50,000 as a show of good faith. In 1961, the $2-million Francisco Grande Hotel and Golf Resort opened. When the facility was completed, a nine-story hotel tower had been built to create the feel of a Major League Baseball stadium. The overhang on the north side of the tower was intended to resemble the brim of a baseball cap, and the swimming pool was in the form of a baseball bat, with an adjacent wading pool in the form of a baseball. Even the parking lot was in the shape of a baseball field, and the flower beds were shaped like baseballs and bats.

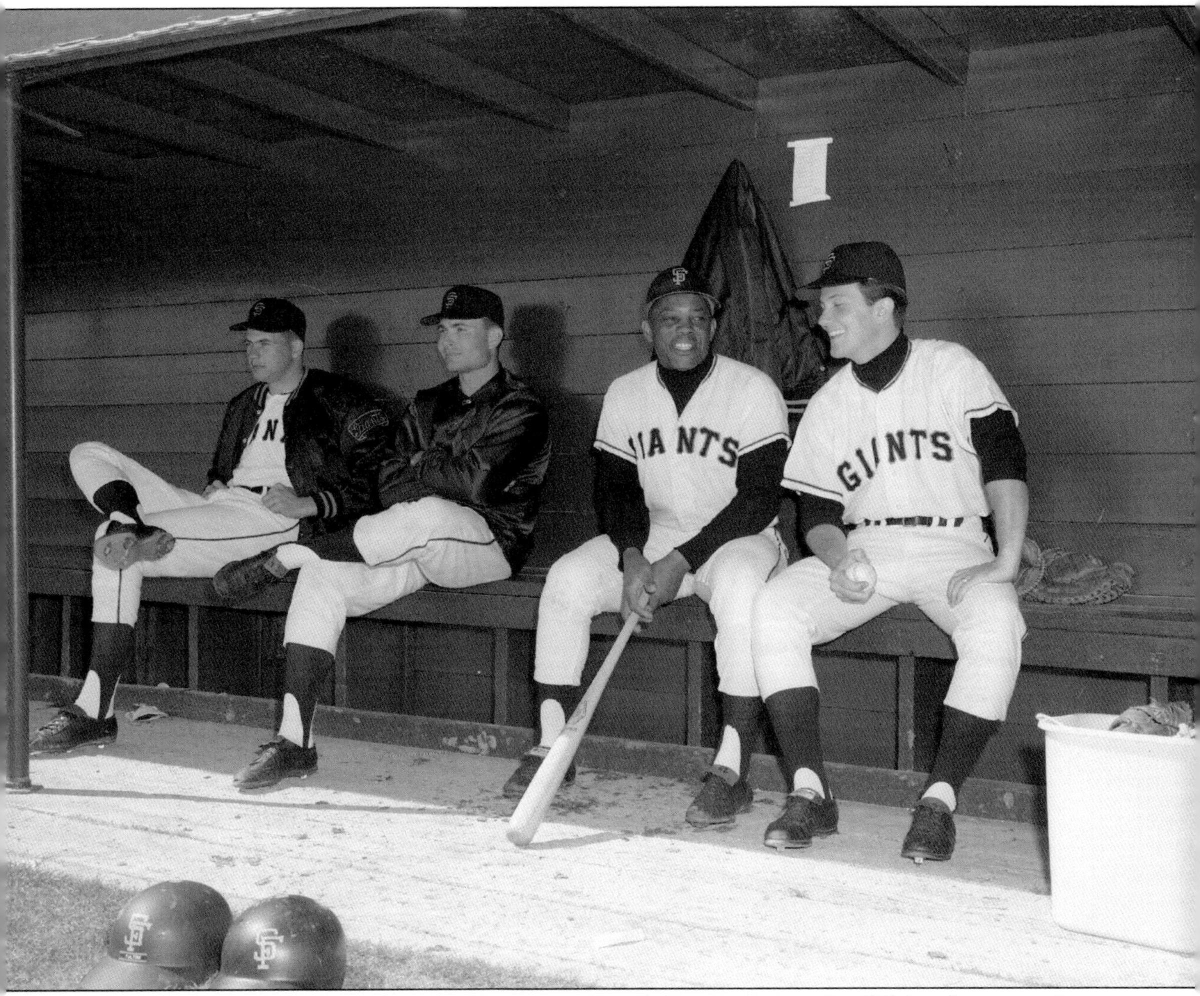

The first baseball game ever played at Francisco Grande Resort featured a 375-foot home run hit by Willie Mays off of another future Hall of Fame player, Gaylord Perry. Several other prominent players on the field that day included Willie McCovey, Juan Marachiel, and the manager of the Giants, Alvin Dark. Pat Boone (far right), a popular crooner of the time, is seated in the dugout next to Willie Mays. In 1962, the Giants went to the World Series, where they lost to the New York Yankees in seven games. In addition to the Giants, the California Angels trained here from 1982 to 1984. The United States Football League's Arizona Wranglers (1982) and the Denver Gold (1984) teams used the facility as a training camp as well. In 2008, the United Football League built a new $20-million complex at Francisco Grande. After one year, the league pulled out of its agreement. However, the city was able to attract the soccer community, and now Grande Sports World hosts a state-of-the art recreational facility that includes a residency program affiliated with a Major League Soccer team.

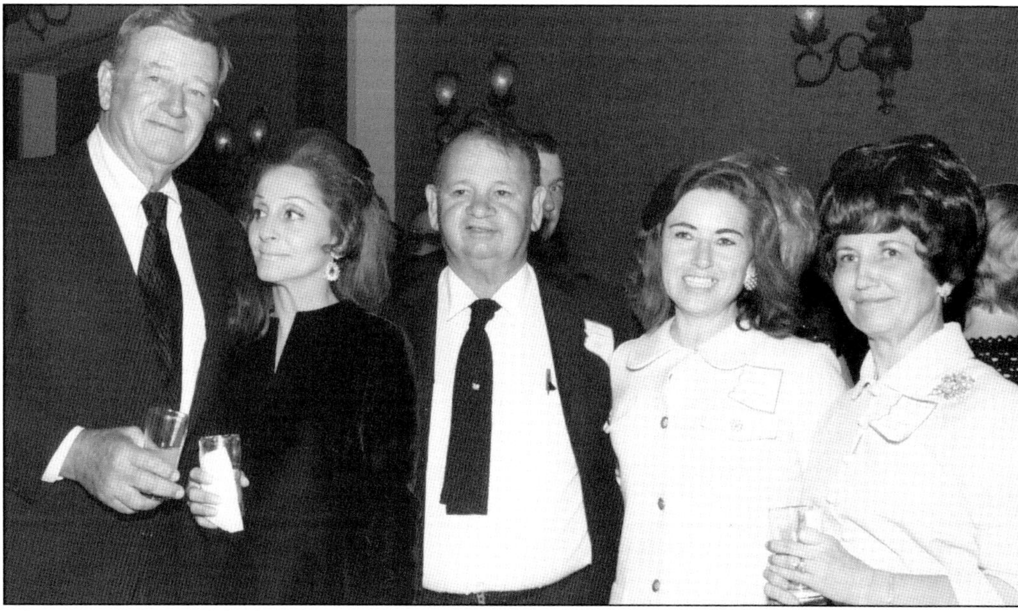

John Wayne, one of the biggest movie stars in the world, spent considerable time in Casa Grande. In 1960, he hired Louis Johnson to run the Red River Feedlot. In 1962, when they became full partners of the Red River Land and Cattle Company, Wayne often visited to check on the enterprise and to see and be seen at various parties around town. Above, he is at his movie-star best at a cocktail party at the 26 Bar Ranch; Louis Johnson is in the middle of the back row and Pilar Wayne is next to her husband. As he and Johnson pose with a prize bull (below), Wayne looks like the cowboy he often portrayed. (The other people are unidentified.) The Duke Lounge located in Francisco Grande Resort is named in John Wayne's honor.

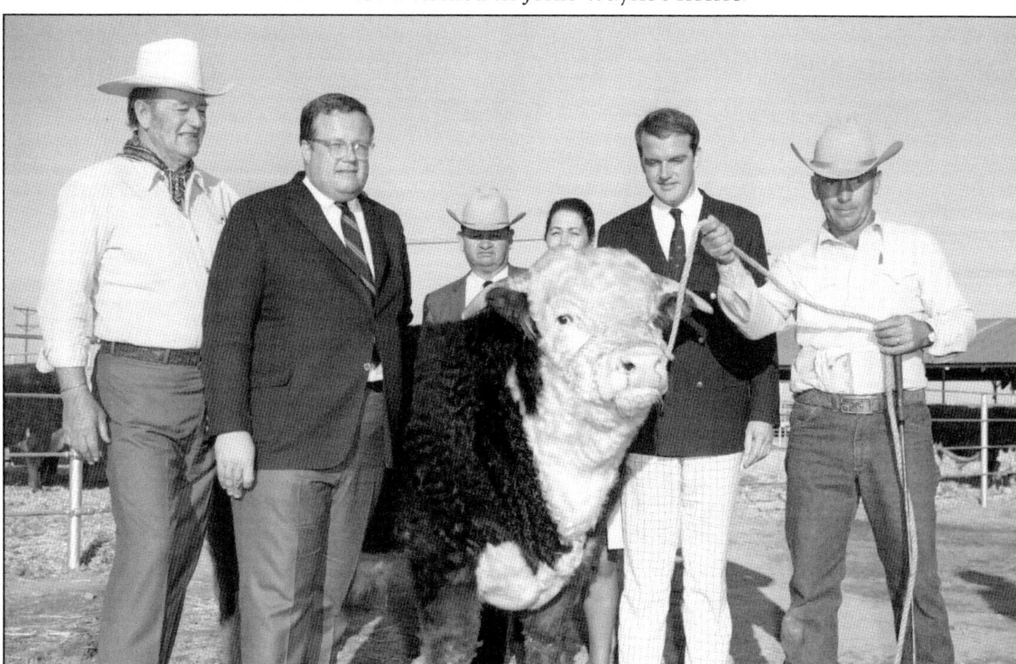

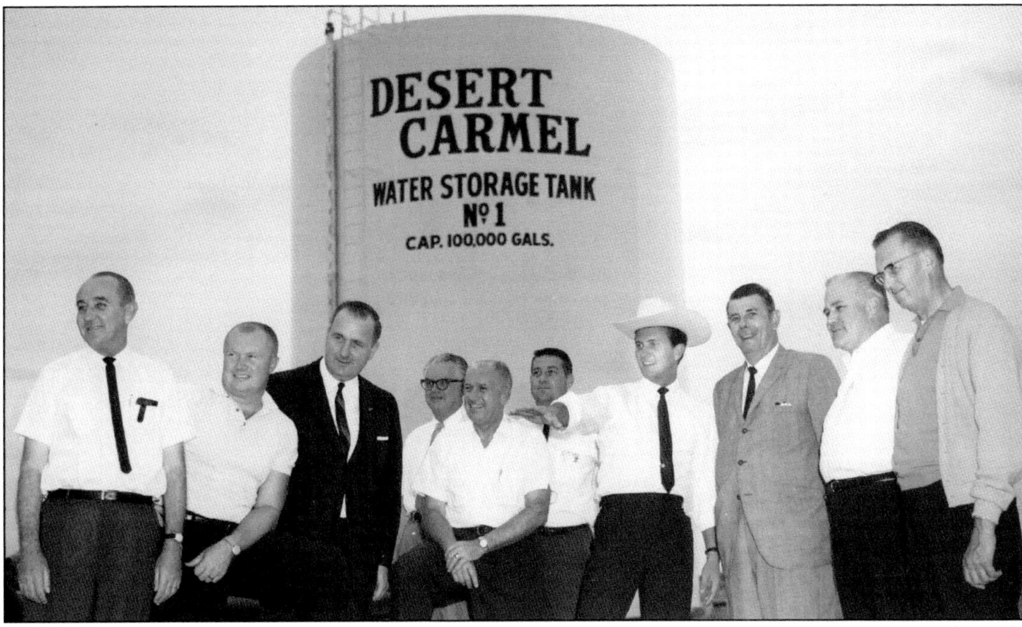

Francisco Grande Resort was not intended to be used exclusively for professional sports activities. With an 18-hole golf course and famed Arizona weather, the resort was frequented by out-of-state travelers and entertainers such as actors Dale Robertson and John Wayne and Pat Boone, the teenage singing idol. Boone spent time with the San Francisco Giants baseball team during spring training and became convinced that the area just east of the resort would be a good place for a subdivision. For several years, he attempted to develop Desert Carmel subdivision, but it proved to be an unsuccessful endeavor. To this day, only a few houses dot the desert at Desert Carmel.

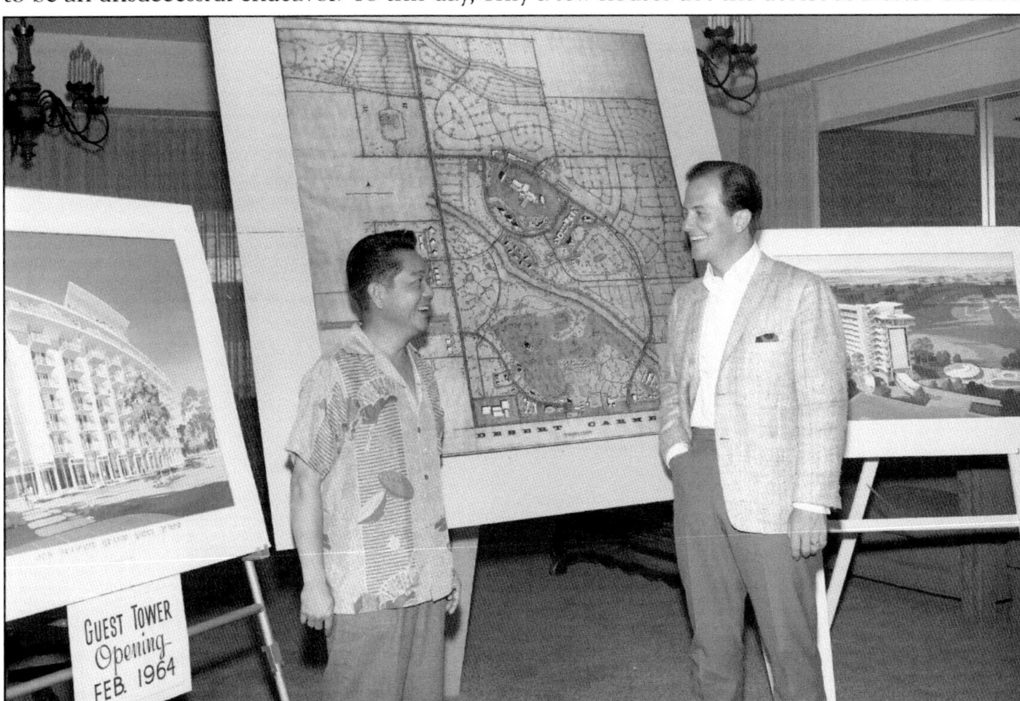

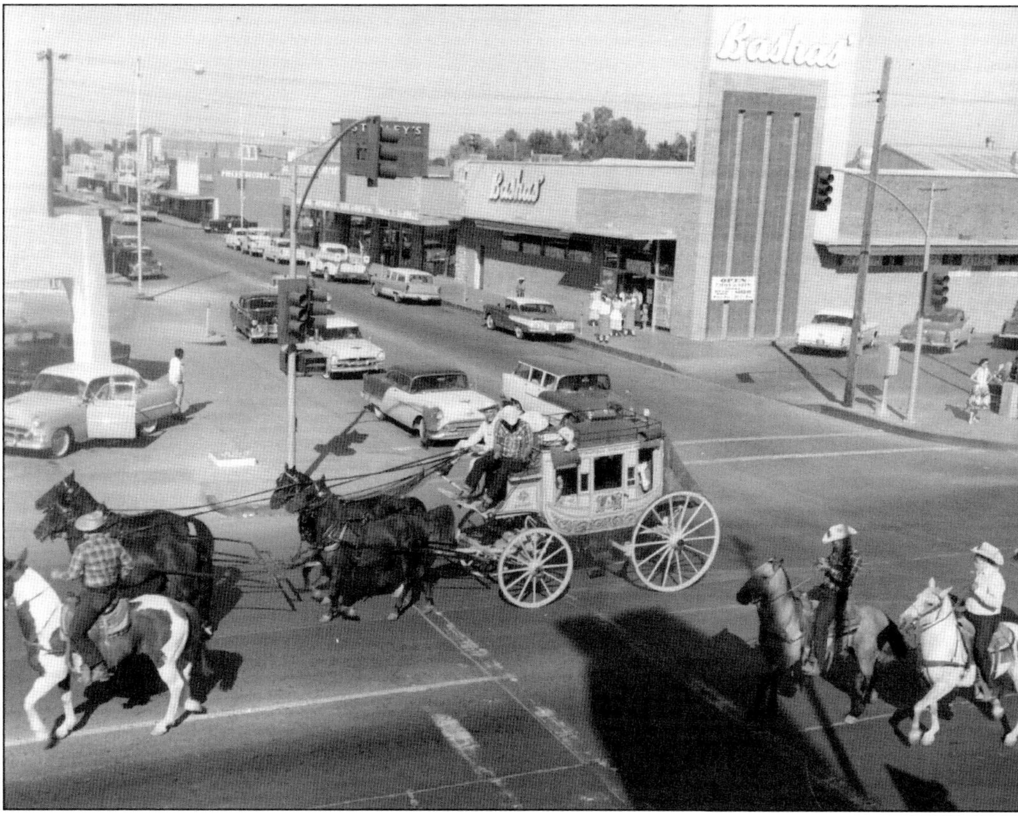

Just as trails to, from, and through Casa Grande began this book, so too can a celebration of part of that history finish the book. In 1958, a celebratory parade honoring the Butterfield Stage Centennial was held (above). Here, at the corner of Florence and Second Streets in downtown Casa Grande, cowboys, stagecoach, and cars present a vivid contrast of the old and new. An overview (below) of the city in the mid-20th century shows what has become of that 1879 railroad stop in the desert. Imagine what it will look like in the mid-21st century.

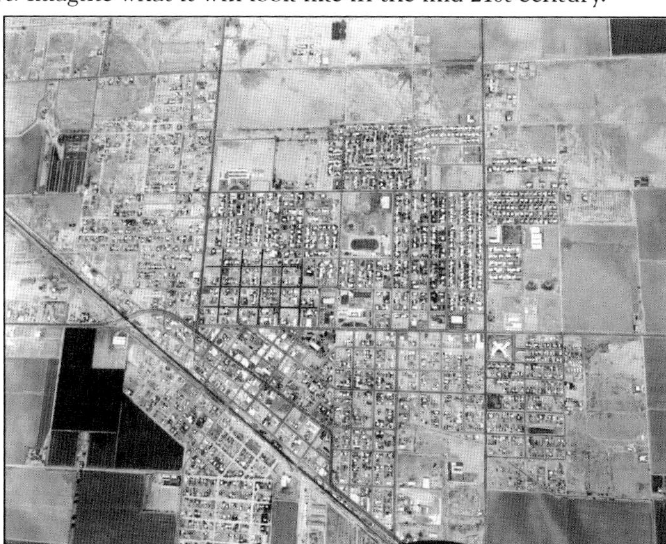

Seven

The Historical Society

The sponsor of this publication is the Casa Grande Valley Historical Society and Museum. Not only the historical society, but many other civic entities owe their existence to the foresight and dedication of a few creative thinkers and planners among the early pioneers of Casa Grande.

In 1913, seven women met at the home of Lillian Peart to organize the Current Events Club. Soon, other women joined, and together they sought not only to learn more about the world, but to provide knowledge of the larger world to the rest of the growing population of Casa Grande. Largely a loose association seeking to improve the literary and artistic culture of their fellow citizens, the group joined the General Federation of Women's Clubs in 1914 and renamed themselves the Woman's Club of Casa Grande. From that modest beginning flowed a plethora of ideas and concrete accomplishments.

The first library was started by the original 15 members of the Woman's Club. They were also responsible for the first hot lunch program for students as well as Meals-On-Wheels for those unable to venture out. They formed a Garden Club, a Junior Woman's Club, and were instrumental in advocating for a hospital. The Woman's Club was the precursor of many of the civic and philanthropic organizations that most Casa Grande residents now take for granted.

In 1962, because of their interest in history and preservation, Flossie Barmes and Barbara Schoen guided the Woman's Club in undertaking another project. As a result, the Casa Grande Valley Historical Society was born in 1963 and incorporated in 1964. The society began in a wing of the Woman's Club, but by the end of the 1960s, it was clear that the collection was outgrowing the space. After a short period of occupation in a small building on Marshall Street, the society was able to purchase the old stone Presbyterian church on Florence Boulevard. This building, recognized as the iconic symbol of the city, has been the home of the historical society ever since.

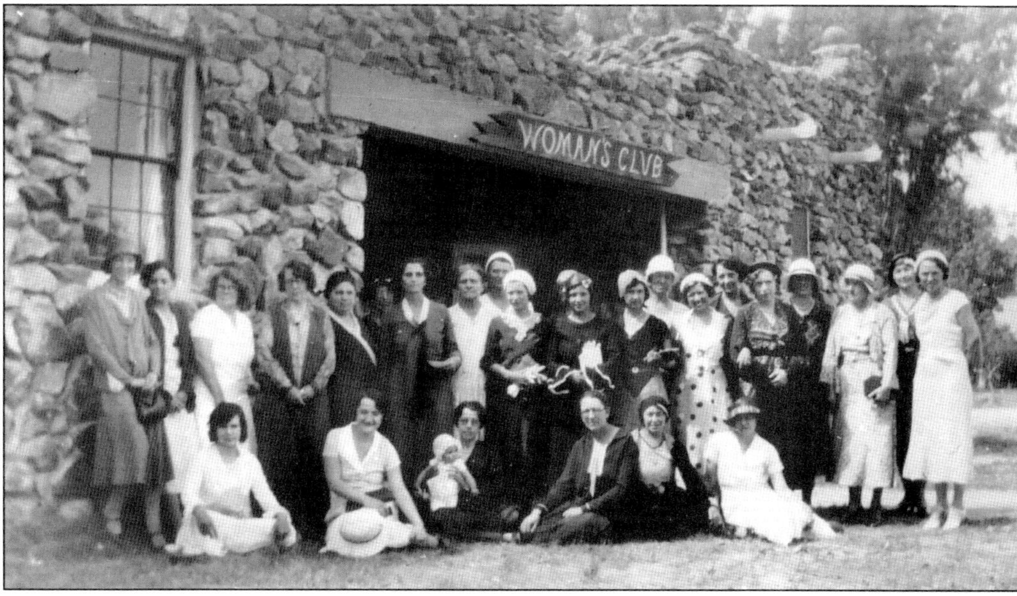

In 1924, each Woman's Club member was asked to contribute rock, sand, or its equivalent to help construct a Hopi-style building designed by Henry Jaastad. It was built by William Sullivan, who was responsible for constructing several other stone buildings throughout the city. By 1925, the building was complete, and the club members posed for this photograph. In 2011, the building, which is now owned by the city, is still located at its original site at the intersection of Florence Boulevard and Sacaton Street. It is in the Arizona and National Register of Historic Places.

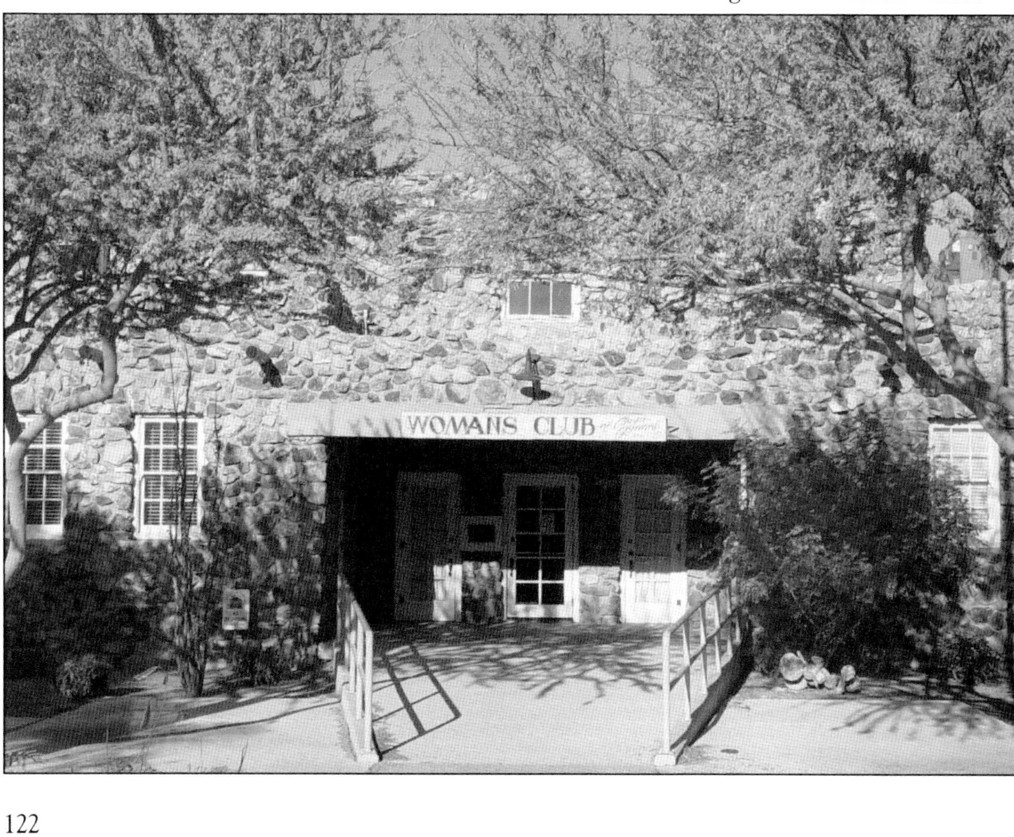

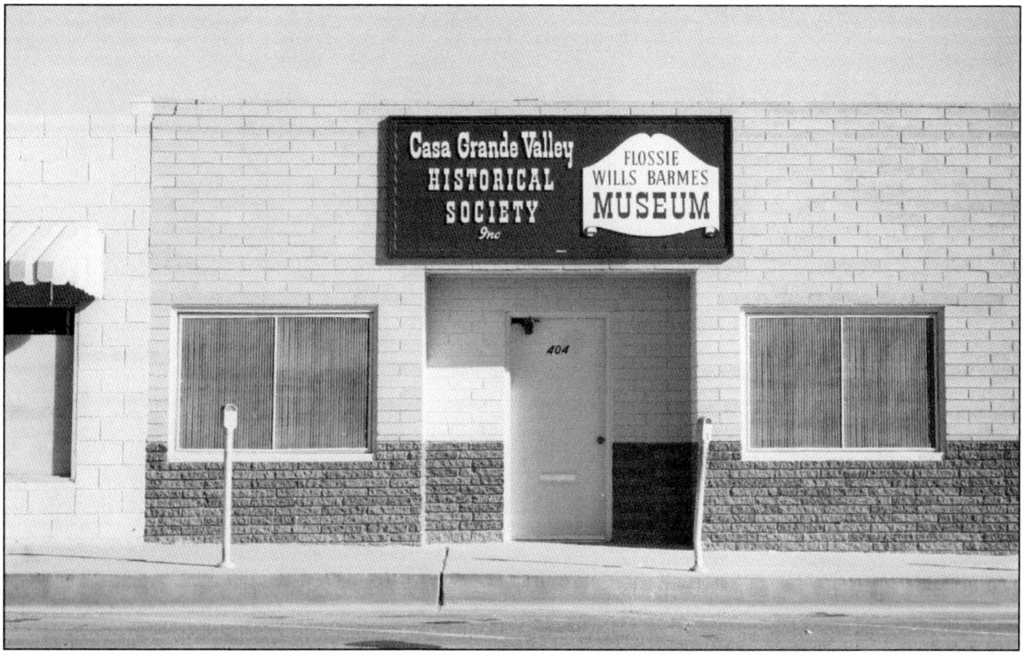

Initially, the Casa Grande Valley Historical Society and Museum was housed in the Woman's Club, until it outgrew the available space. At one time, the museum—named for Flossie Barmes, one of the people most responsible for its creation—was located in this small building at 404 North Marshall Street.

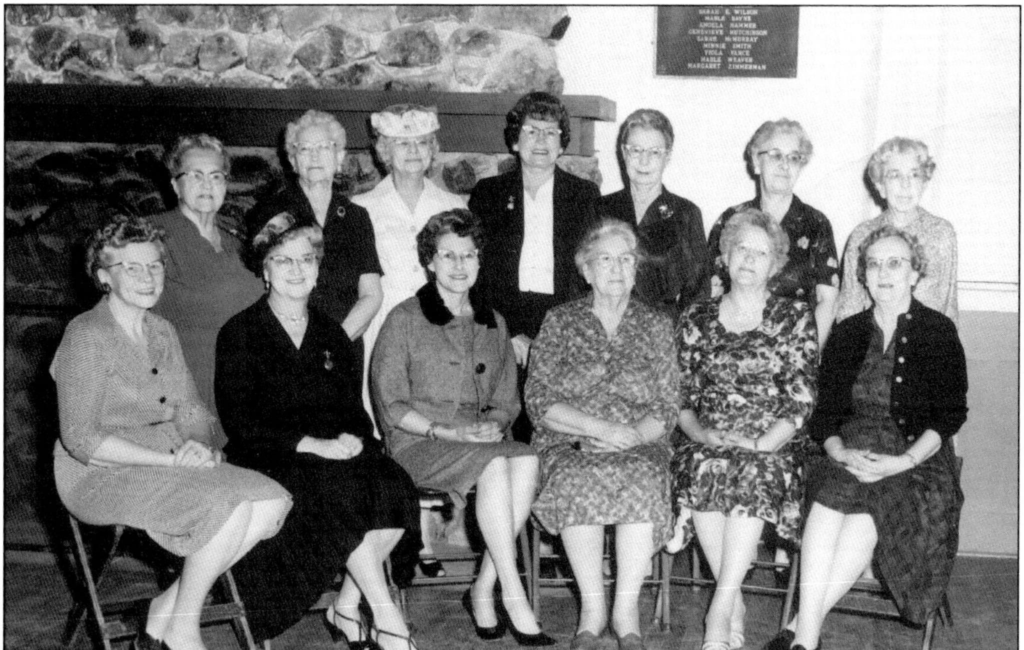

In 1963, this group of past presidents posed for the 50th anniversary celebration of the Casa Grande Woman's Club. Flossie Barmes (back row, far left) and Barbara Schoen (first row, third from left) were the initial motivating forces in the formation of the historical society.

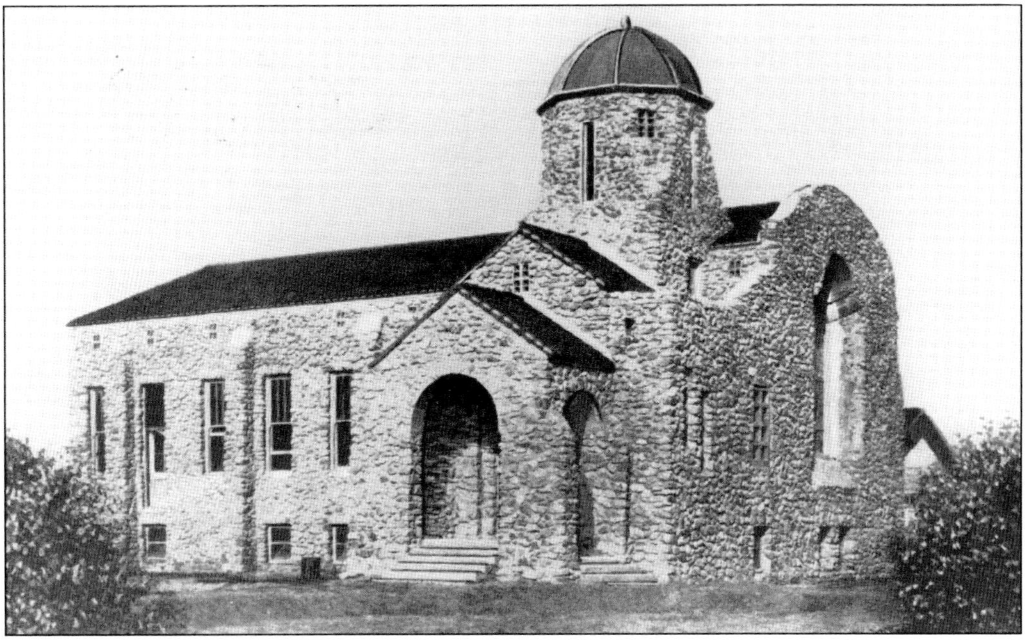

Just two years after it was built, the imposing stone building that was the First Presbyterian Church was already recognized as a well-known landmark. The iconic stone structure has been the home of the Casa Grande Valley Historical Society and Museum since 1977. The building, which was designed by architect Robert Orr and built by Michael Sullivan in 1927, is listed in the National Register of Historic Places. Currently known as Heritage Hall, the old church is now used as a venue for guest speakers, a variety of productions, and even an occasional wedding. An additional building attached to the church served as a mortuary and home for the mortician, Dennis Mays, and his family in the early 1970s. It is now the home of the historical society and museum.

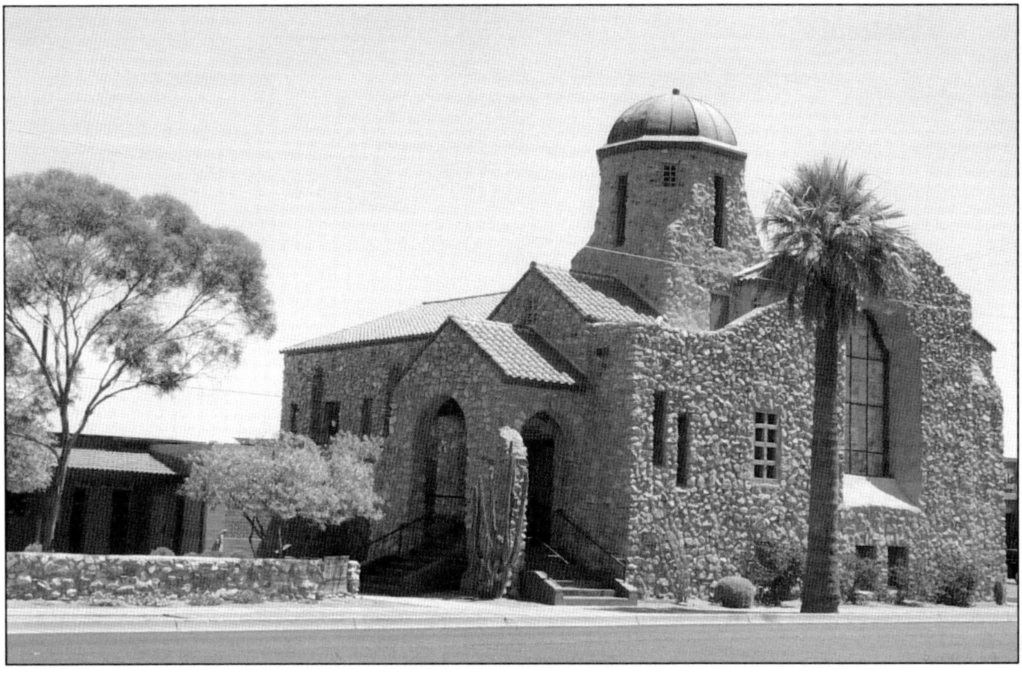

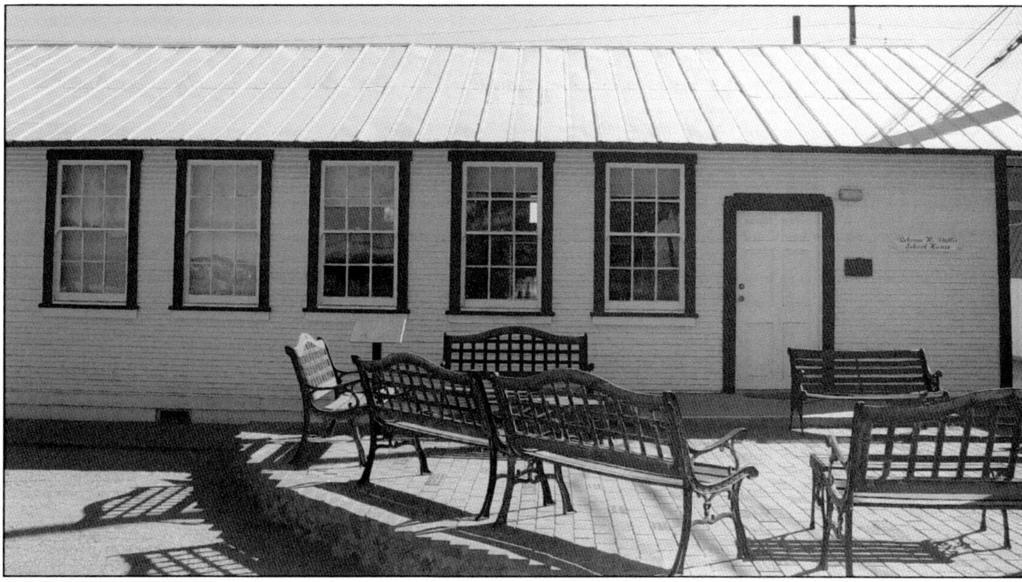

Located on the historical society property is the one-room wood building that was the Southside Colored Grammar School. The simple structure was built in a corner behind the Southside School on the west side of Casa Grande and was used during the years of segregation. The building has been renamed the Rebecca Dallis Schoolhouse after the remarkable African American teacher who taught there for many years. A corner of the room contains students' and teachers' desks typical of the time, as well as study aids. The rest of the room contains artifacts and photographs honoring the contributions of the African American community as they relate to Casa Grande and Pinal County.

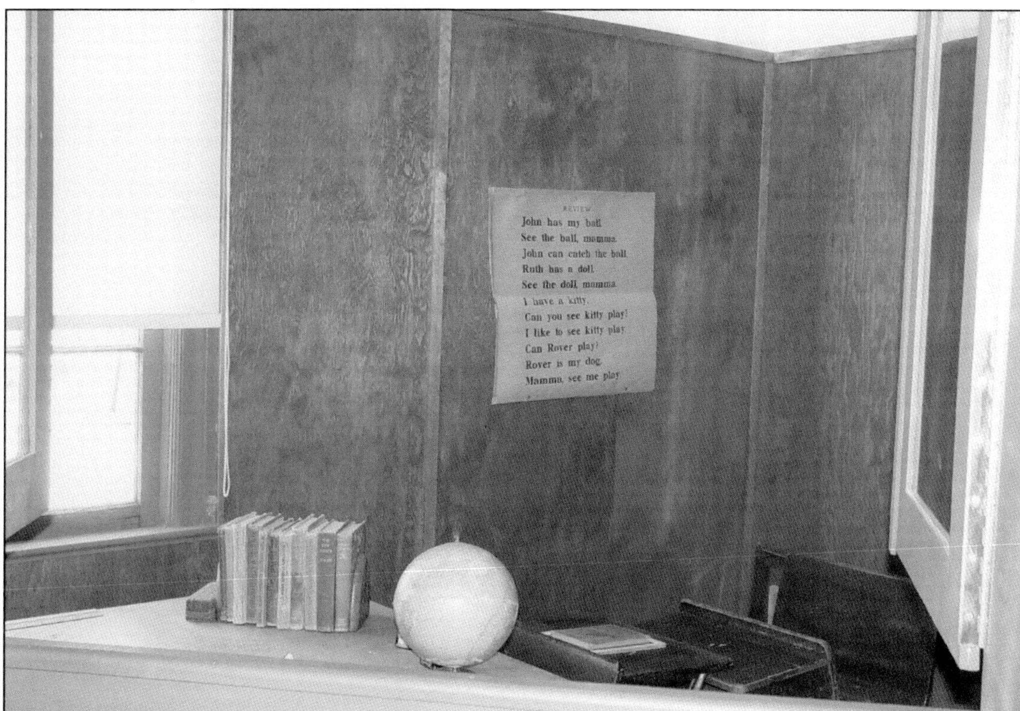

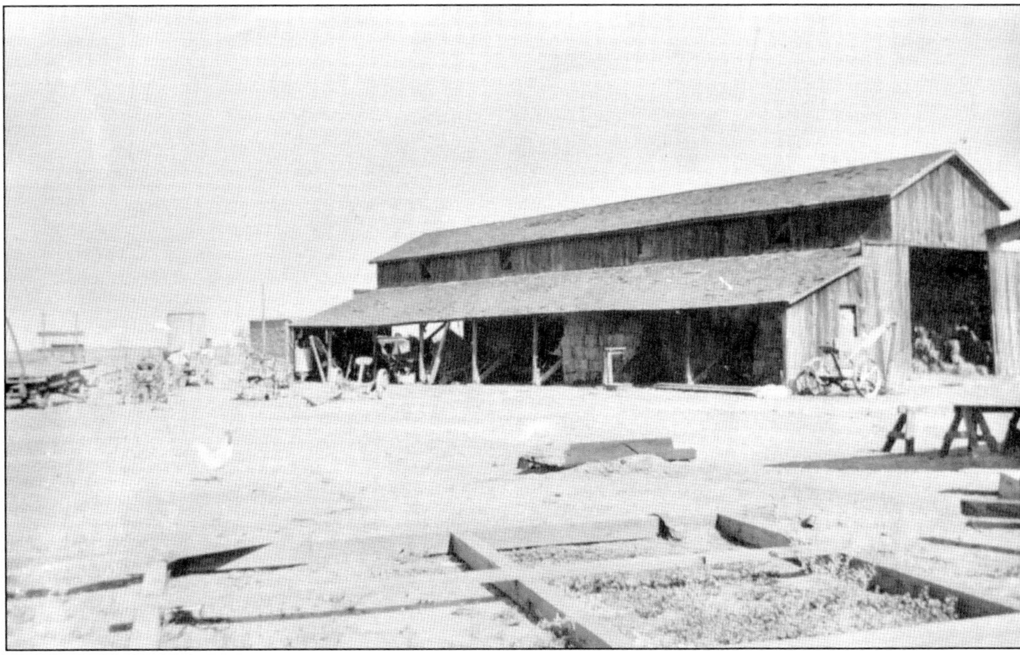

The Trekell family was among the early farmers in the area, and one of the main streets in town is named for them. A replica of their barn, which was typical of those constructed in the area during the 1920s, is located on the museum grounds (below). It houses farm and ranch artifacts and also serves as a special events venue.

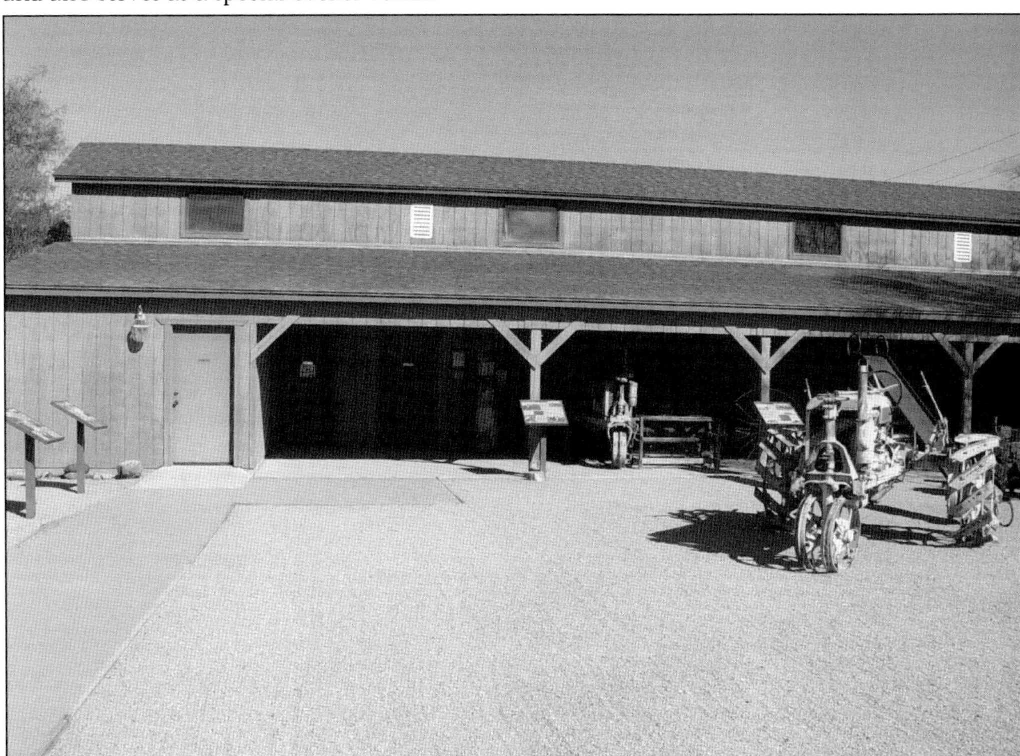

On the right is the historic Weaver Pioneer Cemetery with the grave of Katherine Hamlin as it looked around 1929. When a family member visited the site in 1999, the wood marker was gone.

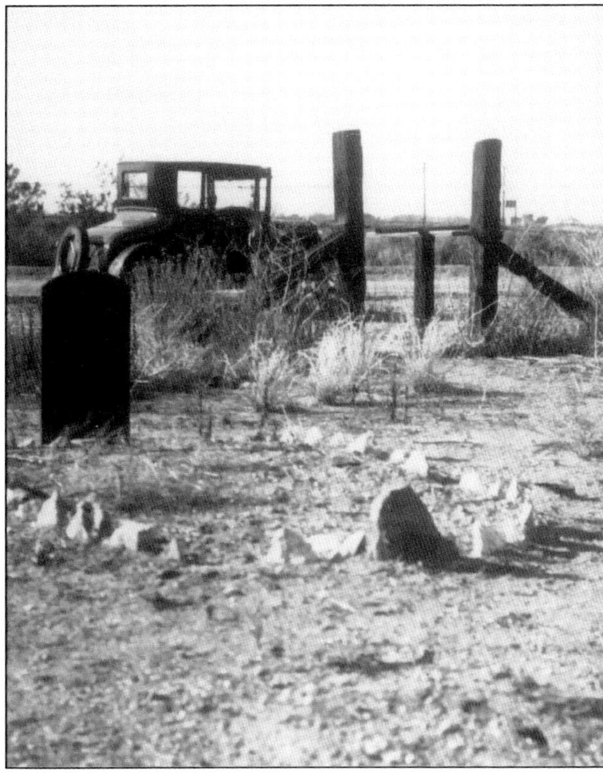

In 2008, the museum was granted ownership of the cemetery, which is located along Peart Road on the southeast side of town. The cemetery contains 52 graves dating from 1830 to 1920. Not all those buried there are members of the Weaver family.

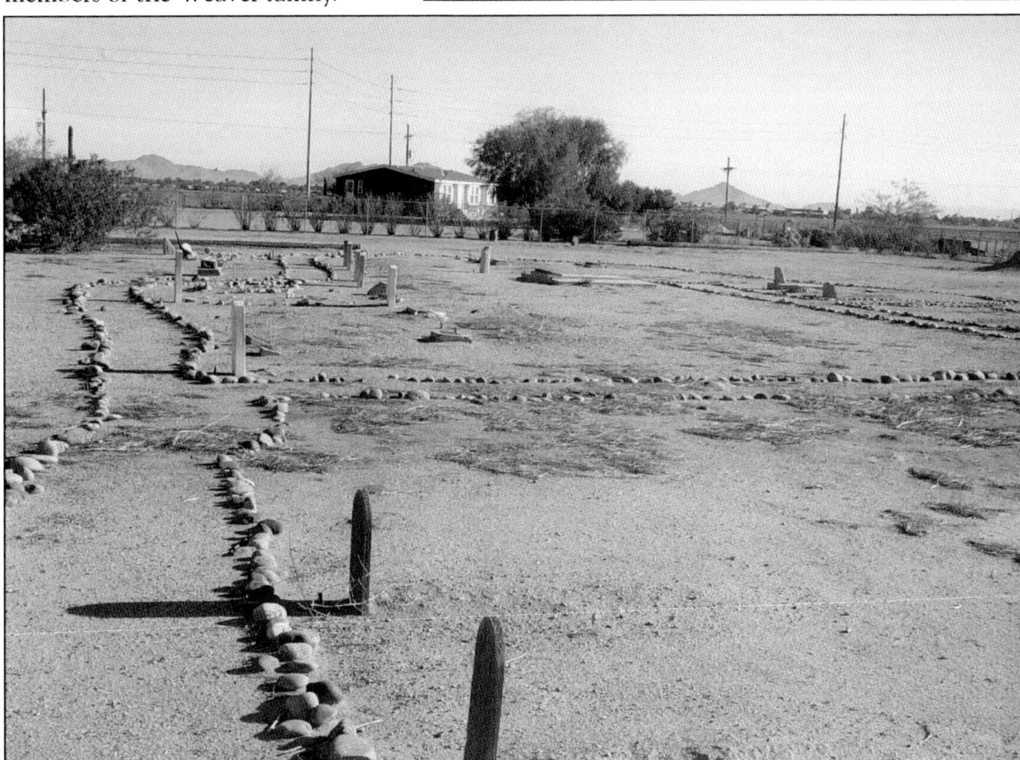